Citizenship in the Arab World

IMISCOE

International Migration, Integration and Social Cohesion in Europe

The IMISCOE Network of Excellence unites over 500 researchers from European institutes specialising in studies of international migration, integration and social cohesion. The Network is funded by the Sixth Framework Programme of the European Commission on Research, Citizens and Governance in a Knowledge-Based Society. Since its foundation in 2004, IMISCOE has developed an integrated, multidisciplinary and globally comparative research project led by scholars from all branches of the economic and social sciences, the humanities and law. The Network both furthers existing studies and pioneers new research in migration as a discipline. Priority is also given to promoting innovative lines of inquiry key to European policymaking and governance.

The IMISCOE-Amsterdam University Press Series was created to make the Network's findings and results available to researchers, policymakers and practitioners, the media and other interested stakeholders. High-quality manuscripts authored by IMISCOE members and cooperating partners are published in one of four distinct series.

IMISCOE Research advances sound empirical and theoretical scholarship addressing themes within IMISCOE's mandated fields of study.

IMISCOE Reports disseminates Network papers and presentations of a time-sensitive nature in book form.

IMISCOE Dissertations presents select PhD monographs written by IMISCOE doctoral candidates.

IMISCOE Textbooks produces manuals, handbooks and other didactic tools for instructors and students of migration studies.

IMISCOE Policy Briefs and more information on the Network can be found at www.imiscoe.org.

Citizenship in the Arab World

Kin, Religion and Nation-State

Gianluca P. Parolin

IMISCOE Research

AMSTERDAM UNIVERSITY PRESS

This work builds on five years of onsite research into citizenship in the Arab world. A grant awarded by the Italian National Research Council (CNR) made the publication of its results possible as *Dimensioni dell'appartenenza e cittadinanza nel mondo arabo* by Gianluca P. Parolin, published in Italian by Jovene in 2007 (ISBN 88-243-1720-0).

Cover photo: Andrea Locati

Cover design: Studio Jan de Boer BNO, Amsterdam
Layout: The DocWorkers, Almere

ISBN   978 90 8964 045 1
e-ISBN   978 90 4850 629 3
NUR   741 / 763

Table of contents

Preface

In European traditions of political thought, the concept of citizenship has provided a crucial link between the ideas of democracy and of the rule of law. In a well-known essay, John Pocock identified the Athenian and Roman roots of citizenship as active participation in collective self-rule and as a legal status of freedom within a territorial jurisdiction respectively (Pocock 1992: 35-55). With the emergence of the concepts of territorial sovereignty in the 17th century and of the nation-state as the basic unit of a global international order since the end of the 18th century, citizenship has acquired a third meaning. It is today often used as a synonym for nationality, which refers to a legal bond between individuals and sovereign states. In its external dimension nationality refers to a rule of mutual recognition between states that entails powers to protect their nationals abroad and a duty to readmit them into their territories. In its internal dimension, nationality does not presuppose democratic participation, but refers to individuals as subjects of a sovereign political authority independent of the nature of the regime.

Since the Age of Enlightenment all three interpretations of citizenship have been combined in democratic revolutions and constitutional transformations in Europe and the American colonies established by European settlers. Representative democracy constitutionally constrained by the rule of law in a sovereign nation-state has become the most widely embraced ideal of legitimate exercise of political authority. As the many dark episodes of authoritarian and totalitarian rule show, this model has not always been successful. Today it faces new challenges by national minorities who claim territorial autonomy, by international migrations that create large populations of non-citizen residents inside state territories and non-resident citizens abroad, and by a broad range of phenomena grouped together under the label of globalisation that are seen to undermine effective state sovereignty.

These developments have triggered a large and still growing new literature on citizenship. This revival of interest in citizenship since the 1980s is multidisciplinary and multidimensional. It has inspired comparative analyses of nationality laws, feminist political theories and sociological studies of citizenship ideals and practices among different groups. Yet there is one pervasive limitation. With very few exceptions this literature is Eurocentric, or more precisely Occidentocentric.

Gianluca Parolin's account of citizenship in the Arab world is a very welcome attempt to fill one of the most significant geographical and historical gaps in the comparative citizenship literature. Drawing extensively on original Arabic sources, Parolin tells a story that is much more complex than the stereotypical images of authoritarian regimes governed by Islamic law. In his analysis, citizenship in the Arab world combines elements of pre-Islamic structures of kinship with the ideal of *ummah* as a religious community and with nation-state sovereignty. Concepts of citizenship derived from these three principles obviously do not correspond, either with regard to territorial scope and inclusion of persons, or with regard to the substantive rights and obligations attributed to individuals. This mismatch results in rather unstable legal constructions that can pull in different directions depending on the demographic composition of the society in question or the direction taken by a particular regime.

Parolin's account leaves little doubt that citizenship laws in Arabic states are commonly characterised by features considered today as illiberal by most Western scholars. Among these are the explicit or implicit link between religious belief and acquisition or loss of citizenship status, the second-class status of naturalised citizens compared with citizens by birth, the principle of perpetual allegiance that prohibits renunciation of citizenship by emigrants, the denial of citizenship to some minorities that are thereby made stateless, the discrimination of women through the dominance of paternal *jus sanguinis* and the unequal treatment of husbands and wives in the acquisition and loss of citizenship through marriage and divorce.

None of these features, however, is unique to the Islamic or Arabic world. As historical comparative studies show, each of these illiberal principles has had its equivalent in a not too distant European past, and some traces survive even in the nationality laws of current member states of the European Union. This should not come as a surprise. First, the imperatives of nation-state building after the break-up of multinational empires created similar problems of minority exclusion from citizenship in the Habsburg, Ottoman, Soviet and Yugoslav cases. Second, ethnicity and religion have also served as bases for national identity and as obstacles for naturalisation in several European countries and continue to do so today in Greece or Denmark. Third, as Parolin shows, international conventions requiring equal treatment of men and women in nationality law, which has had a major impact on national legislation in Europe since the 1970s, have more recently also triggered reforms in some states of the Arab region.

These parallels show that citizenship in the Arab world is certainly not impervious to internal contestation and external influence. However, the gap between a liberal democratic concept and present legislation in these countries still remains very wide and difficult to bridge.

Yet bridged it must be, because in a globalising world, citizenship is no longer a matter under exclusive control of sovereign states. In contexts of migration the citizenship status of individuals becomes a joint product of legislation in two independent states. The Arab world is of special interest in studying the consequences of migration for citizenship because it includes some of the most important sending countries as well as those states with the highest percentages of non-citizen immigrants in the resident population.

Arab sending countries have often tried to exercise political control over their large expatriate populations and to prevent their integration into the receiving society. Yet, eventually, such homeland-driven political transnationalism may result in reverse pressure being exercised by expatriate communities on the governments of their countries of origin (Brand 2006). Citizenship policies of emigration states also affect those of European countries of immigration. Consider, for example, how a principle of perpetual allegiance interacts with the toleration of dual nationality. Only some Western European states still require that applicants for naturalisation must renounce a previous nationality. Austria, Germany, Denmark and the Netherlands currently grant exceptions for immigrants from countries that do not permit such renunciation. The perverse effect of this approach is, however, to create a disadvantage for immigrants from countries with more liberal nationality laws. A more general toleration of dual nationality in Europe would not only avoid such arbitrary discrimination among immigrants, but would also increase pressure on Arab sending states to reconsider the principle of perpetual allegiance.

In the Arab world, pressure for liberalising reforms seems to be currently stronger in contexts of emigration than of immigration. In several of the Arab Gulf states the majority of residents are permanently excluded from citizenship. Citizenship becomes then a minority privilege attached to descent, ethnicity and religion as it was in the Athenian *polis* or the late medieval Italian city republics. In Gulf states governed by autocratic regimes whose wealth is wholly derived from oil revenues, migrants who provide a low-status working class and remain socially fully segregated have hardly any political clout to demand access to citizenship. Yet, as Parolin shows, both Islamic legal concepts pertaining to protected foreigners and modern nationality law may eventually provide some leverage for contesting such exclusionary concepts of citizenship.

Parolin introduces us to a complex body of social, religious and legal norms that have shaped citizenship regimes in the Arab world. It is quite obvious that reconciling these traditions with inclusive and democratic concepts of citizenship is a daunting task. But this challenge is raised by the increasingly dense transnational linkages between European and Arab states created through migration, and it has been occasionally embraced by reform minded Islamic scholars. As Parolin argues, in the Arab world the transformative dynamic of citizenship discourse is currently limited by a traditional focus in legal debates on the status of non-Muslims in Muslim countries and the duties of Muslims in non-Muslim societies. What is still missing are broader reflections on the meaning of citizenship that would include all three dimensions of democracy, the rule of law and the collective identity of the political community. Taking Arab and Islamic traditions seriously and studying them as carefully as Parolin does may be the most useful contribution European scholars can make towards such debates.

Rainer Bauböck
European University Institute, Florence

Foreword

It is a pleasure to welcome the publication of the book *Citizenship in the Arab World*.

The complicated relationship between the concepts of 'nationality' and 'citizenship' has been the subject of many publications in the recent past. Their precise relationship depends very much on the languages and legal systems in which these concepts are operating. In several languages, the term etymologically related to 'nationality' has an ethnic dimension and indicates that a certain person belongs to a nation in an ethnic sense. On the other hand, the term related to 'citizenship' indicates *inter alia* the formal link between a person and a state. In many other languages and legal systems, however, 'nationality' refers to 'the legal bond between a person and a state and does not indicate the person's ethnic origin' (art. 2(a) of the European Convention on Nationality). Thus the term etymologically related to 'nationality' is in the latter case more or less a synonym for 'citizenship'.

Often, the discussion on the relationship between nationality and citizenship focuses on different European languages and legal systems with European roots. It is therefore very enriching that Gianluca Parolin opens his work with a description of the notions related to citizenship in Europe and the Arab world. He considers the roots of the concept of citizenship in ancient Greece and classical Rome and then elaborates on the views on membership in the kin and the religious groups in the Arab world. In such a context, it is extremely interesting to read about the position of non-Muslims – in particular, those belonging to Jewish and Christian minorities – in the Arab world until the end of the 19th and the beginning of the 20th centuries. Fascinating is the description of the development of a law of citizenship in the Ottoman Empire at the end of the 19th century, as well as the emergence of a kind of 'indigenous' nationality in several Ottoman provinces.

Parolin's description of the development of nationality legislation among the independent Arab states in the 20th and early 21st centuries is very informative. He shows the French influence on those nationality laws while pointing out their typical Arab features.

Despite the fact that states in principle are autonomous in nationality matters, we are witnessing a growing discussion on the desirability and feasibility of a certain degree of harmonisation with regard to the grounds for acquisition and loss of nationality. That is particularly the case in Europe, where the already mentioned European Convention on Nationality concluded in Strasbourg (1997) creates some common ground in this field. The dream of the drafters is that the Convention may serve as a starting point for a worldwide convention on nationality. This dream was also incorporated into article 23, which allows non-member states – by invitation – to ratify the Convention. In view of a future worldwide discussion on nationality regulations, Parolin's very detailed comparative description of the grounds for acquisition and loss of nationality in the Arab world is of paramount importance. (With regard to the acquisition of nationality, he distinguishes between attribution and acquisition of nationality, in the narrow sense, in line with the French tradition followed by Arab scholars.) I am very happy with this comparison; there is a real need for up-to-date information on the nationality laws of the countries in the Arab world.

The information on the current situation regarding the nationality laws in the Arab countries will also be very useful to lawyers handling nationality cases involving persons of Arab origin.

To this end, Parolin's volume contains a great deal of important data. The publication of such a book fills an important gap and makes an excellent contribution to the debate. Hopefully, the author will have the occasion to participate in the discussions on the possible harmonisation of some aspects of nationality law, in particular in the Arab world, and to update the information on the developments of these nationality laws from time to time.

Gerard-René de Groot
Maastricht University, Maastricht

Acknowledgements

Sincere and special thanks for their precious help to Steven Gallo, Eliana A. Pollone and Therese M. Sciabica.

Romanisation system

For the romanisation of Arabic, the system adopted in this volume is that used by the Library of Congress. However, for editorial reasons, emphatic letters are assimilated to their corresponding non-emphatic letters and the pharyngeal 'ḥ' is assimilated to the glottal 'h'. The *tanwīn* is superscript. No prime is used.

Introduction

Citizenship is one of the key concepts underpinning both the vision and the philosophical basis of modern Western political thought. A broad range of disciplines employ it in a variety of contexts and with quite different connotations. As a result, the suggestive and multifaceted notion of citizenship proves hard to unravel, and even harder to define.

Identifying the main constituents of the concept, however, is a crucial preliminary step for comparative analysis – especially when comparing systems with fairly different approaches and largely distinct appraisals of such a concept. The purpose of capturing the salient features of citizenship is precisely to transcend the purely descriptive level of definitions and to track their development in the Arab world, thus reaching a deeper understanding of the issues involved.

In the quest for a core notion of citizenship, Aristotle's definition can be viewed as a starting point; both Western and Eastern scholars have used the Aristotelian definition as a basis, at times to refine it, sometimes to extend its scope or even to contest it.

Basic constituents of citizenship

Investigating the social and political nature of man was the innermost and earliest level of inquiry into the texture of human relations in ancient philosophy. In this context, Aristotle was the first to bring man to the centre of the stage and to argue that his distinctive character was his being 'political' (*politikòn*); human beings, unlike animals or gods, are political by nature (*Politics*: 1253a, 2-5). Aristotle opened his treatise on politics with this axiom, thus marking a sharp contrast with the structure of Plato's theory, whose main political work commenced with the definition of justice (*Republic*: 330d). Both authors share a teleological perspective, essentially believing in the primacy of the *polis*, but by assuming man as the cornerstone of the discourse Aristotle somehow surpassed and turned Plato's priority of the *polis* on its head.

Aristotle's axiom influenced generations of intellectuals both in the East and in the West. Nearly seventeen centuries after Aristotle's death,

the famous Arab Muslim polymath ibn Khaldūn still referred to the
opening of the *Politics* in the *Prolegomena* to his work on universal history. Ibn Khaldūn employed Aristotle's opening as the first premise to
the discourse on human civilisation (*al-ʿumrān al-basharī*): 'First: society (*al-ijtimāʿ al-insānī*) is necessary. Philosophers expressed this idea
with the phrase "man is political by nature" (*al-insān madanī bi-l-tabʿ*)'
(*al-Muqaddimah*: I, 1). Man's predicate 'political' (*madanī*) was built in
Arabic on the word used by Arab translators for *polis* (*madīnah*), thus
marking continuity with the Greek linguistic and philosophical
pattern.

According to Aristotle, man (*ánthrōpos*) leads by nature a social life,
whose typical form is the *polis*. Hence, the citizen (*polítēs*) – namely,
the man who actively takes part in public life by exercising political
and judicial functions (*Politics:* 1257a, 23-24) – is the human being who
fulfills his humanity. Before being a member of the *polis*, however,
man is a member of his family (*oikìa*), a minor social unit that Plato
looked at as a hindrance to his perfect city, whereas Aristotle considered it a 'natural' form of membership.

Aristotle's main legacy, however, is the identification of the basic co-
ordinates of citizenship, placing man at the centre and investigating
his relations with the political community. Transcending Plato's duality,
the philosopher pinned down the dependency of the political element
from a certain conception of mankind, in his reconciled vision of man,
body and soul. Following the developments of citizenship through the
ages, evidence can be gathered that major turning points occur precisely when the anthropological model changes; such was the case with
the Aristotelian model, a longstanding shared horizon for the Western
and Eastern political discourse.

In the West, Aristotle profoundly influenced ancient philosophy and
later Christian thinkers; through Scholasticism, Aristotle's conceptions
of man and society pervaded the European culture of the Middle Ages
and beyond, just when the issues of sovereignty and citizenship were
shaping up. Aspects of Aristotle's thought would continue to appeal to
modern philosophy, even when the latter forsook the systemic ideal. In
the Arab world, Aristotle is regarded as the uppermost philosopher
ever since al-Kindī (d. 873 AD), and Avveroes (ibn Rushd, d. 1198 AD)
defined him as '*exemplar quod natura invenit ad demonstrandum ulti-
mam perfectionem humanam*' (*Commentarium magnum*: III, 2, 433).
Aristotle is often remembered simply as the Philosopher both by Scho-
lastic and Arab scholars; Avveroes declared that Aristotle was his first
master, whereas his second master was al-Fārābī (d. 950 AD), author
of the *Virtuous City* inspired by Plato's *Republic*.

The treatise on *Politics*, however, was not included in the *Corpus Aris-
totelicum* of the Arabs. Avveroes himself, known in the West as Aristo-

tle's commentator, ignored Aristotle's *Politics* and wrote a commentary on Plato's *Republic*, just as al-Fārābī did. In the Latin world, too, Aristotle's *Politics* remained unknown until the second half of the 13th century, when the two translations attributed to William of Moerbeke appeared. Therefore, Aristotle's political theories influenced the ancient and early medieval world, both Latin and Arab, only in an indirect way, through other writings of the philosopher. Yet, his influence on ancient and modern political theory is not disputed and proves the underlying importance of the conception of man in the development of political thought.

Some scholars attribute the eclipse of *Politics* to its inherent inability to relate to any political entity other than the Greek *polis*, and the treatise sank into oblivion during the Hellenistic period (Viano 2002). It should cause little wonder, if a closer look into Aristotle's definition is taken; his definition of citizen is firmly and tightly bound to an archetypal political community that Alexander's conquests swept away.

The political community is the other major coordinate of citizenship. If we represent citizenship as an ellipsoid, the individual and the political community are its foci, whereas its main intersection points can be expressed in terms of membership, rights, participation or status, variously considered from the legal, philosophical, political or sociological planes. When the models of each focus change, the entire figure reshapes.

Classical models and early East-West contacts

The relationship between the individual and the political community has been explored everywhere through the ages. However, there are some experiences that have given rise to different models of citizenship: above all, the Greek participatory notion and the Roman status structure. The contrasting paradigms of citizenship in classical Greece and republican Rome affected the development of citizenship theories in the West more than in the Eastern world; when the two models were at their apex, contacts with the Arabs were fairly marginal.[1] The situation partly changed when two more stable political entities were established in northern Arabia: the Phylarchy of the Ghassanids and the Kingdom of the Lakhmids, the former in the orbit of the Byzantine Empire, and the latter allied to the Sassanids. At that point (3rd-7th centuries AD), though, the epoch of the Greek *poleis* and the Roman *civitas* was long over.

In the Eastern Byzantine provinces, neither the Greek nor the Roman classical concept of citizenship took root. In the Greek *polis*, the citizen's political participation was the cornerstone of city life, but for his ecumenical project Alexander preferred the ideal city of Plato's *Republic* to his own tutor's notion of citizen; thus, Hellenism did not spread the Greek idea of citizenship in terms of rights and duties that the individual had to exercise for the sake of the city. By contrast, the Roman concept of the citizen's status (entailing full capacity and subjection to Roman law) was still alive and well at the time of Rome's conquest of the eastern territories, but later died down as citizenship was granted to larger sections of the non-Roman population (especially under Caracalla and Justianian). Hence, Hellenism and the Roman Empire presented a fairly composite picture of citizenship to the Ghassanids, who were to become members of the important Syrian elite of Islam's early Umayyad caliphate.

As for the Persian Empire, it is quite problematical to define the position of the individual *vis-à-vis* authority in the late Sassanid age. The Persian tradition, however, placed the ruler and his rigid class system at the centre; such was most likely the attitude towards the subject that was perceived by the Lakhmids when brought under direct Sassanid control.

When Arabs made more direct contacts with Romans and Persians in the 5th and 6th centuries AD, citizenship did not represent or no longer represented the axis of the political discourse for these civilisations. Only after the Arab-Islamic conquest (*al-Fath*) did Arab scholars come across the different conceptualisations of citizenship in the ancient classics, during the golden age of translations between the 8th and the 10th centuries AD. Greek, Persian and Indian scientific classics were translated and easily taken in by the new, Arabic-speaking culture, but the methods and results of philosophy seemed incompatible with the basic tenets of Islam as they were being framed by Muslim theologians and jurists. Greek philosophy, whose texts reached Arab scholars through later, Neoplatonic readings, proved especially thorny for the Muslim intellectual; among the political works, Plato's dialogues abounded, and the Muslim scholar was thus called upon to take uncomfortable positions on irreconcilable conflicts like the one opposing the king-philosopher of Plato's *Republic* and the Islamic caliph. Legal scholars (*ᶜulamāʾ*) took a clear stance on the issue; philosophy could not play any role in an Islamic system and was to be banned from Islamic learning institutions, where the study of law had to prevail (*ᶜilm al-fiqh*). This did not prevent the flourishing of Arab-Islamic philosophy; however, it was forced to dwell outside the Islamic curriculum and only indirectly did it influence the religious sciences, which were strongly tied to Islamic law.[2]

Different civilisational paths

The Latin and the Arab worlds followed different paths, even if they both drew on Greek philosophy, which supplied categories and terminology later employed to deal with various new issues. In spite of the differences between Latin-Christian and Arab-Islamic results, the themes, the processes and somehow even the terms are analogous; this has always facilitated the comparison between the systems, but at the same time it has made the (op)positions look more extreme. It is hard to determine when the two paths drifted apart; up to the 13th century, anecdotes of Frederick II commending the Islamic caliphal system out of scorn for papal authority (Kantorowicz 1931) prove that a close comparison was still feasible, even if the two worlds were already significantly far removed from each other.

Latin and Arab scholars each searched for a foundation of political authority (sovereignty and *wilāyah*) in moments of power crisis. The masterpiece of literature on Islamic political authority (*wilāyah*) – *al-Ahkām al-sultānīyah* (The Ordinances of Government) – was written by al-Māwardī (d. 1058 AD) at a time when the role of the Abbasid caliph was being challenged by internal and external agents (11th century AD). Likewise, the theory of sovereignty was developed in Europe when local and universal powers were competing. Once fixed, though, the rules of Islamic *wilāyah* remained uncontested, whereas the development of the Western notion of sovereignty and of the underlying concept of citizenship had a much more intricate story.

The Arab-Islamic world did not suffer the kind of destruction brought about by the European Wars of Religion, and was thus not compelled to look for sources of legitimacy other than the religious one, which is the pivot of the *wilāyah*. Timewise, however, when sovereignty started being debated on the banks of the Seine, more than three centuries had elapsed since the waters of the Tigris had gone red with the blood and black with the ink of Baghdad, when the sack of the Mongols had delivered a decisive blow to what was left of the Abbasid caliphate. Even after the caliphate disappeared, Islam inflexibly maintained the ideal of the caliphal *wilāyah* and did not develop any other alternative theory; indeed, every once in a while the prospect of reinstating the caliphate is raised once again.

In the West, the concept of the individual started surfacing in the late Middle Ages against the backdrop of an orderly socio-political system characterised by the presence of local and universal powers. When, in the late 13th century, Aristotle's *Politics* reappeared in a Latin translation, its anthropological perspective of society as an 'orderly body' was adapted by Aquinas and Scholasticism; the famous definition of citizen was also accommodated in Remigio de' Girolami's version (*si non est civis non est homo*) and by Marsilius of Padua in the *Defensor Pacis* (Costa 1999-2001).

The longstanding influence of political Aristotelianism allowed for the continued vertical representation of society, and its vertex was the subject of reflection by intellectuals down to the early 17th century. Thinkers like Bodin or Althusius kept looking at the top of the pyramid, the former championing the principle of sovereignty, the latter of community. However, the individual was still immersed in a tangled web of relations and status within the community.

A major watershed in the history of citizenship was the revolution of the anthropological paradigm operated by natural law; the individual came to the centre of the stage, possessing natural rights prior to and irrespective of his affiliation in a political community. Thus, membership in a political community became a way of ensuring such rights, not their basis. Hobbes, Grotius, Locke and Pufendorf, as well as the various schools of natural law, proposed different solutions on how to frame the power, but all agreed on the individual's centrality and his 'absolute' natural rights. The elements of the political discourse were accordingly reorganised around the subject-of-rights, while holding on to the idea that the individual could escape the brutal struggle for survival only by turning to the 'absolute' power of the sovereign.

In the 18th century attention was paid to the individual, whose essence was encompassed within natural law but whose human existence was neglected, in an attempt to bridge the gap between the *Sein* and the *Sollen*. In a colourful variety of trends and currents, the Enlightenment combined expressions of natural law with corporative visions and republican values; ancient figures and new models were joined with unpredicted results, such as the concept of Rousseau's city. Rousseau, indeed, retrieved the primacy of the city and of membership in a political community (based, however, on the equality of members), drew on the republican legacy of the civil religion and the individual's civic virtue (with the individual, however, as a subject-of-rights) and based it all on the logic of identity (founding a 'common me' with some Hobbesian traits).

The French Revolution proudly proclaimed itself to be a turning point in the history of citizenship, but it actually brought to completion the design of what revolutionaries called the *Ancien Régime*. The individual, his rights and the political community were reshuffled, and the new foci of the ellipsoid became the subject-of-rights and the nation. 'Where is the nation to be found?' asked Sieyès in his *What is the Third Estate?*: in the nation of the twenty million citizens, not of the 200 thousand privileged Frenchmen. Such was the nation, called to establish by law – the full expression of its sovereignty – a new order where the rights of the subjects could take form.

The wind of the Revolution reached the Nile with the fleet of Napoleon, who occupied Egypt in 1798 during the war against the British Crown. The short Egyptian expedition marked the turn of the tide in Euro-Arab relations; after centuries of lateral political and military conflicts and contacts limited to the practical needs of commerce, the two blocs had once again entered into a face-to-face confrontation. Modern historiography currently downplays the alleged consequences of the expedition, but traditional Arab historians considered it one of the main external factors that generated the Arab renaissance (*al-Nahdah*). It was not only the army of the Franks (*al-Ifranj*, a denomination kept from the age of the crusades) that debarked in Alexandria, but also ideas that were alien to the Arab political discourse of the time, which Arabic was not even able to express. The Egyptian historian al-Jabartī (d. 1825 AD), for instance, when relating the expedition, preceded the French names with the title *sītwayān*, a transliterated form of *citoyen*, for lack of a better alternative in Arabic. The singular progression of the European political discourse since the golden age of philosophical interchanges between the Arab and the Latin world can be measured in terms of the lexical gap between the vocabulary of the Revolution and 19th-century Arabic. Concepts lexicalised as citizenship in Europe did not have lexical units in Arabic, and Arabic therefore had to draw on its vast language resources to fill the gap. Terminological choices, however, are not neutral or predetermined, but rather attest to the system's stance on the reception of a foreign concept.

Arabic terminology

The Eastern and Western worlds share a range of images of the political order, the main ones being the figures of the body politic and the pastoral representation of government. Yet conceptualisations of citizen and citizenship are alien to the traditional Arab-Islamic political discourse, and even their expression in Arabic required a lexical effort to find or introduce appropriate referents.

The standard term used to refer to 'people' in Arabic is *ahl*, a term common to all Semitic languages: *ahl* in Aramaic and *'ōhel* in Hebrew. It was first used to indicate the tent, and then, by metonymy, those who dwelled in the tent, i.e. relatives and family. The Arabic *ahl*, as the English 'people', denotes a body of persons who, indefinitely and collectively, constitute a community, but reference to the individual cannot be made. Unsurprisingly, the issue emerged when translators into Arabic approached the classics of Greek philosophy, where references to the individual *polìtēs* are abundant. Arab philosophers also had to address the challenge. A case in point is al-Fārābī's decision to use *ra'īs* to refer to the leader and the neologism *mar'ūs* to refer to the individual who is under the leader's jurisdiction; despite these choices he titled his work *Kitāb ārā' ahl al-madīnah al-fādilah* (The Views of the People (*ahl*) of the Virtuous City).

As far as the pastoral representation of power is concerned, the people under a certain authority are called *ra^cāyā* (herd, singular: *ra^cīyah*), and the ruler is called shepherd (*rā^cī*). The term *ra^cīyah* is not to be found in the Qur'ān, but it does appear in some problematic traditions.[3] In the mid-8th century it was being used, as is proven by the works of ibn al-Muqaffa^c (d. 756) or the Great Qadi abū Yūsuf (d. 798), who devoted a section of his *Kitāb al-kharāj* (The Book of Taxation) to the duties of the caliph as shepherd of the flock. Later on, *ra^cīyah* was still employed for the ruler-ruled dichotomy, the former being responsible to God for the latter. Under the Ottomans, the Turkish variant *raiyyet* (plural *reaya*) came to indicate the common subject as opposed to the entire government apparatus, including its military (*askeri*), bureaucratic (*kalemiye*) and religious (*ilmiye*) classes (Lewis 1988).

Starting in the early 19th century the tendency was to identify the subject as a *tābi^c* (plural *atbā^c*, in Turkish *tebaa*) with respect to his ruler; *tābi^c* is an active participle from the root *t.b.^c* meaning 'to follow', or 'to belong'. In the classical Ottoman terminology, *tābi^c* as 'dependent' or 'subordinate' was already being used to refer both to individuals and to places or functions, but in the 19th century it entered the legal-diplomatic jargon to translate the French '*sujet*'. The Ottoman *tebaa* was thus the individual who owed obedience to the sultan, just like British or Dutch 'subjects' but unlike French or American 'citizens'.

At the turn of the century, the nation-state and its nationality started to emerge in the Arab world. The spread of new ideas needed lexical referents that were not overly bound by traditional views and conceptions. For 'nationality', in the sense of the individual-state relationship, the term employed was *jinsīyah*. This is an abstract term built on *jins*, a borrowing from the Greek *ghènos*, which in Arabic kept the meaning of 'genus', 'race', 'species', and also acquired the meaning of 'gender'. The etymon *ghènos* is itself a stem of *ghèn*, which properly accommodates the role of descent in the attribution of nationality (*jinsīyah*) and stresses at the same time the perpetual nature of membership in the nation-state. Even if the term *jinsīyah* refers to an individual relationship to a state, it did not allow for the individuation of the national; indeed, the first Ottoman Nationality Law of 1869 employed the generic 'Ottoman' instead of 'Ottoman national'.

At the beginning of the 20th century, an Arab neologism – *muwātin* – was coined based on *watan* (originally the place of residence but later also the homeland; Ayalon 1987).[4] *Muwātin* is an active participle to a verb of stem III (*fāʿala*) from the root *w.t.n*; Arab grammarians define the *alif* added after the first radical of the verb as an *alif al-mushārakah*, viz. an *alif* (ā) that gives the verb a sense of sharing. The form **wātana*, therefore, would mean residing in the same place, and its active participle literally means a 'fellow countryman', in contrast to the *ajnabī*, or non-Arab foreigner. Just like 'citizen', *muwātin* relies on a relation with a place (namely the city) more than with an authority. Unlike 'citizen', however, *muwātin* does not immediately entail the idea of a status and rights enjoyed by the subject, but rather the simple distinction between the national and the foreigner. As Lewis put it, *muwātin* relates to a republican more than to a liberal citizenship, it being closer to the concepts of homeland and nation than to the concepts of liberties and rights (Lewis 1988). From the mid-20th century on, some civil and political implications started to be attached to the status of *muwātin*, just as individual political rights began to take root. In legal terms, the equation of 'citizen' and *muwātin* is generally established, even if the contents of citizenship vary according to each country's system. Even more recent is the shift to the abstract term *muwātanah* (citizenship), an expression still not included in many Arab dictionaries.

Subject, membership and rights in the Arab world

Exploring citizenship in the Arab world requires first a disentanglement from all those ideas, images and suggestions that have settled into the concept in the course of European political thought. Identifying the basic or primary constituents of citizenship demands a fairly high degree of abstraction and generalisation in order to include all its different expressions. Along these lines, stating that the discourse on citizenship has involved a variety of combinations of 'subject', 'membership' and 'rights' would embrace the Aristotelian definition as well as the contemporary debate on the new forms of constitutional and supranational citizenship.

The European experience shows that the establishment of 'membership', the rise of the 'subject' and conquest of 'rights' have not been simultaneous, even if they are somehow logically interdependent. Historically, the framing of membership has preceded the surfacing of the subject and the establishment of rights. Thus, approaching citizenship through 'membership' seems a viable and promising option, especially in the Arab world, where 'subject' and 'rights' depend even more crucially upon it.

The traditional Arab social structure was exclusively based on kin. The individual lived as a member of the kin group, and for it. The verse of Durayd ibn al-Simmah (d. 630 AD) is quite clear: 'I am but one of [the tribe of] Ghazīyah, if it strays, I stray, and if Ghazīyah leads the right way, I lead the right way' (*wa-mā anā illa min ghazīya^{ta} in ghawat gha-wayt^u wa-in tarshud ghazīya^{tu} arshud^i*). The kin bond is vivified by kin solidarity (*^{c}asabīyah*), which is – according to ibn Khaldūn (d. 1406 AD) – the fundamental bond of human society and the basic motivating force of history. In a context where an established, common authority is absent, the kin group is the framework by which all the activities of the individual are encompassed. All interpersonal relations are defined in terms of group relations, especially family ties and private justice, two key elements of the group's honour and nobility (*sharaf*). Even religious feelings were framed within the kin group, both the aspect of beliefs and the aspect of communal belonging; on the one hand, the group worshipped its own deities (along with other common deities) while on the other hand the choice of belonging and practising a certain religion rested with the group and not with the individual.

Abrahamic religions also spread in Arabia through group, not individual, conversions, but soon afterwards they tried to replace the kin tie with religious affiliation. Such was the case with Judaism and Christianity. But Muhammad's preaching had to engage with the kin system as well, which at first challenged and later supported him, notably after his successful political and military operations against Mecca. Even before the rise of Islam there is a record of at least one attempt to create a religious community beyond tribal allegiances: the ^{c}Ibād of Hira (a Christian community of Arab Nestorians). It is only after Muhammad's preaching, however, that Arabs who converted to Islam sought to form a coherent political and religious community. The goal of dissolving all particular kin ties in one universal religious community was not thoroughly achieved; indeed, the formative stages of the Islamic community prove on the contrary that traditional bonds were employed to create political unity and disseminate Islam. The gap between the ideal principle and the enculturating compromise can be observed from the standpoint of the reception of several pre-Islamic religious practices and legal institutions. Telling cases in point are the planning of newly-founded cities, the status of non-Arab neo-converts (*mawlàs*), the principle of wedding adequacy (*kafā'ah*) and the restriction of the caliphate to Quraish kinsmen. The way membership in the religious community was regulated also drew on fundamental characteristics of membership in the kin group: automatic, perpetual and exclusive. For many centuries, all the populations of the Middle East – Arab, Arabicised and non-Arabicised – lived in a political context dominated by the logic of religious affiliation. Regardless of all historic distinctive features, Muslims established political systems where Islam was the cornerstone; non-Muslims were treated with a discriminating tolerance that in the long run turned to the advantage of Islam.

The emergence of nation-states opened a new, controversial phase in Arab-Islamic history. The process that led to the creation of modern states in the Arab world followed different paths (Ottoman reforms, mandates of the League of Nations or direct intervention of European powers in atypical protectorates), introducing a new system of international relations no longer based on the principle that each part protects its fellow coreligionists (like France for Eastern Catholics, or Russia for the Orthodox Churches of Greece and the Holy Land), but rather on the premise that each state safeguards its own citizens. During the same years in Europe, vertical 'nationality' (in French *nationalité* and in German *Staatsangehörigkeit*) and horizontal 'citizenship' (in French *citoyenneté*, and in German *Bürgerschaft*) joined in the liberal model state. The Arab course of action was much more tortuous, definitely more complicated than what French scholars suggest by quoting a ruling of a French tribunal.[5] Numerous pointers suggest that the kin and religious orders maintain a certain vitality. Illuminating cases in point can be found in the judicial systems. Upon attainment of independence, tribal courts, confessional judges and state tribunals operated simultaneously almost everywhere in the Arab world. Afterwards, however, the trend changed and state tribunals began to take on the jurisdiction of 'lower' courts; lower courts were abolished by law, and legislation regulating tribal custom and religious law was often passed. Likewise, the need to comply with some Islamic precepts required the adaptation of some rules regarding conflict of laws (or international private law), and a special 'Islamic international private law' (*al-qānūn al-duwalī al-khāss al-islāmī*) was then developed. Membership in the kin group and in the religious community is still a relevant element for modern citizenship, both for the vertical nationality (e.g. naturalisation or stripping of nationality on grounds of kin or religious affiliation) and the horizontal citizenship (e.g. kin group political representation or confessional constituencies).

In the fascinating but extreme variety that characterises the Arab world, is there any reason to group all the multiform realities in a single Arab citizenship? What do the peoples of the foothills of the Atlas, of the Trucial Coast, of the Nile valley, of the banks of the Euphrates or of Mount Lebanon share? On the one hand, most of these people are not even ethnically Arab, since the majority is made up of Arabicised peoples. On the other hand, the majority are Sunni Muslims, but there are other significant Muslim, Christian and Jewish minorities. Moreover, while there is no doubt that actual borders do not include homogeneous areas, it is nonetheless undeniable that language and cultural frontiers run across the Arab world, often making communication and interchange impossible.

Yet, the composite human arch that bridges the Arab Gulf and the Atlantic Ocean does share some political and legal modalities which affect the way individuals lead their public life in the Arab legal environment as well as their relations with the kin group, the religious community and the nation-state. By looking into each one of these three main forms of membership, how they influence each other, reciprocally interfere and combine, some of the major issues of citizenship in the Arab world can be addressed.

1 Membership in the kin group

The first form of membership known by man is membership in the family. This fairly obvious consideration, framed in Aristotle's theory, has long informed Western political theory and its stance on citizenship in particular.[1] In the Arab world the family (in its broader sense of kin group) plays an even greater role and proves to be fairly resilient to external pressures. In order to identify the genuine features of the Arab kin, we need to look through its pre-Islamic patterns, when competing forms of membership were quite trivial.

A telling starting point is how classical Islamic authors represent the Arab social system. Their representation turns out to be discrepant with pre-Islamic sources; historiography accounted for the lack of conformity, and anthropology has developed explanatory models for the Arab social and political order. Once the social context is outlined, the dynamics of inclusion and exclusion from the kin become easily accessible; the kin arranges and handles its internal affairs and the relationships with other groups on the basis of customs, which are by nature fluid.

On the eve of Islam, Arabia presented a widely homogeneous social configuration, despite the different kinds of political organisations.[2] In the heart of the Peninsula, the traditional social order and political life flourished in the absence of a centralised power. But the development of more complex political structures in the northern areas – due to contacts with the Byzantine and Sassanid Empires – did not prevent the perpetuation of the customary social articulations. The same was true in the southern region in the realm of Kindah. Likewise, the same social types are shared by nomadic (*badw*) and sedentary (*hadar*) groups, the two opposed icons of Arab society.

1.1 Representing the social prism

No scientific certainty has been reached on the origins of the Arabs. On the one hand, all the sources available at present date from the Islamic era – that is to say, they are quite late – while on the other hand none of the pre-Islamic engraved inscriptions support the traditional structure presented by Islamic scholars, whose accounts are openly oriented towards a theological end.[3]

To begin with, Islamic historians and genealogists divide the Arabs into three 'layers' (tabaqāt): 'extinct Arabs' (al-ʿarab al-bāʾidah), 'pure Arabs' (al-ʿarab al-ʿāribah) and 'arabicised or arabicising Arabs' (al-ʿarab al-mustaʿribah aw al-mutaʿarribah). According to these authors, among the 'extinct Arabs' are all the tribes that lived in the Arabian Peninsula until God determined to punish them (awqaʿa allāh bi-hādhihi al-qabāʾil al-ʿiqāb) and wipe them out for having disobeyed their prophets (li-annahum ʿasū anbiyāʾahum) and not having followed the straight path (al-tarīq al-sawī) that God had ordered.[4] A distant but clear echo of a motive dear to the Jewish mentality of the Torah can be heard here. The roots of present-day 'Arabity' (ʿurūbīyah) are the 'pure Arabs', descendants of Qahtān or Yaqtān (the Yōqtān that Genesis genealogically links to Noah; Gen. 10:25).[5] The 'arabicised or arabicising Arabs', on the contrary, are believed to be the descendants of Ishmael through ʿAdnān, but in this case the genealogy does not match the Biblical line exactly.[6] The label 'arabicised' is due to the belief that Ishmael spoke Hebrew (sic!) until he got to Mecca, where he married a Yemeni woman and learnt Arabic. Both genealogical lines go back to Sem, son of Noah, but only ʿAdnanites can claim Abraham as their ascendant, and the lineage of Mohammed, the Seal of Prophets (khātim al-anbiyāʾ), can therefore be traced back to Abraham. Contemporary historiography unveiled the lack of inner coherence of this genealogical system and demonstrated that it finds insufficient matching evidence; the distinction between Qahtanites and ʿAdnanites is even believed to be a product of the Umayyad Age, when the war of factions (al-nizāʿ al-hizbī) was raging in the young Islamic Empire.[7]

According to Islamic tradition, Arabs are the kinsmen of ʿAdnān and Qahtān; the descendants of the former (the ʿAdnanites) settled in central and northern Arabia, while the descendants of the latter (the Qahtanites) in the south. In al-Māwardī's classification (later adopted by al-Qalqashandī), five other levels stem from the ʿAdnanites-Qahtanites partition (the shaʿb): the qabīlah, the ʿimārah, the batn, the fakhdh and the fasīlah.

In the author's view, the shaʿb of the ʿAdnanites is made up of two qabīlahs, the one of the Rabīʿah and the other of the Mudar; both are divided into ʿimārahs. In the qabīlah of the Mudar we can mention the ʿimārah of the Kinānah and of the Quraish, and among the Quraish the two batns of the ʿAbd manāf and the Makhzūm. Down the line of smaller groupings of the ʿAbd manāf we find the fakhdhs of the Hāshim and of the Umayyah, and we eventually reach the fasīlahs of ʿAbbās, abū Tālib, or abū Sufyān.[8]

Not all the authors, however, use the same vocabulary or classification. Even al-Qalqashandī presents in his work the different arrangement of ibn al-Kalbī, who introduced a middle partition between the *fakhdh* and the *fasīlah* – the *ʿashīrah* (a small group stemming from a relatively close progenitor) – and used *fasīlah* in the sense of smaller family (*Subh al-aʿshà*: 309). Other Muslim authors employ an even wider terminology and disregard the rigid structures put forward by genealogists; a whole set of terms like *hayy* or *qawm* are used to refer to larger groups, and *bayt* or *dār* for the nuclear family.

Moreover, there is no agreement regarding the placement of the groups in the same categories. For instance, al-Māwardī and al-Qalqashandī consider the Quraish and the Kinānah two *ʿimāras* of the *qabīlah* of the Mudar (ibid.), while for the *Muntaqà* the Kinānah are a *qabīlah* and the Quraish an *ʿimārah* thereof (ed. Wüstenfeld: II, 340). Other patent cases can be found in the works of ibn al-Kalbī, ibn Hazm, al-Jawharī, ibn ʿAbd rabbih, al-Qālī or al-Bakrī.

As noted, all these classifications are the product of later Islamic theory as well as the search for a rigid terminology, typical of the rigorous *ʿilm al-nasab* (a real 'science of lineages') and not of a diverse and politically fluctuating social context. Textual analysis clearly shows that terms like *hayy*, *qabīlah*, *batn* or *fakhdh* do not have precise connotations in Arabic; indeed, al-Qalqashandī, after describing al-Māwardī's hexapartition (which he closely follows), dwells on the point that *hayy* is used strictly for one of the six categories and collectively for the sons of a specific individual. No easier is defining *ʿashīrah* or *raht*, probably a group made up of less than ten kinsmen. Relevant discrepancies can be traced as well when comparing the vocabulary of classical Islamic authors and pre-Islamic poetry, where terms like *ʿimārah* or *fasīlah* never occur (Tyan 1954: 14). Adopting a fixed translation of the Arabic terminology with 'tribe', 'clan' or 'sub-clan' would be inconvenient; on the one hand English lacks so many and such nuanced expressions for such unfamiliar social articulations, and on the other hand the operation would entail choosing between quite different scholarly solutions. Furthermore, Arabic terms convey a certain symbolism such as the somato-anthropomorphic idea suggested by *batn* (belly) or *fakhdh* (thigh).

Anthropology developed different paradigms (like the segmentary model) to explain the Arab social context and dynamics, and recent trends – emerging within the traditional segmentary scheme – openly challenge the rigidity of the classical systematisation of Islamic scholars. The segmentary model was first conceived in the 1940s for the Nuer of Sudan (Evans-Pritchard 1940) and later adapted to Arab social organisation. It builds on a generally uncontested representation of the social order in terms of genealogical relations among groups bound by the principle of common patrilineal descent. Thus, single groups of descent (kin groups), or segments, are key constituents of society, the structure of which is determined by their mutual relations, being a complex of segments engrafted one into the other (Fabietti 2002: 66). In the segmentary model, descendants of a closer ancestor unite against descendants of a more distant ancestor; that is to say that descendants of brothers join against descendants of cousins, and descendants of cousins of the same stock join against descendants of cousins of a different stock, and so forth. Likewise, groups – despite their distance up the genealogical tree – put aside their conflicts in order to face groups that do not belong to the same lineage.

The rigidity of the segmentary model imposed a serious impoverishment on its heuristic potential, even if the model contributed to the abandoning of a certain typological and functionalistic vision and allowed a more penetrating analysis of the political and institutional dimensions of segmentary societies. By favouring a static vision, the intrinsic dynamism of the Arab genealogical system has been largely underestimated, and the resulting limits and flaws have been attributed to the segmentary model itself. Recent ethnographic reports show major variations in the genealogical system surveyed by early scholars; for instance, in the case of the Āl Rammāl (northern Arabia), Montagne's reports of the late 1920s (Montagne 1947) are rather different from Fabietti's reports of the late 1970s (Fabietti 1984). These are incompatible findings that can only be regarded as sagacious genealogical rationalisations if we consider the continuous process of realignment of segments operated by prominent personalities of the group (shaykhs), who conceptually alter the formal order of society according to different political strategies and current opportunities.[9]

A number of factors play a role in easing the operations of segmentary reorganisation in the classical Arab world. First of all, the individual is identified by a given name (ism) and a patronymic (nasab, in the form of 'son of'), while the occurrence of a 'kin name' is fairly exceptional. A 'surname' (laqab) follows the name only when the individual stands out for a distinctive activity or origin.[10] Such a nominal system facilitates the contextual definition of the individual identity, since the relationship with the kin is not enshrined in the name. Secondly, genealogies in the Arab world are an oral knowledge, and only later did Islamic scholars – pursuing religious goals – found a science of lineages (ʿilm al-nasab) that tried to impose rigidity on the social order through writing. Thirdly, it is a knowledge in the hands of an elite (the notables, or shaykhs); the elite determines the major or minor genealogical distance of the segments in a constant process of manipulation – deliberate or unintentional, as Fabietti underlines – by omissions, additions or replacements. In the shaykhs' operation the 'historical' value decreases in order to increase the impact of the rationalisation of the *status quo*, or the prefiguration of future relations among segments (Fabietti 2002: 62-78).

In spite of all the possible hindrances, we can outline and point out some of the characteristics of the complex social organisation of Arabia. To begin with, society is structured in distinct, self-ruling groups of varying size, despite any common origins or real or fictitious common ancestors. Secondly, the key factor is the personal and not the territorial element, the former shaping even urban settlements, like the Quraish in Mecca or the different groups of Yathrib, the future Medina (Lammens 1924b: 296). Finally, all the members of the group share the same religion,[11] as in the case of the Quraish running the sacral functions of the Ka°bah, the Jews of Yathrib and the Christians of the north like the Lakhmids (Nestorians) and the Ghassanids (Monophysites).

1.2   Inclusion by kinship, clientage or slavery

In pre-Islamic Arabia the individual was considered a member of a group by means of kinship, clientage or slavery. Some of these means were particularly effective in the political and legal context of a society characterised by diffuse power, and the emergence of a centralised power has therefore reduced their effectiveness, while others have lasted, even if some distinctions have faded.

Kinship

'Kinship' is the main bond for the Arab kin group. Membership in the group is determined by descent from a real or fictitious common ancestor, and the group itself is known as *banū Fulān*, 'the sons of Tom'.

The first and original member is identified as a *sarīh* (free, pure), in order to tell him apart from the client or the slave. As a general rule, it is by patrilineal descent that membership is established. Applying the principle extensively, every child born to a member of the group is considered a member, even if the mother conceived him in a previous union.[12] In a similar manner, all the children of a widow who are still minor become members of the group of the new husband, but when they come of age they are allowed to be reintegrated into their original group (Robertson Smith 1885: 142). However, if the mother belongs to a group higher in the social ranks, matrilineal descent prevails and the mother's offspring belong to the mother's group.

Only the child born of Arab parents of the same kin group is a full member. Here, too, the term *sarīh* is employed, even if in a second, narrower sense (Tyan 1954: 19). The child of an Arab man and a foreign woman (*a°jamīyah*) is a *hajīn* (ignoble), kept out of the father's

succession and with half the blood money due for the *sarīh*. Inferior to
the *sarīh* is also every child born of parents who do not belong to the
same kin group, and every child born of a mother who is a slave or
was abducted in a *ghazw*, the latter being held in an even lesser regard
and enjoying even fewer rights. Hence the recurrence in Arab poetry
of the boast of being born of a free mother (*hurrah*) or a mother married under payment of a dower (*mahīrah*).

The establishment of artificial descent – adoption (*tabannī*) – also determines membership in a kin group. Largely practiced, adoption could
concern either a free minor whose father had died and whose mother
had returned into her group or a slave who was freed upon adoption.
Adoption had the same legal effects as biological descent with respect
to the name of the *da'īy* (adopted, bastard), marriage bars, inheritance
rules and help-and-assistance duties (al-Mubarrad, *al-Kāmil*: II, 16).

Acknowledging a child born of a slave mother rehabilitates the child,
who would otherwise follow the mother's condition. The acknowledgement is up to the father, who decides to give his name (the *nasab*) to
his slave's child. This is illustrated in the story of ʿAntarah, the hero
that embodies the values of Arab chivalry (*furūsīyah*); for ʿAntarah's
merits and courage, ʿAntara's father Shaddād acknowledges him (*yaʿ-
tarif bi-l-walad*), making him ʿAntarah ibn Shaddād (al-Isfahānī,
al-Aghānī: VIII, 237).

The wife's condition deserves a little consideration as well. Arabs
have quite a distinctive preference for endogamy (marriage within the
kin group), and for the marriage of a man to his parallel cousin (the
daughter of his father's brother) in particular.[13] In the case of endoga-
mic marriage, therefore, no question arises on which group the woman
belongs to, while in the case of exogamic marriage the wife generally
becomes a member of the husband's group; the woman moves in with
her husband (virilocal marriage), and their children become members
of the husband's group (according to patrilineal descent). The blood
bond between the woman and her group, however, still exists albeit
quiescently; in case of divorce, the bond is revived and the woman returns to her group.

Affinity (*musāharah*), on the contrary, does not interfere with the inner structure of the group, even if it is commonly used to foster social
and political connections among different groups.

Clientage

The institution of 'clientage' (*walā'*) emerged to meet with the fundamental need of protection of the individual in the absence of a centralised power (al-Miqdār 1980: 23-72). In the society of the Arabian
Peninsula, characterised by such diffuse power, the individual was not
entitled rights; only his membership in a group ensured him a certain

protection. Outside the group, the individual became a mere outcast who, without anybody to protect him, was at the mercy of any aggressor. Membership in a group was thus a necessary condition (Tyan 1954: 23). All those who were no longer members of any group were in earnest need of finding a patron and becoming clients. Lack of membership was the condition of freed slaves, those who voluntarily rescinded their bond of membership or were excluded from it according to custom, and foreigners who decided to dwell among the Arabs.

The *walā'* occurred between the future client (*mawlà*) and a man of the group. The client was then designated the '*mawlà* of the man', even if the *walā'* was used to bind the whole group to the protection of the *mawlà*. Apart from the clientage that resulted from the manumission of the slave (*mawlà ^citāqah*), 'ordinary' *walā'* was a contract that created reciprocal rights and duties, and the client was indicated as *^caqīd* or *mawlà ^ciqd* (from the root *^c.q.d* of 'contract'). Technically no payment was required, but chronicles relate cases in which the *mawlà*s offered compensations to win the group's support, even if it was a reprobate practice. The ways to contract *walā'* varied according to local traditions, but all of them included some sort of solemnity[14] and were followed by a reciprocal oath, the *hilf*. The term *hilf* comes from the root *h.l.f*, as do the verb *tahālafa*, used to indicate the conclusion of the contract of *walā'*, and the noun *halīf*, a synonym of *mawlà* and *^caqīd*.

In pre-Islamic Arabia, there was almost no distinction between a *mawlà* and a member of the group by kinship. Not so in the Islamic era. Some Arab proverbs confirm the pre-Islamic egalitarian treatment of *mawlà*s, and Islamic tradition attributes these proverbs to Muhammad: 'The client of the kin group is one of their own (*mawālī al-qawm minhum*)'[15] and 'clientage is kinship like kinship by blood (*al-walā' luhmah ka-luhmat al-nasab*)'.[16] Fulfilling the duty of protecting the *mawlà*'s physical safety and property was a point of honour for the group and was celebrated in the literary genre of vainglorious poetry (*fakhr*). These principles, however, were at times coupled with different practices of discrimination between client and full member according to local customs.

Slavery

'Slavery' actually did not entail a true form of membership in the kin group, since the slave was considered the mere property of the master. As a master's property, however, the slave enjoyed the protection of the group, and upon manumission slaves represented the largest source of clients. The slave was such by being born of a slave mother even if the father was a freeman (unless he acknowledged the child) or by being reduced to slavery after a clash among groups or after a case of individual aggression.

1.3   Severance from the group

If membership in a group was a necessary bond, it was not unbreak-
able. The bond could be severed at the individual's will (if he intended
to become a member of another group) or against his will. The group's
prevailing interest could require the estrangement of a member if he
caused internal disturbances, if the group's responsibility for his actions jeopardised their relations with another group or if protecting
him meant the endangering of the group's own existence.[17] In these
circumstances, kinsmen could inflict the penalty of expulsion (*tard* or
*khal*ᶜ) on the member without prejudicing their rights of *tha'r* (vengeance) on the offender. The kinsmen's decision was publicised by a
munādī (announcer), and as a consequence the blood of the *khalī*ᶜ (dismissed) could be shed with impunity (*hadar*). The *khalī*ᶜ could not but
seek protection from another group as a *mawlà* or temporary refuge in
the Meccan sanctuary, thus becoming a ᶜ*ā'idh bi-l-bayt*, secure against
any attack.

1.4   Customary law

In the Arabian Peninsula the legal system consisted exclusively of customary rules. Whether common or limited to a certain area or group,
these customs ruled all the spheres of human life, regulating all social,
political and religious expressions. By their very nature, customary
rules resist every individual attempt at modification; they are within
the province neither of the chieftain nor the assembly of notables.

There are records that attribute the determination of a rule to a specific personality. These records need to be considered with caution;
such records are often not genuine, and even when the innovation was
introduced by a specific person, this person was certainly not acting as
a 'legislator' or a 'reformer'. The new solution had to gain a hold in society to be deemed binding, and here the general esteem enjoyed by
the person and his moral authority may have very easily played a part.
A case in point is the fixation of the blood money (*diyah*) for murder at
one hundred camel heads. Ibn Saᶜd relates that ᶜAbd al-muttalib, Muhammad's grandfather, was the one who raised the *diyah* for murder
from ten to one hundred camel heads (*Tabaqāt*: I, 53-70), but ibn Qutaybah says it was Sayyārah al-ᶜAdwānī, openly criticising ibn Saᶜd's
narrative (*Kitāb al-maᶜārif*: 240).

1.5 Private justice and arbitration

For lack of a judicial system in pre-Islamic Arabia – a natural outcome of the lack of a centralised power – all the controversies were resolved by vengeance (*tha'r*) or arbitration (*tahkīm*).

Resorting to private justice was the general rule in the Peninsula, since no public authority could assure justice. Vengeance (*tha'r*) governed all matters, from murder to injuries, all the way down to torts. Satisfaction was exacted among members of different groups or members of the same group; in the former case vengeance was more common, since the offence roused feelings of the group's solidarity and honour, while in the latter case the dispute tended to be settled without avenging.

Tha'r is not an act of objective justice but rather tends to satisfy a broader moral and physical need,[18] and its exercise is viewed as the fulfilment of an ethical and religious duty.[19] The lawful avenger of blood, the *mawtūr* or *walī al-dam*, solemnly undertakes to abstain from pleasures until he takes revenge, and until then these pleasures become forbidden (*harām*) to him. In the Arab mentality the victim's soul remains in a condition of pain until the murder is avenged; the soul is wrapped in darkness until *tha'r* lights up the tomb. Shame is brought on the *mawtūr* negligent of his duties, and when the lawful avenger of blood does not accomplish his task, other members have to intervene in order to safeguard the group's reputation; poets stigmatise the remiss *mawtūr* or the *mawtūr* who renounces vengeance for settlement or arbitration.

Only a direct supernatural intervention could discharge the avenger from the religious duty of vengeance. This results in a clever manoeuvre to free the *mawtūr* and the group from the obligation: the *taᶜqīyah* or *sahm al-iᶜtidhār*. Prominent personalities from the group form a sizeable delegation that asks the lawful avengers of blood to desist from *tha'r* and accept customary blood money (*diyah*). The offer is rejected if the avengers are determined to take revenge; otherwise, they accept the *diyah* on condition that the deities prove favourable. An arrow (*sahm*) is shot in the sky; if it returns to the ground soaked in blood, the compensation cannot be accepted. This solution, however, did not prevent the poets from voicing their sarcasm.

Vengeance does not follow a rigid procedure, yet a certain degree of ritualisation is present. Firstly, the *mawtūr* has to give public notice of the evidence for vengeance in order to ground his claim and avoid further violence; at this stage the *mawtūr* might swear to abstain from worldly pleasures. When actually carrying out the vengeance, the *mawtūr* utters a sacral formula before the *coup de grâce*. Once accomplished, *tha'r* is publicised to substantiate the termination of the duty and the release from the promise of abstention.

Arbitration (*tahkīm*) developed from the practice of negotiating to fix the amount of composition for murder or injuries (Tyan 1960: 33ff). Thus the resolution of controversies over property, water, commerce or inheritance was subtracted from the province of vengeance, together with the settling of moral disputes like those that originated or were solved in poetry contests (*munāfarah*, or *mufākharah*).

The parties freely choose the arbitrator (*hakam*), who must be an outstanding man of 'honour, uprightness, loyalty, prestige, seniority, glory and divination' (al-Ya'qūbī, *Tārīkh*: 299). In the sources there is no evidence that the *hakam* and the chieftain coincided (not even in Mecca, Lammens 1924a: 158ff); the choice was rather influenced by the religious status, as in the case of the Christian bishops of Najrān (Cheikho 1890-1891: 369), the Jewish *habrs* (Wolfensohn 1927: 21) and the pagan *kāhins* (Lammens 1921: 44). The habit of testing the arbitrator's supernatural faculties increased the identification of the *hakam* with the *kāhin*, the 'diviner' who proved his skills with oracles, sacred arrows or invocations for rain (*istisqā'*).

The very first step to reaching arbitration was the agreement to remit the solution of the controversy to an arbitrator; the parties were often advised to do so, and members of the parties' groups were present throughout the proceedings. Secondly, the object of the controversy was fixed, then an arbitrator was selected; the arbitrator could refuse the task, or accept and impose as a condition the performance of the arbitral decision, and the deliverance of pledges to secure it. Once the arbitrator accepted the task, the parties verified the *hakam*'s faculties in some way – by asking him to find an object that they had previously hidden, for instance (al-Nuwayrī, *Nihāyat al-arab*: III, 127f). Additional hostages (*ruhūn*) could be then handed over to a guarantor (*damīn*), but it is not clear what was to be their destiny in case of non-compliance with the arbitrator's decision. Tyan supposes that the hostages could even be handed to the winner and enslaved (Tyan 1960: 56f). Pleadings were conducted in *saj'*, a rhymed prose used also by the *hakam* for the decision, where it was not uncommon to find references to the supernatural or invocations of the deity.

1.6   The chieftain and the assembly

The lack of a centralised power does not necessarily imply the lack of any form of political and institutional organisation. Actually, such forms of organisation are more 'at ease' when there are no other structures competing with them, and therefore reveal their innermost character. Being intrinsically dynamic, there is no need for inflexible classifications or a rigid terminology, which can turn out to be quite misleading. This is true also for pre-Islamic Arabia, for which a delineation of some of the basic governing principles is sufficient at this point.[20]

The authority of a chieftain is believed to have emerged through the institutionalisation of the leader chosen at times by the group to face a specific threat. Within the broad spectrum of human actions, individuating the leader, or leaders, could range from a mere tacit assent to more explicit choices. Two remarkable cases of clear choices are related in the sources. In the first, ibn Qutaybah says that the Hawāzin bestowed (ta'ahhadū, from the root '.h.d) on Durayd ibn al-Simmah the headship that belonged to his brother 'Abd allāh after the latter died in an incursion (al-Shi'r wa-l-shu'arā': 472). In the second, the banū Hanīfah appointed (tawallū, from the root w.l.y, form II) Hārith ibn 'Abbād after he excelled in the war of Basūs (Cheikho 1890-1891: 271).

When the threat disappeared, the need for a chief disappeared as well. However, the person who led the threatened group was likely to retain a certain prestige among his peers, particularly if the group had been successful. Sources do not provide sufficient data to enable a precise delineation of the path taken by an individual to chieftainship, but their silence, occasionally broken by presumably legendary anecdotes, confirms that by nature it was a process by trial and error. Likewise, there is no record of any conferment of powers, which rather were concentrated in the hands of the leader and were later reabsorbed by the group. This apparently was the delicate phase of transition from emergency to stability.

The chieftain was usually called sayyid or ra'īs, but the essence of his functions (su'dud or ri'āsah) did not reach the level of political authority (mulk); he enjoyed a mere primacy that did not allow him to impose his decisions (ibn Khaldūn, al-Muqaddimah: II, §16). The sayyid could express his opinion (ra'y) but was accompanied by delegations (wafds) to carry out any negotiations with other groups, even if he was personally liable for the payment of blood money.[21] In time of war, the chieftain's powers were considerably increased, and the title of qā'id (commander) was then preferred to the one of sayyid.[22] The chieftain was generally a man of age (hence the occurrence of the title of shaykh as well),[23] temperance (hilm),[24] generosity, courage and military talent.

Regular gatherings of notables are widely recorded, but no detail is given on the composition, entitlements or powers of such assemblies. Belonging to one of these 'assemblies' (variably designated as nādī, nadwah, or mala') was considered an honour, worth celebrating in the encomiastic poetry of madīh. On these grounds only prominent personalities were deemed worthy to sit in the assembly.[25] As for entitle-

ments and powers, the assembly had no decision making power; matters of general interest were discussed and members offered their
counsel or advice (shūrà). These assemblies were consultative and non-
binding in nature. Their existence, however, attests to the need for
communal discussion and sharing of questions that affect the whole
group.

2 Membership in the religious community

The social and political milieu of pre-Islamic Arabia considerably affected the spread of monotheistic religions, which assumed the social order as a vehicle for their diffusion, but soon endeavoured to replace the traditional forms of membership with the sole bond of common faith.

Before the rise of Islam, Judaism was professed by Jews of the diaspora and by Arab converts, and its main centres were located in the coastal region of Hejaz and in Yemen. These communities are thought to have been established after the destruction of Jerusalem in the 2nd century AD, but these are still clouded chapters of Arab history.

An even greater role was played by Christianity, which penetrated Arabia from the north as a result of the missionary efforts of Syriac dissidents, and from the south thanks to the political involvement of Coptic Abyssinia (Rabbath 1980). Known in its Monophysite and Nestorian variants, Christianity evoked interest among the Arabs, as attested in ancient poetry. According to available sources, Monophysites systematically devoted their efforts to preaching to the Bedouins and appointed a bishop for every large camp, thus allowing nomads to retain their customs. Nestorians, by contrast, established an episcopate in Hira (Mesopotamia), where Christians formed a community of ʿIbād ('servants' of God) that transcended the kin order, abolishing descent-based distinctions; this is the first known case of an ideologically defined Arab group that combined tribal organisation with the functions of a religious community.

2.1 The formation of the Islamic community

With Muhammad's public preaching of the revelation, the process towards the formation of a religious community and the creation of a centralised political power in Arabia was set in motion. At its culmination, the Islamic community embraced all those who shared the same faith in Islam, but in the intermediate stages the connection was less rigid and exclusive, and the new political authority correspondingly extended over an area not strictly delimited by religious affiliation.

The process was gradual, though not incremental. Progression was frequently followed by sudden regression, and remarkable policy or strategy shifts were often recorded. The dynamic confrontation between the new creed and the traditional social order, the attempts to bring about a power independent of personal charisma, and the ups and downs of the relations with the other 'heavenly religions' all provide evidence of this course of action.

In the formative period of the Islamic community, we can distinguish three main phases along with the conventional distinction in a Meccan and a Medinan stage; the first phase and the Meccan stage basically overlap, while a second and a third phase can be identified in the Medinan stage, since the early coexistence of Muslims, Jews and pagans in Medina rapidly faded and dramatically ended with the purge of the last Jewish tribe, leaving the field to a holistic community.

In the first phase (from 610 to 622), the background consisted of Muhammad's preaching and his fellow tribesmen's refusal of the message. The new ideas were proclaimed at first in a climate of general indifference. However, as soon as they turned into open criticism and firm condemnation of the moral and social order of Mecca, they generated opposition among the Quraish (al-Maqrīzī, Imtā^c: I, 18). The Islamic tradition tends to emphasise the 'persecutions' that neophytes had to endure at the hands of the Meccans; in the beginning Muhammad's opponents only verbally criticised the former's teachings and prophethood, and the sole form of active hostility seems to have been a boycott (Montgomery Watt 1953: 123). The call to submit to God's will – hence the etymological meaning of Islam – met with tepid reception, and thus Muhammad and his proselytes started leading a life secluded from the rest of the Meccans (some followers even took shelter in the Aksumite Empire, in the so-called 'Hegira to Abyssinia') and took up preaching to other kin groups.

In 619, Muhammad's uncle abū Tālib died, leaving him without protection. In the system of kin group relations, enjoying someone's protection was a vital issue, and the Prophet of Islam had to replace abū Tālib with someone else. He therefore applied to abū Lahab, who turned him down on the grounds of Muhammad's belief that their common ancestor ^{c}Abd al-muttalib was doomed. Since no Quraish was willing to protect him, Muhammad turned to other kin groups in want of protection; at this point, as has been suggested (Montgomery Watt 1953: 138), the horizons of the prophetic mission – originally limited to Mecca and its inhabitants – expanded to reach a larger audience.

Muhammad expected to find support in Ta'if among the banū Mālik as a consequence of their rivalry with the Quraish-allied Ahlāf, but the plan failed and the Prophet of Islam had to leave the city under a volley of stones. Because of abū Lahab's refusal, Muhammad could not even return to Mecca and had to obtain a *jiwār*, a 'pact of protection' (ibn Hishām, *Sīrah*: 251, and al-Tabarī, *Mukhtasar*: I, 1203), at first denied by some tribal chiefs and eventually granted by the *sayyid* of the banū Nawfal (Mélamède 1934: 17-58).

Nomadic groups did not provide better treatment, but Yathrib presented more promising conditions. Yathrib – the future *Madīnat al-nabī* (the City of the Prophet), or Medina (the City by antonomasia) – was a divided settlement: on the one hand, the two main kin groups (the ᶜAws and the Khazraj, both stemming from the banū Qaylah) had been at strife ever since the 6th century, and on the other hand there was a sizeable presence of Jewish tribes (the banū Qurayzah, the banū Qaynuqāᶜ, and the banū 'l-Nadīr).

The first contact with a small delegation of six Khazraj in Mecca for the pilgrimage was made in 620. The following year (621), five of the six pilgrims of the previous year returned to Mecca with another seven people, including two ᶜAws. In ᶜAqabah they committed themselves to avoid some vices and follow the new religion: such is the content of the so-called 'Oath of Women' (*bayᶜat al-nisā'*). With the joining of non-Quraish, Islam crossed the traditional kin boundaries, even if the oath entailed nothing but a religious obligation. After the first *bayᶜah* of ᶜAqabah, Muhammad sent to Yathrib Musᶜab ibn ᶜUmayr, who won to Islam many converts from almost all the kin groups of the settlement.

In 622, a larger group of 75 people from Yathrib returned to ᶜAqabah, where they made the stricter commitment to fight for the Prophet of Islam; the new oath is thus remembered as the 'Oath of War' (*bayᶜat al-harb*). One of Muhammad's uncles, al-ᶜAbbās, is believed to have overseen the operation in order to ascertain if the ᶜAws and Khazraj had properly assumed the obligation of protecting Muhammad. The second oath of ᶜAqabah (the Great *bayᶜah*) produced a qualitative leap in the formation of the community; the mere submission to some moral and religious teachings turned into undertaking to fight under the leadership of Muhammad, also against the kin order. In sharp contrast with the conciliatory attitude earlier recommended, the political element was later confirmed and secured by new revelations, which were believed to authorise war or even prescribe it (ibn Hishām, *Sīrah*: II, 51 and 62ff, and al-Tabarī, *Ta'rīkh*: II, 87ff). The wording implies that armed action is justified only in case of attack, but the attitude of the Quraish was taken as an 'attack' (Q. 22:39, and 2:191).

After having received the second oath of ᶜAqabah, Muhammad encouraged his Meccan followers to migrate to Yathrib, and in the summer of 622 some groups started making the Hegira (*hijrah*). According to Muslim sources, Muhammad remained in Mecca until rumours of a murder plot forced him to leave the city with abū Bakr (Q. 9:40).

When they reached Yathrib the Hegira was fully accomplished. Meccans who migrated, known as *muhājirūn*, severed their kin ties, hence renouncing the protection and the other benefits of membership in the kin group. After the Hegira, embracing Muhammad's prophetic message assumed a distinctively political flavour, and even the spirit of Koranic revelations significantly changed – so much so that Islamic tradition distinguishes between Meccan and Medinan parts of the Qur'ān. Hegira itself was perceived as such a turning point in Islamic history that its date of occurrence was soon adopted to mark the beginning of the Islamic era (AH).

The severance of kin ties involved in the Hegira, though, should not be overestimated, but rather understood in the context of a network of group relations whose boundaries are determined by the presence of the group. Firstly, the matter concerned only the Meccans who migrated, since the Medinans kept leading their lives within the kin order; as a consequence, a polarisation between *muhājirūn* (Meccans) and *ansār* (Medinans) came about because of this difference in status. Secondly, the second oath of ʿAqabah did not provide a suitable organisation for the *muhājirūn*, whose protection and integration therefore had to be achieved through alternative forms of membership other than the traditional ones.

An attempt to engender higher social cohesion was the *mu'ākhā*, a fictitious brotherhood conceived to couple two *muhājirūn*s, or a *muhājirūn* and an *ansār*, with mutual rights of inheritance (Tyan 1954: 131). The *mu'ākhā*'s main aim, though, seems to have been military, since the coupled men had to stand side-by-side in battle and thus refrain from disorderly reactions when facing the enemy (Montgomery Watt 1956: 301). Very little is known about the *mu'ākhā*, which is said to have been abandoned after the Battle of Badr (624), even if the *mu'ākhā* between al-ʿAbbās and his nephew Nawfal ibn al-Hārith was undoubtedly instituted later. A lingering echo of the fictitious brotherhood can still be heard at the time of Muʿāwiyah, who was coupled with al-Hutāt ibn Yazīd when Muhammad marched on Mecca in 630 (ibn Hishām, *Sīrah*: III, 374ff).

With the Hegira the community entered a new phase of its formation, during which the political dimension started shaping up while retaining – in the first Medinan period – a composite makeup. Shortly after the Hegira, Muhammad organised Yathrib's population along legal and political lines in what is known as the *Sahīfah*, or 'Charter of Medina'. Besides controversies over the authenticity of the document,[1] the organisation portrayed is consistent with evidence from other sources; the kin bond was somehow marginalised, but the idea of the bond of the common faith in Islam as the sole basis for the new community had yet to come. The 'community' mirrored in the Charter – transmitted by ibn Ishāq and included by ibn Hishām in his narrative of Muhammad's life, the *Sīrat rasūl allāh*[2] – included: (1) Muslims who migrated from Mecca (the *muhājirūns*) and converts from Yathrib (the *ansārs*), (2) Jews who guarded their religion but had to contribute to the expenses of Muslims in case of war, and (3) pagans who were no longer allowed to apply to non-Muslim Meccans the traditional means of protection for people and goods (*jiwār* or *hilf*). The political and military chief was Muhammad, recognised as the Prophet (*nabī*) and Messenger (*rasūl*) of God; the Charter is said to be derived from Muhammad (art. 1), and any matter of dispute had to be referred to God or to him (art. 23).[3] Such unilaterality is backed by the fact that Muhammad is thought to have been received in Yathrib as an arbiter for tribal disputes and to ensure internal peace (Caetani 1911-1914: III, 27-36).

The organisation provided for in the Charter turned out to be quite unstable, and paralleled the fate of relations with Judaism. The Jews had been initially considered potential allies and converts, but their rejection of Muhammad's preaching exacerbated feelings of hostility. The Arab character of the message was consequently stressed, and Jews were declared falsifiers, corrupters of their own Scriptures and forgers of the pure monotheism that the common father Abraham had introduced in Arabia and that Muhammad was re-establishing and bringing to completion. Changing the direction of prayer (*qiblah*) from Jerusalem to Mecca in 624 was the first hint of the new attitude, shortly followed by the expulsion of the banū Qaynuqāʿ after the Battle of Badr. In 625 the Muslims' defeat in the Battle of Uhud was followed by the siege of the banū 'l-Nadīr, who were eventually forced to leave Medina. The last Jewish tribe in town, the banū Qurayzah, suffered the worst fate; after the Battle of the Trench in 627 all the men were killed, the property was divided and the women and children were taken captive.

The purge of the Jews paved the way for a religiously homogeneous society, and in the third phase (from 627 on) the community (*ummah*)[4] acquired its distinctive and ultimate characters.

In the Qur'ān the word '*ummah*' had been used throughout the second phase to indicate a 'group of people'; Jews and Christians were 'communities' (Q. 23:52), and even Arabs were considered an *ummah* (Q. 13:30) like all those who are righteous (Q. 7:168), or the groups of Jews 'who guide and do justice in the light of truth' and of Christians 'who enjoin what is right and forbid what is wrong' (Q. 7:159 and 3:113-114). When friction with the Jewish tribes of Yathrib unveiled the hindrances preventing the inclusion of non-Muslims in one religious community, the Qur'ān prohibited alliances with Jews and Christians (Q. 5:51) and started referring to a distinct, superior community including only Muslims (Q. 3:104 and 110, and 2:143), while all other communities had to be fought against until they paid the tax, 'being brought low' (Q. 9:29). This marks the beginning of the idea that non-Muslims – even if excluded from the Islamic community and organised in separate groups – can be connected to the *ummah* by a bond of submission.[5]

In the Medinan period closer ties among Muslims were forged and the basis was laid for the organisation of the Islamic community and its legal provisions. In the meantime, a turning point in the ongoing conflict with Mecca was Muhammad's decision in 628 to march with a group of Muslims to his birthplace to perform the *ʿumrah* (the 'minor pilgrimage' that can be undertaken at any time of the year). The Quraish were determined not to allow the Muslims to perform the pilgrimage and intercepted them outside the city's holy territory, in Hudaybīyah, where the parties signed an agreement providing for the Muslims' immediate retreat and the Meccans' consent to allow the Muslims to come on pilgrimage the following year.

According to the Islamic tradition, the Treaty of Hudaybīyah included clauses calling for a ten-year truce between parties, the returning of any Quraish who had left Mecca without his guardian's permission (with no reciprocity of Muslim deserters) and the freedom to establish alliances with other tribes. Such clauses seem to contrast with the growing success of Muhammad, and he had to face widespread discontent among his followers. The truce was initially respected, and in 629 some Medinans performed the *hajj* to Mecca, but the pact was soon denounced on the basis of an attack on a tribe allied with Muhammad. Ready to wage war, Muslims headed for Mecca, but the city surrendered peacefully. Muhammad then circled the Kaʿbah seven times and solemnly proclaimed that 'every claim of privilege, whether of blood or property', was abolished (Montgomery Watt 1956: 261-302), while all the idols in the sanctuary were broken and the stone gods destroyed.

The spread of Islam strategically accelerated in the second Medinan phase, especially after the successful political and military achievements against Mecca. Many tribes that had maintained a neutral stance up to that point deemed it necessary to side with the stronger, and – according to Arab custom – sent delegations (*wufūd*) to Muhammad in order to settle their adherence to Islam and to pay the ensuing tributary duties. The clear political reason behind such conversions to Islam surfaced at Muhammad's death, when some tribes across the Peninsula refused to keep paying their tributes, thus forsaking Islam. Abū Bakr, the first caliph or political successor of Muhammad, had to tackle the issue of dissident tribes, arms in hand, in what became known as the '*Riddah* (apostasy or rebellion) Wars'.

To sum up, after the preaching in Mecca, where the first proselytes (all Quraish) certainly found in the revelation a common and distinctive element that did not, however, disconnect them from their kin relations (610-622), the Hegira led to a short-lived experience in Yathrib of coexistence among Muslims (both Quraish and non-Quraish), Jews and pagans (622-625). The increasing conversions of pagans and the elimination of the Jewish tribes resulted in the formation of a religiously homogeneous community. The Islamic community has maintained such a holistic character ever since, notwithstanding its broad diffusion; nonetheless, it has had to deal with the deep-rooted mentality and rivalry among kin groups (from 625 on).

2.2 Forms of membership in the Islamic community

The full political and religious unity of the Islamic community (*al-ummah al-islāmīyah*) was but an ephemeral event in history. Even so, it has kept the hearts of Muslims beating for centuries (Gardet 1967: 274). At Muhammad's death, the ancient tribal particularism that only Muhammad's personal charisma managed to temporarily subdue vehemently re-emerged, and even the great impetus of the conquests was soon followed by centrifugal forces that gradually tore apart the caliphal empire. Muslims' consciousness of belonging to the same community, however, passed the test of time despite the several internal schisms and the countless political and dynastic upheavals.

Classical Islamic law finally fixed the forms of membership in the Islamic community as well as the status of non-Muslims living under Islamic authority, and the position of those professing heretical doctrines or committing apostasy (individually or collectively).

2.2.1 Muslims

A Muslim is a Muslim by birth or by conversion. Islam presents itself as the natural religion of mankind,[6] and some Koranic verses support such a view (Q. 30:30-32),[7] underpinned by traditions (*hadīth*) relating Muhammad's words, 'No child is born but upon the "natural religion (*fitrah*)". It is his parents who make him a Jew or a Christian or a polytheist'.[8] Such a natural inclination to worship the one God is an inherent disposition that leads men to a pure monotheism (*hanīfīyah*) epitomised by Islam.

Every child of a Muslim man is a Muslim according to Islamic law; here a well-established rule is borrowed from Jewish law, which, however, applies it to the woman with its typical Biblical insight. The combination of the Jewish and the Islamic rule may give rise to a positive conflict of laws; in the case of the offspring of a Muslim man and a Jewish woman, indeed, the child is a Muslim under Islamic law and a Jew under Jewish law. A Muslim woman is obliged to marry a Muslim man and therefore can only give birth to a Muslim child. Thus a Muslim can only generate a Muslim; the man by virtue of a general rule, and the woman by virtue of an impediment to marriage.

At the child's birth, the Muslim father whispers into the newborn's right ear the call to prayer (*adhān*): 'God is great (four times), there is no god but God (twice), Muhammad is the messenger of God (twice), come to prayer (twice)'. On the seventh day, the child is given a name (*tasmiyah*), a sacrifice is offered (*ʿaqīqah*, consisting of two pieces of small livestock for a boy and one for a girl), and alms are distributed.[9] Such birth rites, as well as later rituals like circumcision (*khitān*), though, do not affect the child's religion; he/she is a Muslim because a Muslim begot him/her.

A non-Muslim can convert to Islam by pronouncing the *shahādah* in Arabic (*lā ilāh illā allāh wa-Muhammad rasūl allāh*) – there is no god but God, and Muhammad is the messenger of God – in front of two male adult Muslim witnesses. The *shahādah* represents the basic tenets of Islamic creed, and Islamic theology (*kalām*) is considered a derivation of the *shahādah* itself. The *shahādah* is the Muslim declaration of belief in the oneness of God (*lā ilāh illā allāh* – there is no god but God) and in Muhammad's prophethood (*wa-Muhammad rasūl allāh* – and Muhammad is the messenger of God). Shia Muslims add a third item on ʿAlī's status (*wa-ʿAlī walī allāh* – and ʿAlī is the friend of God), but such an addition is generally regarded as a mere recommendation (*mustahabb*, and not *wājib*, obligatory) and is commonly omitted in the calls to prayer (*adhān* and *iqāmah*).

Just like any freed slave, a non-Arab convert to Islam needed an Arab patron. Here analogy with pre-Islamic practices of clientage is striking. In the Age of the Conquest, this rule created two classes of Muslims: Arabs and non-Arabs. Since the former had a well-established tribal system, only conversion was needed to embrace Islam, while for the latter clientage was a requirement to become Muslims and be attached to an Arab kin group. The inferiority engendered by the non-Arab Muslim's status of client (*mawlà*) led to anti-Arab political and literary movements, like the *Shuʿūbīyah*.

Under Islamic law, the father's conversion results in the conversion of his minor and his mentally weak children. The majority of scholars believe that the mother's conversion produces the same effect, but not Maliki jurists. Children who have not attained puberty can neither validly convert to Islam nor abandon it (al-Zuhaylī 1997: vi, 184). Some

Hanafi and Hanbali scholars, however, on account of both the minor's and the public interest (*maslahah*), admit that the discerning minor (*mumayyiz*) can convert to Islam but cannot abandon it.

2.2.2 Non-Muslims

In Muhammad's early days, a fairly liberal attitude towards religion dominated among the Hejazi kin groups, each having its own idol in the sanctuary of the Ka^{c}bah. Besides polytheists there were two communities for which the religious bond somehow exceeded the kin bond: a larger Jewish and a smaller Christian community. With the rise of Islam a new community took shape (Q. 3:103-104) and was soon declared 'the best of peoples, evolved for mankind, enjoining what is right, forbidding what is wrong and believing in God'(Q. 3:110).

The emergence of the Islamic community overturned previous peaceful relations among religions, imposing a system of ranked religious groups. A tradition (*hadīth*) relates that Muhammad instructed on his deathbed not to leave two religions in Arabia (ibn Sa^{c}d, *Tabaqāt*: II, 44), but an earlier account ascribes this instruction to ^{c}Umar ibn al-Khattāb, the second caliph (Caetani 1911-1914: IV, 351). Despite disputes on the authenticity of the narrative, Jews and Christians in the Arabian peninsula were soon almost entirely uprooted. A case in point is the deportation of the entire Christian population of Najrān in a new settlement in Iraq (al-Najrānīyah; Shahid 1971).

Islam establishes a hierarchy among other religions. At the top of the ladder are the People of the Book (*ahl al-kitāb*): those who received scriptures revealed by God before the time of Muhammad. Among these 'true believers' worthy of tolerance are the followers of monotheistic Abrahamic religions: Jews, Christians and Sabians (Q. 2:62, and 5:69). A later verse mentions also Zoroastrians and lists them ahead of polytheists (Q. 22:17). An initial tolerant attitude towards the *ahl al-kitāb* (Q. 2:136-137, and 22:17) was later replaced by a more adversarial relationship (Q. 9:29), which prevails over the former verses as a result of the application of the theory of abrogation (*naskh*). Nevertheless, the latter verse allowed the extension of the provisions regarding the *ahl al-kitāb* to non-Arab polytheists, thus avoiding the alternative of conversion to Islam or the sword.

Like membership in the Islamic community, membership in non-Islamic communities is determined in accordance with the Islamic view by birth or by conversion, but conversion from Islam to another religion is unacceptable. For Judaism, the child of a Jewish mother is a member of the People of the Covenant (*b^{e}rīth*), while conversion is a far more intricate matter. Conversely, there is no membership in the Christian community by birth. The child of a Christian parent is not a

Christian until the christening (the practice of infant baptism started
spreading by the end of the 2nd century; Aland 1961: 22ff). Islamic
law, however, applies the same Judeo-Islamic perspective of membership by descent to the Christian communities of the Near East, and
does not employ the theory of *fitrah* (Islam as the natural religion of
man). If it did, anyone receiving baptism after puberty would be considered an apostate.

2.3   Partition from the Islamic community

Drawing a line between orthodoxy and heterodoxy in Islam is no easy
task. It is also highly doubtful whether 'orthodoxy' and 'heterodoxy' are
categories that can fruitfully be applied to Islam, since there is no over-
seeing religious authority in the largest denomination of Islam in the
Arab world, Sunni Islam. Sunni Muslims are the 'People of the Sunnah and the Community' (*ahl al-sunnah wa-l-jamāᶜah*), implying that
religious authority is not concentrated in clergy but rather diffused in
the Qur'ān and the Sunnah and their communitarian interpretation developed by generations of scholars (*ᶜulamā'*) and lawyers (*fuqahā'*).

Scholarly views on the slender divide between acceptable dissenting
opinions and heretical doctrines differ considerably. Openly abandoning Islam to embrace another religion is a much easier controversy to
unravel. Rules on collective or individual apostasy apply, and such rules
are the only way of severing the bond of membership in the Islamic
community.

2.3.1   Muslim sects

'And my community will split into 73 sects'.[10] On the basis of this well-
known *hadīth* attributed to Muhammad, Muslim scholars made great
efforts to identify all the sects, since 72 of them were doomed to burn
in the fire and only one was destined to be saved (*al-firqah al-nājiyah*).
Regardless of the authenticity of the tradition and the pious scholarly
efforts, schisms with profound and long-lasting effects occurred shortly
after the death of Muhammad. Four decades had not elapsed when the
first split (*al-fitnah al-kubrà*) marked the end of the early unity of the Islamic community. What began as a political confrontation over the
right to the caliphate turned into the principal religious rift in Islamic
history: on the one side were the supporters of Muᶜāwiyah, the governor of Syria and future founder of the Umayyad caliphate (Sunni Muslims), and on the other were the partisans of ᶜAlī asserting the right to
the caliphate of Muhammad's household, the *ahl al-bayt* (Shia Muslims). Some of ᶜAlī's partisans, however, did not agree on subjecting

ᶜAlī's legitimate authority to arbitration and mutinied (Kharijite Muslims).

One of the most influential Muslim theologians, the Ashʿarite polymath al-Ghazzālī (d. 1111), dealt with the question of orthodoxy and heresy at the end of his *al-Iqtisād fī 'l-iᶜtināq* (The Median in Belief). Al-Ghazzālī's starting point was the proper use of the term *kāfir* (infidel, unbeliever) – broadly the person who denies Muhammad's prophethood or declares Muhammad a liar.[11] He then defined different degrees of *kufr* (infidelity, unbelief). Included among *kuffār* (plural of *kāfir*) were certainly the Jews and the Christians, and in a lower position were also polytheists and followers of other religions that denied prophethood, like Brahmans or atheists. Even Muslim philosophers whose theories clashed with the Qur'ān or only formally admitted Muhammad's prophethood had to be considered infidels. Not so for other Islamic sects or theological schools that truly accepted the tenet of Muhammad's prophethood (like Muslim anthropomorphists or Muʿtazilis); in such cases suspension of judgement was recommended. A Muslim claiming an Islamic religious precept to be nonbinding is not a *kāfir* only if the precept is a minor precept, as in the case of the Muslim who rejects dogma not grounded in the Qur'ān or the Sunnah but simply inferred and non-controversial (by *ijmāᶜ*, consensus). Al-Ghazzālī acknowledged an exception to this rule in the case of a Muslim maintaining that God could send other prophets, even if this dogma is grounded on a Koranic verse (Q. 33:40) and a tradition.[12] The Ashʿarite theologian deemed that the two passages can be interpreted metaphorically.

The Ashʿarite-Ghazzalian doctrine, still prevalent in Arab Islam, was contested by the 'dogmatic integralism' of ibn Taymīyah (d. 1328), whose legacy was later recovered by Wahhabism in the 18th century. According to ibn Taymīyah, dangerous errors and aberrations undermining the true faith permeated the Islamic community and had to be uprooted by resorting to the Hanbali middle path: uncompromising on the principles of divine revelation but tolerant of minor differences. 'As the Prophet said – wrote ibn Taymīyah –: "The Muslim is brother of the Muslim".[13] How then can it be permitted to the community of Muhammad to divide itself into such diverse opinions that a man can join one group and hate another one simply on the basis of presumptions or personal caprices, without any proof coming from God? [..] Unity is a sign of divine clemency; discord is a punishment of God'.[14] On the other hand, however, members of deviant Islamic sects should be treated as collective apostates. In a *fatwà* on ᶜAlawis (or *al-nusayrīyah*), for example, ibn Taymīyah affirmed, 'They are greater disbelievers than Jews and Christians. Nay, they are greater disbelievers than most of the *mushrikīn* (polytheists), and their harm to the *ummah* of Muhammad

(PBUH) is greater than the harm of the disbelievers who are at war with Muslims'. Ibn Taymīyah had a similar opinion on the Druzes (durūz), and stated that both groups were so far beyond the confines of Islam that even the food they prepared was forbidden to Muslims and it was unlawful to have intercourse with their women or to accept their repentance. In other words, the only way to treat them was physical annihilation, which is something that the Mamluks, through ibn Taymīyah's prodding, tried to do during his lifetime.

2.3.2 Collective apostasy

The narrow line of demarcation between Muslim sects and apostate groups has hardly ever been drawn out of sheer dogmatic considerations. Political reasons have often motivated the decision to declare that a Muslim sect had forsaken Islam and thus to apply the rules of collective apostasy. At an early stage, collective deviations were dealt with in a practical way, while a definite theory on collective apostasy was developed by later scholars. Nevertheless, collective apostasy has always been declared on a case-by-case basis.

The first splinter groups appeared on the Islamic scene at an early date. Shortly after Muhammad's death, some factions refused to recognise Muhammad's political successors, claiming that they had submitted only to Muhammad and that with his death their allegiance had duly ended (Caetani 1911-1914: III, 346ff). These factions withheld their financial contribution (the Islamic alms tax or zakāh), but they did not otherwise challenge Islam, even if some leaders asserted their prophethood. Abū Bakr, the first caliph, contended that they had not merely submitted to Muhammad but had joined the Islamic religious community, and defying the caliphate meant breaking from the community, thus committing apostasy (riddah). He declared war on the rebels. The Islamic tradition labelled these campaigns the 'Wars of Apostasy' (hurūb al-riddah), and later scholars depicted them as the first jihād against the infidelity of Arabs (Sachedina 1988: 53-90).

The three major hotbeds of the rebellion were al-Yamāmah, northern Hejaz and the city of al-Sanᶜā' in Yemen, and the main dissidents were Musaylimah of the banū Hanīfah in al-Yamāmah, Sajāh of the banū Tamīm in northern Hejaz, and al-Aswad al-ᶜAnasī in Yemen. Musaylimah proclaimed himself prophet, and therefore Muslim authors remember him as the 'Liar' (al-kadhdhāb). His memory was yet alive in 1862 when William Palgrave visited Nejd. The English scholar reported that Musaylimah was still remembered as a prophet and some of his 'burlesque imitations' of the Qur'ān were still recited (Palgrave 1865: I, 382). After two unsuccessful expeditions, he was defeated by Khālid ibn al-Walīd in the conclusive combat of the 'Garden of Death' (hadīqat al-mawt) in 633.

Islamic law later developed a set of rules pertaining to the treatment of factions that were considered to have collectively abandoned Islam. The territories inhabited by collective renegades were to be declared dār riddah (home of apostasy) and thus subjected to even harsher regulations than the ones prescribed for the dār al-harb (home of war, i.e. non-Muslim governed territories). According to the 8th-century Hanafi jurist al-Shaybānī and the 11th-century Shafi'i jurist al-Māwardī, no truce can be concluded with them, nor can money be accepted from their hands for allowing them to live in their land, and they cannot even be taken captives. On this last point, however, al-Māwardī mentions al-Shāfiʿī's stricter position and abū Hanīfah's soothing exemption for the women who took refuge in the dār al-harb.

Under the Abbasids (750-1258) some converts who were reckoned still to be followers of Manichaeism were accused of being zindīq, zandaqah being the condition of those who formally embraced Islam but covertly guarded their previous beliefs, thus representing a serious threat to Islam. Zandaqah was included in the category of apostasy, and the third Abbasid caliph, al-Mahdī (ruled 775-785) ordered the death of all the suspect crypto-Manichaeans. In time, blunt accusations of apostasy were addressed to many Sufis. One of them, the Persian mystic Mansūr-e Hallāj (d. 922), was first called a zindīq for his Manichaean-related theory on the mystic union, and later executed for denying the obligation to perform the pilgrimage to Mecca (hajj) for those who meet God in their hearts. A century later, however, many Copts forced to convert under the Fatimid caliph al-Hākim (d. 1021) were later allowed to revert to Christianity without being punished for apostasy.

Intolerance of and discrimination against deviant factions is not merely a set of historical rules and past practices. Two present-day cases in point are the Ahmadis and the Bābī-Bahā'īs, which are both movements that arose in the 19th century in non-Arab Muslim lands. On the other hand, however, some groups managed to maintain their inner atypical beliefs while being outwardly mainstream Muslims. An interesting case is that of the Donmeh (from the Turkish word for convert, dönme), or Sabbatean crypto-Jews. The Donmeh follow the path of the self-proclaimed Jewish messiah Shabbatai Zevi (d. 1676), a Jew who converted to Islam in the 17th century but covertly continued practicing Jewish rituals. Notwithstanding the closely knit social network sustained by the rigorous practice of intermarriage, the Donmeh fully integrated into Turkish society and are thought to have made a considerable contribution to the rise of the Young Turks.

Ahmadis are the followers of Mīrzà Ghulām Ahmad (d. 1908), a religious figure from Qadian, Punjab. Mīrzà Ghulām Ahmad's claims of being the *mujaddid* (the reformer) and later also the Messiah and the Mahdī (the guided one) sparked great controversy among Muslims, and he and his followers were branded as heretics. Nevertheless, Ahmadis consider themselves Muslims, and Mīrzà Ghulām Ahmad named his movement the Ahmadi Muslim Community (*Jamāᶜat-i Ahmadīyah Muslimah*). The community split into two branches soon after the death of Mīrzà Ghulām Ahmad. The *Jamāᶜat-i Ahmadīyah Muslimah* and the *Ahmadiyah Anjuman Ishāᶜat-i Islām* vary in their interpretations of Ahmad's teachings and claims (especially on the return of Jesus, the status of Mīrzà Ghulām Ahmad, the finality of Muhammad's prophethood, the caliphate and the *jihād*), but members of both branches are labelled as collective apostates. In 1922 in British India, the Madras High Court ruled that anyone who accepted the prophethood of Muhammad and the supreme authority of the Qur'ān would be treated as a Muslim in the eyes of the law.[15] Hence, a Muslim becoming an Ahmadi was not an apostate. The situation changed after the establishment of the Islamic Republic of Pakistan. In 1974 the Pakistani Parliament introduced in the Constitution the definition of the term 'Muslim' and a list of groups that are, legally speaking, non-Muslim. The amendment thus explicitly deprived Ahmadis of their identity as Muslims.[16] A decade later, Ordinance XX of 1984 was issued to further restrict the activities of Ahmadis. In particular, the Ordinance added two sections to the Pakistani Penal Code of 1860, punishing the Ahmadis for misusing Islamic epithets, descriptions or titles (PPC 298 (b)), or for calling themselves Muslims, preaching or propagating their faith, outraging the religious feelings of Muslims or posing as Muslims (PPC 298(c)). Act III of 1986 (also known as the 'Blasphemy Law') raised the penalty for remarks disrespectful of Muhammad from fine or imprisonment to death (PPC 295(c)); Ahmadis' beliefs in the prophethood of Mīrzà Ghulām Ahmad are *per se* considered defilements of Muhammad's name. The Muslim World League had already classified Ahmadis as a sect of apostates in 1974[17] and recommended severe measures against them.[18]

Similarly, the Muslim World League condemned the Bahā'īs in 1988. Bahā'īs, however, do not consider themselves Muslims, but rather believe in different 'manifestations of God' and in the idea of progressive revelation. The Bahā'ī faith developed in 19th-century Persia, growing out of Shaykhī doctrines rooted in Shia Islam. In 1844 a 25-year-old Shirazi, Sayyid ᶜAlī Muhammad, declared that he was the forerunner of the Mahdī, or his 'door' or Bāb. The Bāb and his followers were persecuted by the Muslim hierarchy and the Bāb was eventually executed because his teachings contradicted the finality of Muhammad's prophethood, a central point of Islamic faith. In 1852 one of the Bāb's persecuted followers, Mīrzà Husayn ʿAlī Nūrī, claimed to be the fulfilment of the Bāb's eschatological prophecy and assumed the name of Bahā'ullāh, the Glory of God. The Bahā'ī doctrine is highly syncretistic, and its core tenets are the 'three onenesses': the oneness of God, the oneness of religion and the oneness of humankind. Bahā'īs propagated out of Persia and are currently one of the world's most widespread religions. Since the Islamic revolution in Iran, Bahā'īs have been virulently persecuted, allegedly on grounds of belonging to an 'organisation-enemy' of the Islamic Republic. The Bahā'īs' relations with Israel, where their World Centre is located, are often cited as evidence of their disloyalty. In the Arab world and in a Sunni context, Bahā'īs are not treated in a more conciliatory manner. In 2003 the Islamic Research Academy of al-Azhar confirmed its previous orientation, declaring the Bahā'ī faith 'a form of intellectual epidemic' (min nawʿīyāt al-awbi'ah al-fikrīyah). In Egypt, Bahā'ī places of worship are still banned (Law 263 of 1960),[19] and the opportunity of seeing their own religious affiliation (al-bahā'īyah) indicated on official documents sparked great excitement in the Bahā'ī community, but the Supreme Administrative Court in December 2006 overruled the decision of a lower court.[20]

2.3.3 Individual apostasy

Joining Islam is fairly easy, but abandoning it has severe consequences. The Qur'ān asserts that God despises apostates (murtadd), and a harsh punishment for apostasy (riddah or irtidād) is envisioned for the afterlife (Q. 2:217-218). The idea is reasserted in other passages (Q. 3:85-91 and 137, 4:115, and 16:106), but by no means does the text prescribe worldly punishment for turning from Islam.

All Islamic legal schools, however, agree on the point that apostasy needs to be punished, even if they hold different views on how it should be punished. Maliki, Hanbali and Jaʿfari jurists list apostasy as a hadd crime, i.e. a capital offence punishable by a pre-established punishment found in the Qur'ān. Hanafi and Shafiʿi jurists do not regard apostasy as a hadd crime, but nevertheless share the common view that it should be punished by death.[21] Capital punishment is based upon two hadīths. According to the first, Muhammad said, 'Whoever changes his religion, kill him',[22] and according to the second, the blood of a Muslim can be shed only in three cases: '(1) in retaliation for murder, (2) for having committed adultery (3) or for having reverted from Islam and left the community'.[23]

According to Islamic law, apostasy is not limited to the abandonment of Islam for the sake of joining another religious community, but can also be perpetrated by committing a sacrilegious act or professing a non-mainstream belief. Scholars listed examples of sayings or acts that are regarded as implications of unbelief, but general rules providing established criteria have not been constructed (Peters-De Vries 1976: 3).[24] Different examples can be grouped into categories of offences against monotheism (e.g. asserting that there are other gods besides God, or worshipping an idol), Muhammad's prophethood (e.g. rejecting Muhammad's claim to be a prophet, or proclaiming him/herself a prophet) or other beliefs (e.g. denying the obligatory status of ritual prayer, or contemptuously disposing of a copy of the Qur'ān). The acts entailing apostasy must be proved by the testimony of two witnesses (a generic accusation is not sufficient) or by confession.

In order to perform a legal act of apostasy, the Muslim must be adult (bāligh), in full possession of mental faculties (ʿāqil) and acting out of free will (mukhtār). If the Muslim was not born a Muslim, Maliki jurists require an unambiguous and explicit conversion (husn al-islām clause, viz. under no constraint, when sober, with witnesses and the parents' assent if the person is not of age). As far as age is concerned, the consensus (ijmāʿ) is that minors can apostatise only after having reached the age of discernment. According to Shafiʿi doctors, minors cannot apostatise until they come of age, while jurists of other schools hold that discerning minors (mumayyiz) can commit apostasy, even if their coming of age must be awaited in order to invite them to repent and, in case of persistence in their apostasy, to execute them. Apostasy must be deliberate. The individual is not held responsible in the case of constraint, delirium, mental illness or misinterpretation of sacred law (namely, believing that something prohibited is permissible).

When apostasy has been legally established, the apostate is exhorted to re-embrace Islam (istitābah) before sentencing; exhorting the apostate is obligatory (wājib) for all schools, except for Hanafis who deem it merely recommended (mandūb). The apostates are given three days to reflect. The possibility of revocation and repentance (tawbah) is acknowledged by Sunni scholars, whereas Shia Jaʿfaris accept repentance only of an apostate born an unbeliever (murtadd millī) and not if born a Muslim (murtadd fitrī). Magicians (sāhir), heretics (zindīq) and recidivists are excluded from istitābah; their apostasy is legally irrevocable, since there can be no reasonable certainty that they earnestly returned to Islam.

Apostasy entails the death penalty. A closer consideration of the different treatments afforded to male and female apostates, together with a cross comparison of Islamic and Jewish prescriptions on the punishment (and to whom it should apply), helps cast light on the proportion of capital punishment for apostasy in Islamic law, notwithstanding the absence of a clear Koranic basis for it.

Hanafi and Ja'fari scholars rule out the killing of the female apostate. She should be imprisoned until she returns to Islam, and during imprisonment she should be beaten at prayer time every day (Ja'faris) or every three days (Hanafis). The milder treatment is explained with reference to the woman's weakness, which renders her unable to pose a serious threat to the Islamic state (al-Jazīrī 1988: IV, 426). A *hadīth* is often quoted to prove Muhammad's disapproving of the killing of a woman: 'She was not fighting those who are fighting'.[25]

The apostate must be executed by the sword. Scholars reached such a conclusion without any explicit indication in the sources. Earlier, a tradition reports that ibn ʿAbbās rebuked ʿAlī for having burnt a group of apostates,[26] reminding him of Muhammad's words, 'Do not punish anybody with God's punishment'.[27] ʿAlī's act would have been regarded by Jews as fully compliant with the prescriptions of Deu. 13:13-19 (NJB) on collective apostasy, but apparently it hurt Muslim sensibility. Another *hadīth*, narrated by ʿĀ'ishah, relates that Muhammad prescribed that the Muslim 'who comes up and fights against God and His messenger must be killed, crucified or expelled from the territory'.[28] This *hadīth* is a variant of the aforementioned tradition concerning the three cases in which the shedding of a Muslim's blood is permitted. Here, however, other options are given, such as crucifying or exiling the man, and it is clearer that the sanctioned conduct is revolting and fighting against God and His messenger, not just abandoning Islam.

The execution by the sword, in the absence of any textual evidence in the Islamic tradition, gains special meaning if compared with parallel Jewish rules. The Torah does not impose a punishment for apostasy, but the Deuteronomic code provides for the killing of those who entice a Jew to forsake Judaism and serve foreign gods. It is incumbent upon close relatives to denounce the enticers and stone them to death (Deu. 13:7-12, NJB).[29] What is condemned is the enticement to deviate 'from the way' or 'from God', expressed by the causative form (*hiphʿîl*) of the root *n.d.h* (deviate).[30] In the case of a whole city having decided to serve foreign gods, its men and cattle must be smitten with the edge of the sword (*lᵉ-phî hārebh*), their city laid under the curse of destruction (*hahᵃrēm*) and its loot burnt with fire (Deu. 13:13-19, NJB). Some analogy can be drawn here with ʿAlī's action and ibn ʿAbbās's reproach, since the Biblical 'herem' of the city was the consecration to the Deity of persons and things to be utterly destroyed. Further on, the Deuteronomic code prescribes the stoning to death of the man or the woman 'who does what is wrong in the eyes of Yahweh your God by violating his covenant, who goes and serves other gods and worships them' (Deu. 17:2-3, NJB).[31] Disobeying the priest (*hak-kōhēn*) or the judge (*hash-shōphēt*) is equally punishable with death (Deu. 17:12, NJB), as is rebelling against the orders of the political authority, according to the oath of the Reubenites, the Gadites and the half tribe of Manasseh on behalf of the people about to enter the Promised Land (Jos. 1:16-18, NJB). According to the Talmud, the death sentence can be imposed only by a Biblical authority (*Sanhedrîn* 82b),[32] but the ruler can put a rebel to the sword (*Sanhedrîn* 49a).

On the one hand, the Islamic rules on the execution of the apostate by the sword match the Jewish rules on the punishment of the rebel by the political authority, while on the other hand the notions of apostasy sensibly vary in the two traditions. Judaism punished the enticement of deviant conduct and the service to foreign gods, whereas Islam initially punished every individual forsaking it and posing a threat to the Islamic state. Later on, Muslim scholars agreed that apostatising included even just professing heretical doctrines, which *per se* menaced the Islamic state and therefore needed to be sanctioned by death.

Besides its penal features, apostasy has relevant civil consequences, too. The rights of apostates to dispose of their patrimony are held in abeyance pending their repentance. If they do not repent, all their acts are null and void. The apostate lacks the capacity to inherit, and the marriage contract is immediately nullified (*faskh*). Unlike the father's conversion, the father's apostasy does not have any effect on his minor children, who remain Muslims. The legal status of the apostate has been sagaciously described as a situation of 'civil and social death' (Gibb-Kramers 1974).

2.4 Characters of the confessional system

2.4.1 Personality of Islamic law

Islam shaped a confessional legal system based on personality, i.e. Islamic law applies to Muslims (exclusively), wherever they are. This general rule is coupled with the pre-eminence of Islamic law over all other sacred or positive laws. Territoriality thus reclaims some terrain, since *sharīʿah* rules apply even if only one of the parties is a Muslim. Moreover, jurisdiction and applicable law overlap: only an Islamic judge can apply Islamic law, while controversies between members of the same religious community are left to the authority of confessional courts, which apply their religious law (also called *sharīʿah*). Even non-Muslims temporarily residing within Muslim territories (known as *mustaʾmins*) bring suits regarding their personal status to the courts of the religious community to which they are associated, and the court applies its confessional law even if the non-Muslim does not abide by such a law at home. The Islamic judge, however, tends to extend his jurisdiction well over the paramount principle of personality of confessional laws. For instance, he will adjudicate among non-Muslims if they do not all belong to the same denomination (*tā'ifah* or *millah*), and will apply Islamic law with some noteworthy exceptions (e.g. he will not dissolve the marriage if one party is Catholic). One can therefore envisage what might be called a 'general jurisdiction' of the Islamic judge that stops just short of the internal matters of other non-Muslim communities.[33]

2.4.2 Jurisdiction of the Islamic judge

Confessional jurisdictions concerned with personal status matters of members of the same religious community is a rule supported by solid textual evidence in Q. 5:42-48. According to Muslim commentators of the Qur'ān, the situation that occasioned the revelation of these verses was a case of adultery between two Jews of Khaybar that Muhammad was called upon to solve. He ordered their stoning to death in compliance with the Biblical prescription (Deu. 22:22-29, NJB). The Koranic passage requires Jews to be judged by the Torah (Q. 5:43-45), Christians by the Gospel (Q. 5:46-47), and Muslims by the Qur'ān (Q. 5:48), and ends with the admonition: 'To each among you have we prescribed a law and an open way. If Allah had so willed, He would have made you a single people, but (His plan is) to test you in what He hath given you: so strive as in a race in all virtues. The goal of you all is to Allah; it is He that will show you the truth of the matters in which ye dispute' (Q. 5:48).

No matter where Muslims are, they must be judged according to Islamic law by an Islamic judge (Cardahi 1937: 603). Eluding this constitutes apostasy.[34] The absence of territorial limits to the application of Islamic law is considered a consequence of Islam's universalism (Khadduri 1966: 6), but its implementation is hindered by the fact that Muslims do not hold the power throughout the world. For this reason, Muslim scholars developed the theory of the world division in two main blocks: the *dār al-islām* (home of Islam) and the *dār al-harb* (home of war). In the former the ruler is a Muslim (even if the majority of the population is non-Muslim), while non-Muslims rule the latter. Relations between the two blocs are regulated under the law of *jihād* or war (*qānūn al-jihād aw al-harb*) or the broader Islamic *jus gentium* (*al-qānūn al-islāmī li-l-umam*), temporarily devised to govern international relations with non-Muslim political entities on more than war terms alone (Rechid 1937: 371ff; Armanazi 1929 and 1930).[35]

2.4.3   Status of non-Muslims in the dār al-islām

Non-Muslims can live on Islamic territories (*dār al-islām*) according to two different legal statuses: the *dhimmah* or the *amān*. These are only made available to non-Muslims who belong to the People of the Book (*ahl al-kitāb*, a denomination originally including mainly just Jews and Christians but later extended to other categories like Zoroastrians, Mandeans and Sikhs). Polytheists and renegades, however, are still excluded (ibn Qayyim al-Jawzīyah, *Ahkām ahl al-dhimmah*).

*Dhimmī*s are free non-Muslim subjects permanently living in a Muslim-ruled land on the basis of a covenant (*ʿahd*) or a perpetual safe-conduct (*amān muʾabbad*), under the protection of God and His messenger (*bi-dhimmatⁱ āllāhⁱ wa-rasūlih*). By virtue of such a protection, the *dhimmah*, Muslims say that non-Muslims have the same rights and duties of Muslims.[36] The protection of *dhimmī*s from Muslims, foreigners (*harbī*s) and other *dhimmī*s rests with the caliph or imam. ʿAlī is remembered to have said, 'They paid the tax (*jizyah*) for their blood to be like our blood, and for their belongings to be like our belongings' (*shams al-dīn* ibn Qudāmah, *al-Sharh al-kabīr ʿalà matn al-Muqniʿ*). There are four ways a non-Muslim belonging to the *ahl al-kitāb* can become a *dhimmī*. The first is by entering a protection covenant (*ʿahd al-dhimmah*).[37] The covenant should be established between the caliph (or his deputy) and the leaders of non-Muslim communities, in consideration of the general interest (*al-maslahah al-ʿāmmah*) of Muslims, with provisions for the payment of the *jizyah*, and is non-expiring. The second way is by acquiring land that is *kharājīyah*, i.e. land on which *kharāj* is levied, *kharāj* being the land tax imposed on lots belonging to non-Muslims of the *dār al-islām*. In the third, a non-Muslim foreign woman (either *harbīyah* or *mustaʾminah*) can become a *dhimmīyah* by marrying a Muslim or a *dhimmī*. And lastly, the minor children and the women related to the *dhimmī* become *dhimmī*s themselves on the basis of the family ties.

*Mustaʾmin*s, on the other hand, are non-Muslim foreigners (*harbī*s) who only temporarily reside in the *dār al-islām* thanks to a short-term safe-conduct (*amān muʾaqqat*). The short-term safe-conduct can be personal or general. The personal *amān* (*khāss*) can be granted by any adult, mentally sound Muslim to one or a group of *harbī*s (non-Muslim foreigners), while the general *amān* (*ʿāmm*) can be granted only by the caliph or his deputy to an unspecified number of *harbī*s. The *amān* allows the *mustaʾmin* to reside in the *dār al-islām* up to one year, together with his minor children and all the women related to him. During this period, the *mustaʾmin* is afforded the protected status of *dhimmī*s without having to pay the *jizyah*, which will be imposed if he exceeds the time limit of one year without returning to the *dār al-harb*.

From a legal standpoint, *dhimmīs* – unlike *musta'mins* – are considered subjects of the *dār al-islām*, even if they enjoy fewer legal and social rights than Muslims and have to endure many restrictions imposed by Islamic law.[38] The breach of any of these laws will result in the loss of the status of *dhimmī* and of the ensuing residence rights. When a non-Muslim foreign woman (*harbīyah*) marries a Muslim or a *dhimmī*, she becomes a member of the 'people of the home of Islam' (*ahl dār al-islām*), being a *dhimmīyah*. Likewise, if a *musta'min* converts to Islam, his minor children become Muslims and his wife a *dhimmīyah*, with no possibility for the latter to go back to the *dār al-harb*, since her husband's conversion does not have any effect on the marriage, which is still valid and falls under the new provisions of Islamic law. The basic underlying principle is that the woman follows her husband's status upwards, and the minor children their father's. However, since Islam sits at the top of the hierarchy, and prevails over all other confessions (*al-islām ya'lū wa-lā yu'là 'alayh*), if it is the woman who decides to convert to Islam, her minor children will become Muslims and the marriage will be dissolved. If both parents apostatise, their minor children will remain Muslims.

2.5   Islam and the kin group

Islam proudly claims to have obliterated every trace of the ancestral system of the previous era, depicted as the 'Age of Ignorance' (*'asr al-Jāhilīyah*). Even so, several features of the pre-Islamic mentality and kin organisation linger, overtly or covertly, even under Islamic disguise.[39] At the origins of different institutions or in the multifaceted political processes, the observer can detect the deep-rooted and long-lasting trends – briefly, the 'legal and political Arab milieu' – that dominated the scene before the rise of Islam but afterwards had to face competing forces.[40]

'The believers are but a single brotherhood' (Q. 49:10). The evocative power of the brotherhood that Islam wants to establish among Muslims cannot be ignored,[41] as well as the assertion of the superiority of the bond of faith over the bond of blood (Q. 9:23). However, the pre-Islamic kin order adamantly persisted. Its weight can be measured to some extent in the structure of the settlements founded during the expansion outside the Peninsula (§5.1.) as well as in the regulations pertaining to the early conversion of non-Arabs (§5.2.), in the rule of wedding adequacy in classic Islamic law (§5.3.) and in the restriction of the caliphate to Quraish kinsmen (§5.4.).

2.5.1   Planning newly founded cities

In the planning of cities founded along the routes of the conquest that followed Muhammad's death, the permanence of kin distinctions is patent. Cities like al-Kūfah (Mesopotamia), al-Basrah (Shatt al-ᶜArab), al-Fustāt (Egypt) or al-Qayrawān (northern Africa) were all founded as military camps that soon became stable settlements. The settlement was partitioned and allotted to different kin groups by the *tamsīr* or *takhtīt*; at the centre of the plan were the main mosque (*al-jāmiᶜ*) and the palace (*dār al-imārah*), while in the surroundings were arranged minor units (*dār*s or houses) grouped in *ᶜashīrah*s, each having its own mosque, and an outer open area for the group's meetings and burials (*jabbānah*). Settlements were thus divided into military and administrative units (e.g. five *akhmās* in al-Basrah, seven *asbāᶜ* in al-Kūfah) under the command of a person (the *ra's al-khums* in al-Basrah, for instance) who was responsible for the unit at war as well as for keeping order in peacetime. The *ra's* usually belonged to the larger kin group, but smaller groups nonetheless had representatives among the peers (*al-ashrāf*).

A large kin group like the Kindah had a dozen mosques in al-Kūfah as well as in al-Fustāt, Damascus or Hims. In highly urbanised regions like Syria, however, the partition plan was much laxer, whereas in new locations like al-Fustāt broad open areas were left between kin lots. Founded on the site of the ancient Diridotis (Teredon), the city of al-Basrah was divided into only five kin constituencies and soon hosted a large number of non-Arab local *mawlà*s (Caetani 1911-1914: III, 292-309 and 769-784, and Massignon 1954: 154-174), while al-Kūfah had a much more heterogeneous configuration, being divided into fifteen streets or *minhāj*s along which were arranged the lots of eminent nomadic tribes (the Tamīms, and the Asads), Hejazi kin groups (the Thaqīfs, the Sulayms, the Juhaynahs, and the Muzaynahs) and a sizeable Yemeni community (Massignon 1934-1937: III, 337-360). Still much later, when the Abbasid caliph al-Mansūr (ruled 754-775) built the new capital city of Baghdad on the model of Persian cities, he set up units and unit leaders like those in the primitive Muslim settlements. In the cosmopolitan Baghdad, however, units were ethnically or geographically homogeneous rather than grouped on the mere basis of kin,[42] since outside the peninsula the ethnic bond began replacing the kin bond in the age of the Marwanids during the second Umayyad period (64-132 AH/684-750 AD).

2.5.2   Status of non-Arab neo-converts (mawlàs)

Well-known to the customary law of pre-Islamic Arabia, clientage (*walā'*) gained special relevance with the rise of Islam when it became the only gate to Islam for non-Arabs and showed the enduring strength of kin bonds in the Arab social order. Both before and after the advent of Islam, any non-Arab on Arab territory – whose boundaries dramatically expanded after the conquests of the first century AH (632-750 AD) – had somehow to be brought into the Arab kin system, and one way to do it was by having recourse to the *walā'* to form a fictitious blood relation.

In pre-Islamic times, non-Arab kin groups enjoyed a peculiar status. They maintained their kin relations while being placed under the protection of Arab kin groups. No effective membership was involved. Some Jewish tribes were strong enough to avoid this arrangement, but many paid tributes to Arab tribes and became their clients.[43] As a result, the kin relations of minor groups grew weaker, but even so they were not completely disbanded. Similarly, freed slaves became clients of their former masters but did not become members of their kin group, in view of the fact that tainting the kin with non-Arabs was a highly despicable act for the Arabs. Non-Arabs were not even accepted as confederates; the *hilf* – a merging alliance – applied only to other Arabs or to non-Arabs who had a full kin status (Goldziher 1889: I, 105f).

As a result of the Arab-Islamic conquest, Arabs had to cope with huge masses of non-Arabs in their midst. If non-Muslims could be treated on the same terms as other clients (maintaining their internal organisation under Islamic hegemony and paying a tribute), converts on the other hand needed to be absorbed into the Arab-Islamic society. 'Having lost their genealogies (*ansāb*), suffered a defeat, or even having been enslaved' (al-Balādhurī, *Futūh al-buldān*), non-Arab converts were not suitable confederates (*halīf*). In order to overcome the deadlock, the notion of an Islamic *walā'* was developed. Every non-Arab wishing to become a member of the Arab-Islamic society had to find a patron (a superior *mawlā*). Freed slaves had a readily available patron in the person of the former master, unless he refused to undertake the task, leaving them in need of another patron.

Muslim scholars drew heavily on the pre-Islamic tradition to elaborate the doctrine of Islamic clientage, which consisted of different forms (*walā' al-muwālāh*, *al-tabā^cah*, or *al-khidmah*) including a novel 'clientage by conversion' (*walā' al-islām*), but it is precisely this original form of clientage that illustrates the attitude of Islamic law towards the previous social order and kin or ethnic distinctions. An oft-quoted *hadīth* states: 'Whoever converts at somebody's hands, the latter is the patron of the former',[44] thus providing some textual evidence for the theory. Under *walā'*, an outsider related to a social order conceived in terms of kin relations. The patron's main duty was to afford protection to the client (the inferior *mawlā*) and pay or receive blood money (*^caql* or *diyah*), but in return he had some rights to the *mawlā*'s belongings. The client, on the other hand, did not have to pay or receive the patron's *diyah* and did not inherit from him. Broadly speaking, the Arab patron provided an access to the new privileged society of the conquerors, while the non-Arab Muslim convert rendered him services, offered his help and swelled the civilian and military ranks of the patron.

Under the Umayyads, non-Arab converts or *mawlās* technically enjoyed the same status of Arab Muslims,[45] even if depending upon their patrons. However, *mawlās* were victims of cultural bias and were considered on the same footing as slaves. Hypotheses on the reasons for this have been advanced by scholars based on literary works from that period. Ibn Thābit (d. 674) and Dhū 'l-Rummah (d. 735) believed that they were discriminated against for being mainly peasants and not warriors, while according to al-Nābighah al-Jaʿdī (d. 670) it was for having been brutally defeated or for being largely freed after having been enslaved during the conquest. Muslim and non-Muslim sources seem to confirm the latter hypothesis, given the huge number of prisoners captured in the campaigns (ibn Khayyāt, Sebeos, Bar Penkaye and Michael the Syrian). Prisoners were generally enslaved and other slaves had to be supplied one-off or yearly under the terms of surrender (al-Tabarī, *Taʾrīkh*). War slaves and their offspring came thus to outnumber freeborn clients by far, and the term 'slave' was improperly used to address any *mawlā*. According to the sources, discrimination was not merely episodic; rather, severe ill-treatment of *mawlās* was the rule. Above all, a *mawlā* was barred from any task involving authority, viz. he could not act as imam, judge or governor (Goldziher 1889: I, 109 and 116), and his career was therefore in his patron's retinue. However, the *mawlās*' numbers, higher education and aptitudes soon earned them influential positions in the new polity. With the exception of government, non-Arab Muslims rapidly dominated the intellectual scene and played a major role in the formation of Islam (al-Hasan al-Basrī), Islamic law (abū Hanīfah, al-Awzāʿī and Tāwūs), Koranic studies (abū ʿUbaydah), Muhammad's biography (ibn Ishāq) and even in the collection of pre-Islamic Arab poetry (Hammād al-Rāwiyah). Arabs realised the *mawlās*' cultural refinement, and by the late Umayyad period *mawlās* were charged with the education of the caliph's descendants and with judiciary functions.

Yet *mawlās* enjoyed a privileged status, especially when compared with non-Muslims of the countryside. Many of the latter would venture to abandon their lands, attracted by the lure of joining the ranks of the Arab conquerors by converting to Islam and enlisting. The conversion thus consisted in migrating (performing the *hijrah*) to the garrison towns. ʿUmar II took in these converts, but other Umayyad caliphs sent them back to their villages or allowed them to stay provided that they kept up their fiscal duties as non-Muslims.

With the Abbasid revolution (750 AD), Arabs were finally deprived of the social and political privileges that they still retained. After the decline of 'Arab privileges', an Arab patron was no longer required for the non-Arab who wished to embrace Islam. Freed slaves would remain clients of their former masters, but freeborn non-Arab converts and the offspring of freed slaves were not bound to clientage. On the other hand, however, Arab superiority and the new political hue of the *walā'* maintained a key position under the Abbasids.

Muslim scholars of the classical age framed a comprehensive theory of clientage under Islam. All schools agree that clientage can stem from an act of emancipation (hence named *walā' al-ʿitq*), whereas only Hanafis, Jaʿfaris and Zaidis allow that it can be established by contract (*walā' al-muwālāh* or *tadammun bi-l-jarīrah*). For Hanafis and Jaʿfaris the clientage contract is independent of the act of conversion, while Zaidis hold that clientage is a consequence of conversion and cannot be established separately by contract. There is widespread consensus among jurists that *walā'* has to be regarded as instituting fictitious kin[46] and therefore cannot be transferred by sale, donation or inheritance, while such transfers were acceptable under pre-classical law. The transfer of rights and duties attached to clientage follows special provisions similar to kin transmission (Brunschvig 1976). But even though Sunni schools assert that *walā'* creates kin relations (*taʿsīb*), only the patron inherits from the *mawlà* (in case of *walā'* of emancipation, not *walā'* by contract), and the *mawlà* is a mere 'passive' member of the patron's kin group. In legal terms, *walā'* is a relation of dependence chiefly prompted by the individual's detachment from his own group, even if it does not lead to the acquisition of the full status of member of the patron's group (Crone 1980, 1987 and 1991).

Classical Islamic law generally does not attach any importance to the servile or non-Arab origins of the individual, but there is a relevant exception: non-Arabs and freed slaves cannot marry Arab women according to Hanafis, Shafiʿis, the majority of Hanbalis and some Zaidis. Malikis, while claiming that such unions are legal, let the Arab woman divorce a freed slave if he was believed to be an Arab. Only Ibadis, Twelvers and Ismailis clearly do not discriminate between Arabs and non-Arabs, freeborns and emancipated, for marital law purposes. This leads to some further considerations on the principle of wedding adequacy in Islamic law.

2.5.3   The principle of wedding adequacy (kafā'ah)

The absence of ethnic and social distinctions among Muslims is an ambitious goal hindered by the inveterate practices of the Arabs and of the other peoples who embraced Islam.[47] Jurists rearranged these traditional concepts in the discipline of family law, the cornerstone of social order. In pre-Islamic Arabia, both spouses were required to be on a par in terms of lineage and social status, while Islam waived the requirement for the man, who can marry a woman inferior to him. None of the Sunni schools ignored the issue of wedding adequacy (*kafā'ah*), but all addressed it in different ways according to the various theoretical and legal premises assumed by each legal school (*madhhab*). On the one hand, Hanafis presented a wide-ranging list of *kafā'ah* cases, whereas, on the other hand, Malikis downplayed its significance. Some scholars argue that differences need to be traced back to the different Hanafi and Maliki socio-geographic milieus; the former was characterised by sharp social divides between Arabs and non-Arabs in the cosmopolitan al-Kūfah, while the latter flourished in a much more homogeneous Hejazi society (Lynant de Bellefonds 1965: II, 171-181). However, the similarity of the operational rules of all Sunni schools suggests caution in assessing the dissimilarities of the scholars' ornate theories (Aluffi Beck-Peccoz 1990: 145).

With regard to kin relations, almost all schools require the man's adequacy to the woman's lineage (*kafā'at al-nasab*), thus reinforcing the practice of endogamy so deep-rooted in Arab customs. Being of Quraish, Arab and non-Arab descent are the three main levels of lineage requirements for *kafā'ah*, with further intermediate kin distinctions. Stricter doctrines can be found among Druzes, Zaidis and Zahiris, or in contexts where the presence of noble lineages is highly felt (like in Somalia, Cerulli 1919).

According to the Hanafi doctrine, the adult woman can contract a valid marriage without the assistance of her tutor (*walī*), but the contract is revocable (*ghayr lāzim*). Both the woman and her *walī* can ask the judge to annul the marriage (*faskh*) for the husband's lack of *kafā'ah* until the first signs of pregnancy appear. In the case of the Asādah of Hadramawt, a group that claims descent from ʿAlī, any member can contest a marriage on account of *mésalliance* (Anderson 1954: 23 and Ziadeh 1957: 515f). In Maliki law, the involvement of the woman's *walī* in the marriage is compulsory, and the woman cannot contract it by herself; consequently, the *kafā'ah* doctrine applies only if the husband concealed his inferior condition to the woman's tutor. The *walī*'s control over the man's *kafā'ah* – prescribed by Malikis but not necessary for Hanafis and Shafiʿis – is compensated by the possibility of annulling the contract. Even if they frame the problem differently, Muslim scholars share the same concerns for the protection of *nasab* and the law sanctions it, regardless of the clear Koranic condemnation.

2.5.4 Restriction of the caliphate to Quraish kinsmen

Nasab is also the seventh and last condition required for attaining the caliphate. The caliph must be a member of the Quraish, like Muhammad. Shafi'i jurist al-Māwardī (d. 1058) stated that the point was backed by an explicit textual ruling (*nass*) and by general consensus (*ij-māᶜ*). Conversely, he openly criticised the theory of the Muʿtazili doctor Dirār ibn ᶜAmr (d. 815), who maintained that anybody could be caliph, and that if one had to choose between a Quraish and a black man, the latter should be preferred, since it would be much easier to remove a black from office if he contravened divine law.

'You should listen to and obey your ruler even if he was an Ethiopian slave whose head looks like a raisin'.[48] This *hadīth* is given different interpretations. Muʿtazilis and Kharijites argue that it prevents the insertion of any restrictive clause based on kin, while mainstream Muslim scholars contend that the tradition refers to the caliph's appointees and not to the caliph himself, since there is little sense in the caliph being a slave (ibn ᶜĀbidīn, *Radd al-mukhtār ᶜalà 'l-Durr al-mukhtār* and ibn Nujaym, *al-Ashbāh wa-l-nazā'ir*).

Al-Māwardī quoted another tradition to further substantiate his theory: 'This matter will remain with the Quraish'.[49] Soon after Muhammad's death, Abū Bakr is reported to have cited this *hadīth* at the Saqīfah meeting when the *ansār*s were about to elect a Medinan caliph. According to al-Māwardī, the *ansār*s recognised the authenticity of the tradition and abandoned the idea of having two caliphs, one for the Medinans and one for the Meccans. Abū Bakr was then elected first caliph by acclamation, and proclaimed: 'We are the commanders and you are the ministers'.[50]

2.6 Islam and Arabness

In a broader perspective than the kin group – but with a very similar approach – the relations of Islam with its dominant ethnic group are also quite complex. Islam and Arabness are so closely knit that it is almost impossible to disentangle the respective contributions and influences, both in the past and at present. To explain the complexity of the relationship, scholars have resorted to different paradigms. The sole ambition of this section is to draw some attention to the meaning of membership in an ethno-religious community like the Arab-Islamic *ummah*.

2.6.1 Koranic prescriptions and early Islam

The Qur'ān adopts a clear stance on kin relations. 'Of no profit to you will be your relatives and your children on the Day of Judgment: He will judge between you: for Allah sees well all that ye do'[51] (Q. 60:3) was already revealed after the truce of Hudaybīyah in 628. But after the ʿumrah of 629 it was spelled out that the only possible distinction to be made among men was on the basis of piety (taqwà), in stark opposition to the attitude of the Quraish and the other polytheist Arabs: 'O mankind! We created you from a single (pair) of a male and a female, and made you into nations and tribes, that ye may know each other (not that ye may despise [each other]). Verily the most honoured of you in the sight of Allah is (he who is) the most righteous of you. And Allah has full knowledge and is well acquainted (with all things)' (Q. 49:13).[52]

Most commentators, however, do not infer from the superiority based on piety or righteousness that belonging to a certain tribe or nation is of no consequence. In the fairly unequivocal Koranic passage, the majority of Arab Muslim scholars conversely find a divine sanction of the original differentiation between Arabs divided into tribes (qabā'il), and non-Arabs divided into nations (shuʿūb).

As mentioned above, in early Islam the dominance of the Arab tribal mentality led to imposing the obligation upon non-Arab converts to seek the protection of members of Arab kin groups, in open contrast with the brotherhood and equality among Muslims stated in the Qur'ān. Certain mosques were reserved for mawlàs in order not to have them mix with Arabs, and it is narrated that the cruel al-Hajjāj used to wound the hands of the Nabateans to tell them apart from Arabs, and that he banned non-Arabs from entering al-Kūfah. Similarly, it was possible to have non-Arab Muslim slaves, but enslaving an Arab Muslim was not approved of (al-Shāfiʿī, Kitāb al-Umm).

2.6.2 The first Shuʿūbīyah

Opposition to the discrimination against non-Arabs soon emerged, and non-Arabs demanded the enforcement of the principle of equality among Muslims regardless of their belonging to shuʿūb or qabā'il. The movement assumed the name of Shuʿūbīyah, and since its inception it was endorsed by schismatic Muslims like the Kharijites (who refuse the restriction of the caliphate to Quraish kinsmen, asserting that even a black or a woman could be caliph if fit).

Later on, in the 2nd century Hijri (8th century AD), the term Shuʿūbīyah came to be used for a movement that not only rejected Arab privileges (whence the epithet of People of Equality, or ahl al-taswiyah, in al-Jāhiz's *Kitāb al-bayān wa-l-tabyīn*), but also advocated non-Arabs' superiority. Shu'ubites were chiefly Muslims of Persian origin, but there are indications of Shu'ubite literature by Arameans, Copts and Berbers as well.[53] Direct Shu'ubite sources were lost in time, but some of their allegations can be recovered from their adversaries' works (mainly al-Jāhiz and ibn Qutaybah). Different historiographical interpretations are given to the *Shuʿūbīyah* (Gibb 1962, Goitein 1966), but the core issue was probably the status of Persian officials in the new Empire. The latter ones were bound by *walāʾ* to Arab conquerors, and their liberty and social mobility were therefore severely hindered. A vivid account of the society of the time is given by al-Jāhiz in the epistles *Dhamm akhlāq al-kuttāb* (Censure of the Conduct of Secretaries) and *Fī madh al-tujjār wa-dhamm ʿamal al-sultān* (In Praise of Merchants and Dispraise of Officials). The author heats up against the *Shuʿūbīyah*, which he considered a real menace to Islam (al-Jāhiz, *al-Hayawān* and *Fakhr al-sūdān ʿalā 'l-baydān*).

The decline of the movement at the end of the 3rd century Hijri (9th century AD) was due – according to Gibb – to three main factors: (1) the merging of the pre-Islamic, Arab and Islamic traditions into a new, common 'culture' (*adab*), (2) the rise of the *muʿtazilah* with its rigid monotheism and (3) the foundation of the *Bayt al-hikmah*, centre for the translation and diffusion of the works of Greek philosophy, deemed effective tools against dualist doctrines (Gibb 1962: 69-72). In this context, ibn Qutaybah (d. 889) played a key role in accommodating the Persian tradition and the Arab-Islamic ideas through his various works.

2.6.2 Other opposition movements to Arab dominance

If animosity between Arabs and non-Arabs died down in the Muslim East at the end of the 3rd century Hijri, it built up in the Muslim West two centuries later. In the al-Andalus of the 5th century Hijri (11th century AD), however, Arab dominance was challenged by Berbers and Slavs. In the case of the Andalusian *Shuʿūbīyah*, the manifesto – ibn Gharsīyah's epistle – is still extant (Goldziher 1899 and Monroe 1970).

Hanna and Gardner see in the first and second *Shuʿūbīyah*s the same roots of later movements such as Ottomanism and Westernisation (19th century), or Internationalism, Regionalism and Socialism (20th century). All of these endeavoured to defy Arab dominance, instead triggering stronger affirmations of Arab particularism (Hanna & Gardner 1966). Some serious objections can be raised against this speculation, although it is enough to consider the theoretical distance between modern opposition movements and Early Islam *Shuʿūbīyah*s, or the significant differences of their respective actors and goals. Nonetheless, a map of the movements challenging Arab dominance could be traced down to present-day Kurdish and Berber claims, and the experience of the first *Shuʿūbīyah* has proven highly influential through the centuries. Many Arab-Muslim authors have vigorously condemned such movements, preaching a return to the unifying force of Islam (al-Sammāk 1990).

Among the many anecdotes there is one about Saladin that is worth mentioning. In 1169, Salāh al-dīn al-Ayyūbī had the caliph's first black eunuch beheaded for complicity with crusaders. He then replaced the black eunuch with a white eunuch, and dismissed all the other black eunuchs. The black troops in Cairo rose up against the execution of the man – whom they considered a spokesman and a champion of their rights – driven by 'racial solidarity'. The term ibn al-Athīr employed for 'racial solidarity' is the neologism *jinsīyah*,[54] based on *jins* (kind, genus, race). Centuries later and with no apparent relation to this early anecdote, *jinsīyah* was used to convey a 'new' idea of membership, membership in the nation-state.

3 Membership in the nation-state

3.1 The emergence of nation-states and nationality

Centuries after the formation of the Islamic community (*al-ummah al-islāmīyah*), a new form of membership (nationality or *jinsīyah*) in a new form of political organisation (the nation-state or *al-dawlah al-waṭanīyah*) took shape in the Arab world. The concepts of nation-states and nationality ties initially penetrated the vast Arab territories under Ottoman suzerainty during the decline of the Empire, and started taking root in the second half of the 19th century. The Sublime Porte felt urgent need of a secular membership bond to do away with capitulatory privileges and consolidate its control over the non-Turkish provinces. It is thus from this point that the search for the origins of nationality and citizenship in the Arab world must start. The Ottoman dismemberment and the creation of nation-states sped up the process, which culminated in the attainment of independence after World War II.

3.1.1 Ottoman decline

3.1.1.1 Capitulations (imtiyāzāt)
The main *raison d'être* of capitulations is that non-Muslims must be granted protection by the Islamic ruler in order to live in the *dār al-islām*. The practice developed on the one hand from the *dhimmah* covenants (*ʿahd al-dhimmah*) entered into by the imam and the leaders of non-Muslim subject communities, and on the other hand from the general safe-conducts (*amān ʿāmm*) that offered protection to non-Muslim foreigners. In both cases the Islamic ruler imposed restrictions on non-Muslims while dictating specific regulations applying to their protection, taxation and jurisdiction. These restraints and prescriptions, however, were later regarded as privileges.

The practice of producing written protection covenants is attested down to the 12th century, but reached its apex in the Ottoman capitulations (*imtiyāzāt*). Ottoman capitulations included provisions regarding the security of persons and goods, the exercise of consular jurisdiction and the exemption from collective responsibility. In line with the *dhimmah* procedure, capitulations were contracted between the Sublime Porte and European powers, but the Ottoman chancery followed the *amān* model. Ottoman capitulations were adopted by decree (*marsūm*) and generally had no time limit (Pélissié du Rausas 1910).

Since the Ottoman capitulations provided the breeding ground for the development of the concept of citizenship in the Arab world, their characteristics need to be carefully considered. In granting privileges to non-Muslim foreigners (*harbīs*), Ottomans endeavoured strictly to comply with the Islamic provisions of *fiqh* (according to the official Hanafi *madhhab*).[1] Foreign merchants resident in Ottoman ports and cities started forming recognised communities (*millet*), and their representatives obtained patents (*berāt*) from the Sultan, just like the leaders of *dhimmī* communities. Ever since the 17th century, European powers called for full extraterritoriality of their merchants' communities, but the Porte continued treating these communities as regular *millets*. On personal status matters between members of the same *millet*, religious and consular courts have always had full jurisdiction in compliance with Islamic conflict of laws rules (de Maslatrie 1866), whereas cases involving Muslims and criminal issues were left to Ottoman courts. However, provisions regarding judicial guarantees for *musta'mins* standing trial in Ottoman courts were progressively included in capitulations.

Capitulations were abused both by Ottoman subjects wanting to evade the Porte's authority and by Europeans trying to escape consular jurisdiction. Europeans converted to Islam as a means to do forum shopping, since Ottoman courts had full jurisdiction over foreign Muslims (if not otherwise expressly stipulated).[2] However, the major problem that Ottoman authorities faced was the extension of capitulatory privileges to Ottoman subjects, and from the 18th century onward the Topqapı was no longer able to stand up to European claims.[3]

Capitulatory privileges were much greater than the ones enjoyed by *dhimmīs*, and many of the latter contrived to enhance their status by assuming the function of dragoman. With the remunerated assistance of complaisant ambassadors and consuls, Ottoman non-Muslim subjects obtained their appointment by *berāt*, by which the Sultan extended some diplomatic immunities, commercial and fiscal privileges, as well as exemption from the poll tax (*jizyah*) levied on ordinary Ottoman subjects (*raᶜāyā*).[4] After a failed attempt to put an end to the practice, Selīm III himself (ruled 1789-1807) decided to grant privileges to his non-Muslim subjects for 1,500 piastres. The new privileged class (*Awrūpā tüjjārı*) was soon joined by a class of Muslim merchants (*khayriyye tüjjārı*) upon whom the same franchises were conferred for 1,200 piastres.

In the 19th century the situation of the capitulatory system grew even weaker for the Ottoman Empire, and the abolition of capitulations became a primary goal for the statesmen of the *Tanzīmāt*. In 1867 the Porte issued a *firmān* laying down equal conditions for subjects and foreigners, reserving the right to unilaterally modify the ʿuhūd-i ʿatīqah (capitulations, but literally the 'old covenants'). European powers vehemently protested the decision, and ʿAlī Pāshā even envisioned the adoption of the French Civil Code in order to quell the European dissent (Davison 1963: 252). The capitulations, however, were abolished only after the dismemberment of the Empire.

To curb the worst capitulatory abuses, in 1869 ʿAlī Pāshā signed the first Ottoman Nationality Law, intended to determine on whom the Sultan's authority could be exercised. Citizenship was thus initially framed as an issue pertaining to the exercise of political authority, outside the realm of Islamic law. ʿAlī Pāshā's legislation ensured that every change of nationality had to be approved beforehand by the Ottoman government. In the same year, the Sultan sent the European powers a memorandum denouncing the illegality of many capitulatory provisions (viz. the status of the 'protected', fiscal exemptions, extraterritoriality of consular jurisdictions, difficulties in successfully prosecuting criminal offences committed by foreigners, etc.), and issued a further regulation (*nizāmnāme*) on the status of consuls, which was as vigorously criticised as the memorandum.

3.1.1.2 Tanzīmāt *and Ottoman nationality*

At the beginning of the 19th century the Ottoman Empire was a vast mosaic of nations, communities, and privileges on its way to dismemberment. A comprehensive plan of reforms, know as *Tanzīmāt* or 'reorganisation', was initiated in 1839 to combat the decline of the central bureaucratic apparatus. The reforms, affecting various sectors of state bureaucracy (from the military to the economic administration, from the educational to the fiscal system), kept swinging uneasily between two models: on the one side, traditional confessional communitarianism (i.e. the *millet* system), and on the other side, forced denationalisation and Ottomanisation (ʿothmānlılıq). The measures inspired by the first model aimed at reorganising from the inside the major religious communities in order to limit their autocracy and internal corruption, whereas Ottomanisation intended to advance the equality of Ottoman subjects regardless of their ethnic or religious affiliation, rarely obtaining the desired result (Arabs fiercely opposed the policy of Turkification (*tatrīk*) associated with Ottomanisation).

Thirty years after the *khatt-ı sherīf* of Gülkhāne, the first Ottoman Law on citizenship was enacted in 1869 (Law 19 January 1869), even before the Fundamental Law (the *qānūn-i esāsī*) of 1876, and marked a historical milestone in the entire reform process. The Ottoman legislator adopted the principle of paternal *jus sanguinis* (art. 1). The individual born on Ottoman soil by foreign parents could only apply for Ottoman nationality three years after having come of age (art. 2). Acquisition by naturalisation required a continued residence of at least five years (art. 3), or was granted for individual merits (art. 4). A final provision dictated that all residents in the Ottoman dominions had to be considered Ottoman nationals and would be treated as such until their different nationality was legally established (art. 9); a Ministerial Circular of 26 March 1869 explained that the Law was non-retroactive (Young 1905-1906: II, 225), and the Decision of 20 April 1869 of the Nationality Commission confirmed that those holding another citizenship before 1869 could keep it (*Marie Debbas* case).

Among the modes of acquisition of Ottoman citizenship, conversion to Islam was not listed. This was a radical break with the tradition, which the new Law did not uproot, but had rather laid a secular system over it. The Council of State and the Council of Ministers, however, would continue to consider the conversion to Islam as a sufficient reason for the exceptional granting of citizenship of article 4; a significant innovation was that citizenship by conversion could be demanded but not imposed, as it was earlier (Salem 1907: 51-52). On the other hand, the introduction of the concept of secular citizenship proved so disorienting that Ottoman and Persian authorities had to sign a treaty to clarify that Persian residents of the Empire were to be treated as foreigners, even if they were Muslims (Ottoman-Persian Treaty of 14 December 1873, art. 6). Technically, under the 1869 Law, Ottoman Muslims and Ottoman non-Muslims belonged to the same political community on equal footing (even if the *millet* system was still standing), and the notion of the Islamic unity of the *ummah* was somehow shelved.

3.1.1.3   *Imperial provinces and indigenous nationality*

During the Ottoman decline of the 19th century, some of the Empire's dominions became fully independent (like Greece), some came under European sovereignty (like Algeria) and others gained certain autonomy under Ottoman political and religious suzerainty. In the latter provinces, the 1869 Ottoman Nationality Law was applied, but a set of local rights and duties was restricted to provincial citizens. Only natives of the province, for instance, were eligible for local enfranchisement and enlistment, at the exclusion of other Ottoman citizens. So in addition to Ottoman nationality, the notion of 'indigenous nationality' (*al-ra'awīyah al-mahallīyah*) emerged in the autonomous provinces.[5]

The institution of an indigenous nationality served not only the needs of assigning rights and duties to natives but was also used as a means to express the yearning for independence. Rights and duties were even assigned to individuals irrespective of their being Ottoman nationals. By the turn of the 20th century, Arab lands – where religious affiliation was the only known form of membership beyond the kin group – suddenly witnessed the rise of two new forms of secular membership, an overarching Ottoman nationality and a local indigenous one. Ottoman and local legislation introduced a secular nationality, but for the concept of full citizenship to take root in the Arab world an *évolution psychologique* was needed (Ghali 1934: 71). Somehow, the two World Wars, the establishment of nation-states and the patriots' common struggle for independence all contributed to creating modern forms of solidarity and a sense of belonging to a new political community: the nation-state.

3.1.2   Ottoman dismemberment

The 1918 Armistice of Moudros marked the end of Islamic political unity under Ottoman rule. Some territories, like Persia or Morocco, had already avoided Ottoman suzerainty, and others had been withdrawn from the Porte's control by European colonial aspirations, but the peace treaties of Sèvres and Lausanne completed the partition of the Empire – the entity that had come closest to the ideal of the Islamic unity ever since the Abbasid golden age.

Ottoman nationality ceased to exist, leaving the ground clear for the new, full-fledged nationalities drawn by the treaties. In the interwar period, the Turkish Republic abolished all capitulations, adopted the Swiss Civil Code and enacted a progressive Turkish Nationality Law in 1928 (Law 28 May 1928). While the nationality law in Turkey was only part of a general reform seeking to establish a secular nation-state for all its citizens, in the former Arab provinces nationality legislation was the main effort towards secularism, largely lacking a true citizenship spirit.

In Ghali's view, three factors heavily influenced the way the Arab dominions of the Ottoman Empire were detached: (1) the Arab Revolt of 1916, (2) the Sykes-Picot Agreement of 1916 and (3) the Balfour Declaration of 1917. The first affected the drawing of the geo-political map of the area by raising the Arabs' aspirations for Arab unity and the creation of Arab nation-states, the second by defining the British and French spheres of influence and control in the Near East, and the third by pledging the United Kingdom's support to the establishment of a national home for the Jewish people in Palestine (Ghali 1934: 83-94).

3.1.3   Peace treaties and nationality of detached territories

The nationality clauses of post-war peace treaties were designed to ease
the arrangement of former Ottoman subjects across the newly drawn
political boundaries and to allow for the regrouping of different nationalities living in former Ottoman lands. In 1920 the plenipotentiaries
who gathered in Sèvres signed the first peace treaty laying the basis for
a definition of nationalities of the defeated Empire, while solidifying its
partition. The Treaty of Sèvres was not ratified by Turkey for territorial
claims, but the rules on nationality were not contested and were thus
later transposed into the Treaty of Lausanne of 1923.

The nationality provisions of the Treaty of Sèvres were organised in
a general section (art. 123-130), and in a special section for Egypt, Sudan and Cyprus (art. 102-106, and 117) due to their particular international status. The basic principle of the treaty is that Turkish subjects
habitually resident in territories detached from Turkey became *ipso facto*, in the conditions laid down by the local laws, nationals of the state
to which the territory was transferred (art. 123). Habitual residence was
preferred to the place of birth (the principle previously adopted in international agreements). In the English version the subjects had to be 'habitually resident', but *'établis'* in the French one; the discrepancy gave
rise to speculations on the precise meaning of the qualification. The
English 'habitual residence' was somehow less exacting than the
French *'domicile'*, defined in article 102 of the Code Napoléon as the
'lieu du principal établissement'. A clear-cut solution was never found,
and scholars and national legislators followed either interpretation
(Bentwich 1926: 97; Fauchille 1921-1926: I, 865).

The Treaty of Sèvres also granted former Ottoman subjects the right
to opt for Turkish nationality (art. 124) or the nationality of the state
the majority of whose population was of the same race as the person
exercising the right, if the person was over eighteen years of age, was
habitually resident in a territory detached from Turkey and differed in
race from the majority of the population of such a territory (art. 125).
The right of option had to be exercised within one year of the treaty's
coming into force (art. 125), and the place of residence had to be transferred within the succeeding twelve months to the state for which the
person had opted (art. 126). The fairly short term to transfer the residence seems to have seriously undermined the right of option but was
dictated by the desire of implementing in due time the policy of regrouping nationalities so dear to Wilson. Moreover, the state for which
the former Ottoman subject opted could not refuse its 'returning
national'.

A very controversial clause was the one regarding the nationality of
Jews. In the spirit of the Balfour Declaration, article 129 provided that

Jews of other than Turkish nationality who were habitually resident within the boundaries of Palestine (as determined by article 95) on the treaty's coming into force became *ipso facto* citizens of Palestine to the exclusion of any other nationality.

The Sèvres provisions for Ottoman dismemberment were particularly harsh on Turks (especially with regard to the partition of Anatolia), and even the former wartime Allies soon proved not to be too keen on enforcing them (Temperley 1920-1924: VI, 7). Turkish revolutionaries vigorously rejected the treaty and called for the political unity of all the Turkish lands in the National Pact (*misak-ı milli*) of 1920. The treaty was terminated and the diplomats returned to the negotiating table in Lausanne, where the new peace treaty was signed in 1923.

The Conference of Lausanne only had to adapt the Sèvres clauses on nationality to the new territorial arrangements and to add some minor tweaks. The section on Egypt was no longer included, since the country gained independence in 1922, and Hejaz was no longer mentioned due to the particular international status of the region. Turkey renounced all rights and titles on the Dodecanese islands in Italy's favour (art. 15), and recognised the annexation of Cyprus proclaimed by the British government (art. 20), while negotiators integrated the Convention on the Exchange of Populations between Greece and Turkey of 1923 (art. 142).

The Treaty of Lausanne largely reproduced the Sèvres provisions on nationality (art. 30-36). The term for exercising the right of option was extended to two years, acknowledging that twelve months was too short a period for such a momentous decision (art. 31-32). On the other hand, however, the treaty subjected the right of option for non-Turkish nationalities to the consent of the receiving state (art. 32). While upholding the principle of the 'habitual residence', the treaty allowed for natives of a certain detached territory who were resident abroad at the time of the treaty's coming into force to exercise the right of option for the nationality of the territory they were natives of, with the consent of the government exercising authority therein (art. 34).

In the region's troubled post-war years, peace treaty provisions for setting boundaries and dividing populations were interwoven with implementing the national legislation of the new nation-states. The shaping of nationality laws and the emergence of independent states was thus a challenge that the Arab world faced fairly late, and resorted to foreign models in order to meet it.

3.1.4   The French model

In drafting legislation on nationality, Arab legislators largely followed the French model both before and after reaching full independence.

The general framework and the specific solutions demonstrate strong correspondence with the slow but continued development of the French rules on *nationalité*. As is often the case in the circulation of models, some of the French rules encountered a responsive legal environment and took root, even surviving the disappearance of the original model, while others simply could not, due to profound resistance.

In the 20th century, almost all leading Arab jurists studied in Europe and most of them earned doctoral degrees in France, thus keeping alive and consolidating the influence of the French legal mentality. Arab scholarship on nationality in particular draws heavily on French works and invariably quotes French scholars like Niboyet, Battifol and Lagarde.

Even the decision to consider nationality as within the domain of international private law (conflict of laws) reveals a profound French influence. Until the *revirement* of the French Court of Cassation in the late 1950s, for instance, the Egyptian Council of State followed previous French orientation in considering it a matter of public law, but then adapted to the new course of French jurisprudence (al-Wakīl 1965: 61). Unlike their French colleagues, however, Arab scholars overlooked the relation of citizenship to public law.

French citizenship rules were initially included in the *Constitutions*. In the wake of the Revolution, every individual born on French soil was a French citizen, as were those born of a French father outside France if the father still cherished the desire to return to France (*esprit de retour*). The *jus soli* thus prevailed and was maintained in the revolutionary Constitutions of 1791, 1793 and 1799 (Vanel 1945 and 1946 and Lefebvre-Teillard 1993: 223).

The Code Napoléon (1804) marked a turning point by introducing provisions on citizenship in the Civil Code and by establishing the dominance of the *jus sanguinis* (CodeNap, art. 8). A child of foreign parents could apply for French citizenship after having come of age, if a resident of France (CodeNap, art. 9). Legislation on naturalisation was passed in the first half of the 19th century, but only in 1851 was a general reform enacted which reinstated the *jus soli* for a child born in France of foreign parents who themselves were born in France (double *jus soli*). The Law of 1851 served as the main source of inspiration for the Ottoman Law of 1869, the first nationality law in the region. In 1889 the discipline was reintegrated in the Civil Code and the cases of attribution were sensibly expanded for national defence reasons.[6] The equality of rights envisioned in the Code Napoléon suggested stricter citizenship requirements (as the *jus sanguinis*), while the equality of duties required an enlargement of the citizenry base on which defence duties were imposed in the late 19th century (Bruschi 1987: 46).

In the interwar period legislation was passed restricting the rights of naturalised citizens, but after World War II citizenship was entirely reformed and placed in a Nationality Code (*Code de la nationalité*), passed on 19 October 1945 and destined to become '*une véritable somme du droit de la nationalité*', according to Lerebours-Pigeonnière (Lagarde 1997: 39). The Code, consisting of 151 articles and scrupulously regulating the attribution, acquisition and loss of French nationality, inspired most of the national legislators that attained independence in the postwar years. In 1973 a reform incorporated the solutions to the issues that had been raised by the courts in the meanwhile. It removed all the provisions that came under the *domaine réglementaire* under the 1958 Constitution and included adaptations to the major civil law reforms (i.e. equality of spouses, equality of filiation, attainment of majority and the new adoption regime).

A ten-year debate over citizenship and migration led to the adoption of a new law in 1993, which repealed the Code of 1973 and reintroduced nationality provisions in the Civil Code, since nationality is '*un élément d'individualisation de la personne, au même titre que son état civil*', according to the report attached to the bill and presented to the French National Assembly. The Law of 1993 is also inspired by a liberal vision based on the elective concept of citizenship – '*la nation n'existe que par le consentement de ceux qui la composent*' – a polity open to those who want to become members of it but requiring some *liens objectifs* with the community. It is also characterised by a more conservative perspective with an 'obsessive fear' of fraud against migration laws (Lagarde 1997: 42).

3.1.5   Independent states and nationality legislation

3.1.5.1   Egypt

Nationality has been a key concept for the formation of the modern nation-state in Egypt. Even under Ottoman suzerainty, the set of rules applying only to Egyptians gave rise to the theory of the 'indigenous nationality' and laid the basis for the creation of a strong national identity. Later on, nationality legislation was the first step towards a secular entity (1926-1929), followed by the abolition of capitulations (1937) and the institution of general state courts (1955).

By the end of the 19th century, the Egyptian indigenous nationality was fully shaped. Local legislation usually referred to the 'Egyptian' in order to grant a right or impose a duty, to the exclusion of all other Ottoman subjects. Public functions and jurisdictions were reserved for local subjects, as was the application of military conscription rules or the Indigenous Penal Code. Every piece of legislation, however, adopted a different definition of the person it would apply to, the definition of the indigenous being therefore 'multiple, complex and contradictory' (Badawi Pacha 1926: 12). Egyptian Syrians, for instance, had to enlist but were not allowed to vote.

Indigenous nationality only complemented Ottoman nationality, the latter being conditional to the former (Messina 1928: 161), and the Egyptian was treated internationally as an Ottoman subject. When Egypt ceased to be an Ottoman province, the indigenous status turned into full-fledged nationality, but legislation regulating Egyptian nationality was only adopted in the late 1920s after the country reached full independence.

Egyptian nationality was first regulated by the Decree-Law (*marsūm bi-qānūn*) of 26 May 1926, the main purpose of which was to sort out the status of former Ottoman subjects in the country. Ottoman subjects had long been established in Egypt, contributed greatly to its economic and cultural growth and were deeply assimilated, but some of them (chiefly Syrians, Jews and Armenians) found new home countries as a consequence of the Empire's partition. The 1926 Decree-Law defined the Ottoman as the subject of the Porte on the eve of the 1923 Treaty of Lausanne (art. 1), thus leaving out Tunisians, Albanians and Tripolitanians. Along with the peace treaties, the 1926 Decree-Law referred to 5 November 1914 as the watershed for Egyptian nationality. Diplomats at the peace conferences had regarded the day the Allies entered into war with the Ottoman Empire as the day Ottoman suzerainty over Egypt and Cyprus had ended. Ottoman subjects residing in Egypt on or after 5 November 1914 and up to the coming into force of the 1926 Decree-Law were to be considered Egyptian nationals *de plein droit*. On the one hand, the 1926 legislation recognised the right of option for other territories but required birth (or birth of a parent) on the territory opted for and the residence transfer to the country of option within six months (art. 4), even if allowing for return within the following five years and the reacquisition of the Egyptian nationality. On the other hand, former Ottoman subjects, if resident in Egypt on or after 5 November 1914, could acquire Egyptian nationality (art. 6-7). The Ottoman subjects who had never taken residence in the country could transfer their residence to Egypt within a year and acquire its nationality after five years (art. 9).

The 1926 legislation severely restricted the provisions of the 1923 Treaty of Lausanne concerning the right of option for other nationalities by requiring birth on the territory instead of the mere community of race, reducing the term for the exercise of the right and discouraging the option. At the same time it was sharply criticised by capitulatory powers, who claimed their right to veto all Egyptian legislation affecting the status of foreigners through the General Assembly of the Mixed Court of Appeal.

Egypt wanted to reassert its sovereign right to regulate the status of nationals and foreigners, and issued a new Decree-Law on 27 February 1929. The 1929 Decree-Law drew on the 1926 stipulations but redressed some restrictions as to the right of option, especially by allowing former Ottoman subjects who had opted for a foreign nationality to keep their residence in Egypt, unless ordered otherwise.[7] The pre-eminence of *jus sanguinis* was upheld (art. 5), while a particular case of double *jus soli* was introduced for the child born in Egypt of a foreign father born in Egypt but ethnically belonging to the majority of the population of a country whose language was Arabic or whose religion was Islam (art. 6(4)). Even if it was not an application of *jus soli*, birth in Egypt entitled the individual permanently residing in Egypt to claim Egyptian nationality at the age of majority (art. 7). The 1929 Decree-Law included provisions on naturalisation (art. 8-11), loss and deprivation of nationality (art. 12-13) and the nationality of married women (art. 14). An Egyptian woman married to a foreigner was deprived of her Egyptian nationality provided that her husband's national law granted her the husband's nationality, whereas the foreign woman marrying an Egyptian had Egyptian nationality imposed upon her (art. 14(1-2)).

The 1929 legislation granted Egyptian nationality to those who were already assimilated, or those deemed to be easily assimilable because of their ethnic or religious origins. At the same time it provided for various cases of deprivation for those considered unworthy of Egyptian nationality. Unlike the 1928 Turkish Nationality Law, which absorbed all foreign elements into the national community through the *jus soli*, the 1929 Egyptian Nationality Decree-Law allowed for the absorption of foreign elements only if there was a common cultural, linguistic or religious background (Saba 1931: 100ff).

The 1929 Decree-Law remained in force until it was repealed by Law 160/1950, which made use of earlier legislation but sensibly limited the access to Egyptian nationality to foreigners by repealing the double *jus soli* (*al-mīlād al-mudā'af*). It also abandoned the principle of unity of nationality within the family by allowing a foreign woman married to an Egyptian to waive Egyptian nationality (art. 9).

Just after the 1952 Revolution, a new law on Egyptian nationality (Law 391/1952) was passed. Its purpose was to require a stronger attachment to Egypt (i.e. continued residence from 1 January 1900, regardless of Ottoman nationality) and to secure the protection of the national community (*himāyat al-jamā'ah al-watanīyah*) from disloyal nationals, like Zionists and others convicted for treason (*khiyānah*) against Egypt (art. 1). Nationality could be withdrawn to protect the security and integrity of the state (*bi-qasd himāyat amn al-dawlah wa-salāmatihā*), and nationals who left the country for six months, with no intention to return to Egypt, lost their Egyptian nationality (art. 19). The 1952 legislation increased the discretionary powers of the government with regard to the acquisition and deprivation of nationality.

The short-lived federative experience with Syria under the United Arab Republic (UAR) demanded a new, common legislation on nationality. The provisional constitution of March 1958 referred to the national Syrian and Egyptian laws in force at the time (art. 3), but later in the year the UAR Nationality Law (Law 82/1958) was issued by decree of the President of the Arab Republic of Egypt. Central to the 1958 Law was membership in the Arab community (al-ummah al-ʿarabīyah). The expatriate citizen (al-muwātin al-mughtarib), a member of the Arab community who was neither a resident nor a national of an Arab state, was assimilated to the UAR as a national and could be naturalised under more lenient provisions. Like in the 1952 Egyptian legislation, discretionary powers were quite broad, and the government's consent (muwāfaqah) was required for any change of nationality status.

When the federation was terminated on 28 September 1961, Syria promptly issued a new Legislative Decree in October 1961, while Egypt did not adopt a new law until 1975. In the meanwhile, the Egyptian courts ruled that the provisions of the 1958 UAR Nationality Law applied only to Egyptians after Syria's breakaway (infisāl).

The 1975 Egyptian Nationality Law (Law 26/1975) limited access to Egyptian nationality by narrowing the scope of jus soli and extending the residency requirements for naturalisation. The Interior Minister has to consent to the acquisition, even if cases of loss or deprivation are reduced and regulated. Under the 1975 Law, Egyptian nationality is passed on by filiation even outside the country (perpetual nationality). In 2004 a law extending the rule of jus sanguinis to maternal descent was passed (Law 154/2004), thus allowing children of Egyptian mothers and foreign fathers to acquire Egyptian nationality just like the children of Egyptian fathers.

3.1.5.2   Iraq

Established as a kingdom under British rule (1921), and detached from Turkey by the peace treaties (1923), Iraq was the first Ottoman dominion to reach independence (1932) and to join the League of Nations (same year). Iraqi nationality was also the first nationality regulated after the Treaty of Lausanne went into effect. The Iraqi legislature, unlike its Egyptian counterpart, was bound under the provisions of the Lausanne treaty.

The 1924 Iraqi Nationality Law (Law 42/1924) was inspired by the desire to increase the Iraqi population by favouring the option for Iraqi nationality and hindering its renunciation. The watershed for the 1924 Iraqi Law – just like the 1928 Transjordanian Law – was 6 August

1924 (day of the deposit of British ratification instruments for the Treaty of Lausanne). Ottoman subjects habitually resident in Iraq on that date were considered Iraqi nationals, habitual residence being presumed from residence since 23 August 1921 (the day Faysal I was crowned King of Iraq). For the exercise of the right of option for Turkish nationality – the only option open to Arab Ottoman Iraqis – the 1924 legislation further restricted the Lausanne provisions by requiring a permit issued by an Iraqi official (established by Royal Decree 80/1926), and the consent of the Turkish government (art. 4). Conversely, the 1924 Law adopted a broader notion of 'native' to allow all former Ottoman subjects residing abroad to opt for Iraqi nationality even if not ethnically belonging to the majority of the Iraqi population (art. 7). For the attribution of nationality, the 1924 Iraqi Law assigned a prominent role to *jus sanguinis* (art. 8) and a residual role to *jus soli* (art. 9). For acquisition by naturalisation, on the other hand, only a three-year residency was requested. The Iraqi Nationality Law of 1924 – later amended several times[8]– was the first piece of legislation in the Middle East to promote an 'open' concept of nationality.

Three months after the military coup of ᶜAbd al-salām Muhammad ᶜĀrif (February 1963), a new Iraqi Nationality Law was enacted (Law 43/1963) but soon amended after the reorientation that followed the internal November coup (Law 206/1964). The Baathist bloodless coup of 1968 led to new amendments to the 1963 Law in 1968 (Law 147/1968), in 1970 (Law 60/1970), in 1972 (Law 131/1972) and – in a pan-Arab spirit – in 1975 (Law 5/1975), while loss of Iraqi nationality was modified in 1980 shortly after Saddam Hussein's takeover (Law 207/1980). Decisions by the Revolutionary Command Council, on the other hand, dealt with the status of Iraqi Jews (*qarār* 1293/1975), stipulated new conditions for naturalisation (*qarār* 180/1980; persons of Iranian origin were expressly excluded by *qarār* 518/1980) and determined the deprivation of citizenship on account of disloyalty (*qarār* 666/1980).

3.1.5.3   Palestine

Unlike other mandates of the League of Nations, the 1922 Mandate for Palestine clearly provided for the enactment of a Palestinian Nationality Law, and special provisions to facilitate the acquisition of Palestinian citizenship by Jews taking up permanent residence in Palestine had to be included (art. 7). The establishment of a national home for the Jews in Palestine was a goal of the British Mandate incorporated in the Mandate preamble but was limited to the territory west of the Jordan River (art. 25). In the eastern territory, known as Transjordan, the British government set up a separate administration and installed the Hashemite Emir ᶜAdb allāh, elder son of Britain's wartime Arab ally the *sharīf* Hussein of Mecca.

The wording of article 7 included both the terms 'nationality' and 'citizenship', the former to refer to the relationship between the individual and the state, the latter to indicate the membership of the same individual in the polity regardless of the 'ethnic-communitarian' affiliation which the problematic etymon of nationality could suggest. The underlying assumption was that different nationalities (chiefly Arabs and Jews; Oppenheim 1927: I, 526) had to coexist within the western territory included in the Mandate, 'it being clearly understood that nothing should be done which might prejudice the civil and religious rights of existing non-Jewish communities in Palestine' (1917 Balfour Declaration, faithfully reproduced in the 1922 Palestine Mandate preamble). 'Or the rights and political status enjoyed by Jews in any other country', concluded the Declaration (and the Mandate preamble). Zionist authors inferred from the wording of article 7 that a Jewish nationality in Palestine was established for all world Jews (Brickner 1930).

The British government waited for the signing and the enforcement of the Treaty of Lausanne to regulate Palestinian nationality. Two years later, on 24 July 1925, King George V gave his assent to the Palestine Citizenship Order-in-Council. The Order-in-Council chose as a watershed for Palestinian nationality 1 August 1925, the day of its coming into force, but the choice was inconsistent with the entry into force of the treaty on 1 August 1924, thus generating problems of coordination (sect. 1). For instance, all former Ottoman subjects who left Palestine before 1 August 1925 and did not possess a provisional citizenship certificate issued in 1922 for the elections to the Legislative Council became stateless. They had lost their Turkish nationality due to the Treaty of Lausanne (art. 30), and could not be attributed Palestinian citizenship (Ghali 1934: 215). The situation was addressed and solved by a 1931 Order-in-Council.

The provisions of the Treaty of Lausanne on the right of option could not be applied to Palestinian nationality. Arabs could not claim to differ by race from the majority of the population of other detached territories, while Jews could not claim to belong by race to the majority of the population of Palestine (art. 32). The 1925 Order-in-Council, however, omitted the latter condition for the former Ottoman subjects residing abroad and wishing to opt for Palestinian citizenship (art. 34), but required birth in the territory as well as a preliminary six-month residency in Palestine (sect. 2).

The rules on the attribution of Palestinian nationality were inspired by the 1914 British Nationality and Status of Aliens Act, except for the *jus soli*, which was relegated to a minor role. Even if closely related, a positive conflict of nationalities between the 1914 Act and the 1925 Order-in-Council could arise; for example, an individual born in the United Kingdom of a Palestinian father born in Palestine was a British citizen under the 1914 Act and a Palestinian national under the 1925 Or-der-in-Council. Moreover, British citizens taking up Palestinian citizen-ship did not have to renounce their British citizenship, since in British legal mentality dual citizenship was permissible.

The controversial clause of the Treaty of Sèvres granting immediate and inescapable nationality to Jews habitually resident in Palestine on the entry into force of the treaty (art. 129) was left out of the Treaty of Lausanne. The conditions for naturalisation in the 1925 Order-in-Coun-cil included: (1) a two-year residency in Palestine during the three years before the application, (2) good behaviour and knowledge of any of the three official languages (Arabic, English or Hebrew) and (3) the inten-tion to take up permanent residence in Palestine after acquiring Pales-tinian nationality (sect. 7). In the eyes of newly immigrated Jews the two-year residency requirement was nonsense, but the Order-in-Coun-cil provided for no distinction between the Palestinian-born and the naturalised Palestinian citizen (sect. 8).

After the 1948 Arab-Israeli War, the Gaza Strip (*Qitāᶜ Ghazzah*) fell under Egyptian rule while the West Bank (*al-Diffah al-gharbīyah*) was annexed in 1950 by the Hashemite Kingdom of Jordan. From that mo-ment on, legal pluralism has been the distinctive feature of the Palesti-nian system. Elements of Ottoman law, British Mandate legislation, Egyptian and Jordanian law were all applied in the West Bank and the Gaza Strip, as well as Israeli law after the military occupation that fol-lowed the 1967 Six-Day War.

After the foundation of Israel in 1948, Palestinian citizenship en-tered its 'hyphenated phase' (Kassim 2000: 204ff). Due to their differ-ent status, different citizenship rules apply to (1) Palestinians from the West Bank, (2) Palestinians from the Gaza Strip, (3) Palestinians living in Israel, (4) Palestinian refugees[9] who took shelter in the West Bank or in other Arab countries or (5) Palestinians of the diaspora.

The Palestinian Liberation Organisation (PLO), recognised by the Arab League in the 1974 Rabat summit as the sole legitimate represen-tative of the Palestinian people, negotiated with the Israeli government in 1993 the Oslo Accords that established the Palestinian National Authority (PNA). The PLO's definition of the Palestinian national was enshrined in the 1964 Palestinian National Charter (*al-Mīthāq al-qawmī al-filastīnī*), adopted by the first Palestinian Conference: 'Palestinians are Arab nationals who, until 1947, normally resided in Palestine re-gardless of whether they were evicted from it or have stayed there. Any-one born after that date of a Palestinian father – whether inside Pales-tine or outside it – is also a Palestinian' (art. 5). In the mid-1990s, a draft Palestinian Nationality Law was circulated but never voted in. The Basic Law (*al-qānūn al-asāsī*) passed by the Legislative Council in 1997 and promulgated by the PNA president in 2002 only stipulated that Palestinian nationality has to be regulated by law (art. 7).

As for non-Jewish Palestinians of Israel, the 1952 Israeli Nationality Law required a demanding proof of residence that caused many of them to be considered stateless residents. Later amendments (1968, 1971 and 1980), however, eliminated major cases of statelessness. The 1952 Israeli Nationality Law completed the 1950 Law of Return, which grants Israeli nationality to every returning Jew, and the 1950 Absentees' Property Law.

At present, the situation seems to be evolving towards the establishment of two states in Palestine: Israel and the territories under the PNA control (Israel disengaged from the Gaza Strip in 2005 but keeps a military presence in the West Bank). This means the existence of Israeli citizenship on the one hand and an *in fieri* Palestinian citizenship on the other.

3.1.5.4 Jordan

The Emirate of Transjordan was an autonomous political division of the Mandate for Palestine, and the British government limited its oversight to financial, military and foreign policy matters. Under the 1928 Anglo-Transjordanian Treaty and the Organic Law for Transjordan, administrative and legislative powers were vested in the Emir (OLT, art. 16), assisted by an elective Legislative Council (OLT, art. 25).

The 1928 Organic Law required Transjordanian nationality to be regulated by law (art. 4), and a Tranjordanian Nationality Law was approved on 23 April 1928. The 1928 legislation defined the uncertain status of Transjordanians between 1925 and 1928. After the coming into force of the Treaty of Lausanne they could no longer be considered Ottoman subjects, while the Mandate provisions on Palestinian nationality (namely, art. 7) and the 1925 Palestinian Citizenship Order-in-Council did not apply to the territory east of the Jordan River. For the establishment of Transjordanian nationality, the same watershed of the 1924 Iraqi Law was adopted (6 August 1926, the day of the deposit of British ratification instruments for the Treaty of Lausanne), and 'habitually resident' were those Ottoman subjects who had their usual place of residence in Transjordan during the twelve months preceding the same date (art. 1). The 1928 Law regulated the right of option in full compliance with the Lausanne provisions (art. 2-4) and facilitated the option of former Ottoman subjects living abroad just like the 1925 Palestinian Citizenship Order-in-Council (art. 5). The attribution of Transjordanian nationality was based on *jus sanguinis*, but could be also based on double *jus soli*, unlike Palestinian nationality (art. 6). The 1928 Law was amended twice in 1944 by laws 18/1944 and 24/1944.

During the 1948 Arab-Israeli War, King ʿAbd allāh seized the West Bank. This triggered a large Palestinian migration to the territory across the river, which became in April 1949 the Hashemite Kingdom of Jordan. An additional law of the Transjordanian Law of 1928 was passed in December 1949 (*qānūn idāfī li-qānūn al-jinsīyah* 56/1949), declaring all the residents of Transjordan and the West Bank – which was annexed in 1950 – Jordanian nationals. In 1988 King Hussein of Jordan declared the full legal and administrative disengagement from the West Bank (*fakk al-irtibāt*), and consequently transferred all responsibility for 'liberating the occupied Palestinian lands' to the PLO (King Hussein's Speech of 31 July 1988). The implementation of the *fakk al-irtibāt* was regulated by a Declaration of the Jordanian Prime Minister Ziyād al-Rifāʿī (20 August 1988), where he spelled out that West Bank residents had to be considered Palestinian, not Jordanian, nationals (art. 2), i.e. stateless.

A new Jordanian Nationality Law was passed in 1954 (Law 6/1954). Provisions for naturalisation were later amended in 1956 (Law 21/1956), as well as those for acquisition in 1963 (Law 7/1963), those for loss of nationality in 1958 (Law 50/1958) and those for dual nationality in 1987 (Law 22/1987).

3.1.5.5 Lebanon

In the territories under French Mandate, the establishment of Lebanese and Syrian nationalities was accomplished in two stages. Two decisions of the French High Commissioner dealt with the right of option in the first stage, while in the second other two decisions rescinded the 1869 Ottoman Nationality Law and regulated the Lebanese and Syrian nationalities, taking into account local particularism, the high birth and migration rates.

The French High Commissioner issued the first two decisions (*arrêté* in French, or *qarār* in Arabic) on 3 August 1924 (2825 and 2825-*bis*). These acknowledged the pre-existence of a Lebanese and Syrian nationality (*nationalité*, or *tābiʿīyah*), interpreted the '*établissement*' clause as the '*domicile*' of the Code Napoléon and assumed as a watershed 30 August 1925 (day of the entry into force of the Treaty of Lausanne for the territories under French Mandate).

Two other decisions (15/S and 16/S), adopted on 19 January 1925, correspondingly regulated the Lebanese and Syrian nationalities on the basis of the *jus sanguinis*, but unlike other legislation in the region they attempted to keep all possible residents and expatriates attached (Transitional Clauses, art. 10). Longer residency was required for naturalisation, but language knowledge was not compulsory. Compared with the domestic French nationality rules, the 1925 Decisions 15/S and 16/S proved to be more 'open'.

Decision 15/S of 1925 is still the fundamental text on Lebanese nationality, even if repeatedly amended. Provisions on naturalisation were modified by act of law on 27 May 1939 (rescinded by the Legislative Decree 48/1940 on 31 May 1940), while the former clauses on naturalisation (Decision 15/S, art. 3) were repealed by Decision 122/LR of 19 June 1939. Naturalised Lebanese nationals were disqualified from public office for ten years by the Law of 7 June 1937, whereas the loss of Lebanese nationality was regulated by the Law of 31 January 1946. Issues related to nationality and marriage were addressed by the Law of 11 January 1960, which amended Decision 15/S, art. 4-7. All efforts exerted during the civil war and the 1990s to pass a new, organic Lebanese nationality law proved unsuccessful.

3.1.5.6   Syria
Unlike Lebanon, in independent Syria the French Mandate legislation on nationality (Decision 16/S) was repealed and replaced with Law 98/1951, Legislative Decree (*marsūm tashrīʿī*) 21/1953, Law 82/1958 (during the UAR experience), Legislative Decree (*marsūm tashrīʿī*) 27/1961 and finally Legislative Decree (*marsūm tashrīʿī*) 276/1969 of 24 November 1969. The 1969 Decree was issued after the takeover by radical neo-Baathists and the promulgation of the Provisional Constitution of May 1969. However, the enacting regulations were issued in 1976 (Interior Minister's Decision 92/1976) when Hāfiz al-Asad's corrective movement had already shed the party's extremists. The 1969 Legislative Decree affords a distinctive preferential treatment to Arabs who wish to acquire Syrian nationality. For Syrian legislation the world is thus divided into three categories: Syrian nationals, Arabs and foreigners (*ajānib*).

3.1.5.7   Saudi Arabia
In November 1916, Hussein, the *sharīf* of Mecca, proclaimed himself King of Hejaz with British support and led the development of a state structure in that western region of the Arabian peninsula. The Hashemite army was defeated in Jeddah in 1925, and in early 1926 ʿAbd al-ʿazīz ibn Saʿūd, the Sultan of Nejd, declared himself King of Hejaz. Hejaz was much more advanced than Nejd, and the nationality legislation enacted by ʿAbd al-ʿazīz in September 1926 applied only to the former.

The 1926 Hejazi Nationality Regulations were inspired by the traditional forms of religious affiliation: open to Muslims (art. 4) and rigidly based on *jus sanguinis* (art. 2). A Hejazi national was a resident of Hejaz ever since the downfall of the Ottoman Empire in the Great War (art. 1). No clear watershed was assumed by the 1926 legislation, but it did consider as Hejazi nationals all those residing in Hejaz or bordering regions 'in close proximity to' its date of enactment (24 September 1926), provided they did not carry any other passport (art. 10). Thanks to an odd application of the *jus soli* (art. 3), Hejazi nationality was granted to the child of foreign parents born on Hejazi soil only during the child's stay in Hejaz (art. 9).

In 1930 a new piece of legislation, fairly close to that of 1926, was issued to regulate the nationality (*tābiʿīyah*) of both Hejaz and Nejd. In 1932 the Kingdom of Saudi Arabia was formed, but it was not until 1954 that Saudi nationality was regulated by the *nizām al-jinsīyah al-ʿarabīyah al-saʿūdīyah* issued with the *irādah malakīyah* 8/20/5604 of 22 *Safar* 1374 AH. Under the 1954 regulations, a Saudi national is (a) a former Ottoman subject (in 1914) resident in the Kingdom at its formation (1926), (b) a former Ottoman subject born on Saudi soil who resided in it from 1914 to 1926 and (c) every individual who resided in the Kingdom from 1914 to 1926 and had no other nationality (art. 3). Regular attribution of Saudi nationality is based on *jus sanguinis* (art. 7), and the principle of unity of nationality within the family is implemented (art. 12-14). Religious affiliation was never explicitly mentioned in the text, but all jurists agree on considering it a 'tacit condition' of Saudi nationality (al-Qāsim 1977: 76).

Firstly amended in 1961, naturalisation rules (art. 9) were significantly amended in 2004 by Royal Decree 54/M of 29 *Shawwāl* 1425 AH. Under the new provisions, Saudi nationality can be granted to foreigners resident in the Kingdom for more than ten years (art. 9, and 12). The Enacting Regulations issued by Ministerial Decree 74/WZ of 9 *Rabīʿ al-awwal* 1426 AH (18 April 2005) provided for a point score system for naturalisation (art. 8). Other 2004 amendments affected the nationality of a foreign woman marrying a Saudi national (art. 16) and the nationality of a Saudi woman marrying a foreign national (art. 17).

3.1.5.8 Gulf states

Despite firm British determination to regroup all emirates of the Trucial Coast into one political entity, territorial and dynastic disputes blocked the project. Different states thus individually declared independence.

Kuwait was the first Gulf Emirate to proclaim its independence in 1961. From 1948, however, Kuwait had defined the 'original Kuwaiti' as: (a) every member of the ruling family, (b) every resident of Kuwait since 1899, (c) every child of a Kuwaiti father and (d) every child born on Kuwaiti soil of an Arab or Muslim father. These provisions stood out among other regional legislation for the unique role played by *jus soli* in the determination of *de facto* Kuwaiti nationality.[10] In 1959 an Emiri Decree (*marsūm amīrī* 15/1959 of 5 December 1959) established

Kuwaiti nationality and regulated its attribution, acquisition and loss. The 1959 Decree assumed 1920 as a watershed for Kuwaiti nationality, since in that year the citizenry gathered to resist the attack of ᶜAbd al-ᶜazīz ibn Saᶜūd's troops in the battle of Jabrah, a turning point in the shaping of Kuwaiti national identity. In 1960 Emiri Decree 5/1960 on the determination (*tahqīq*) of Kuwaiti nationality was issued, whereas the basic rules were repeatedly amended in a restrictive sense around the beginning of the 1970s (laws 70/1966, 30/1970 and 41/1972). In particular, the political rights of naturalised citizens were postponed from ten to twenty years after the naturalisation decree in 1966 (Law 70/1966) and then to 30 years in 1986 (Decree-Law 130/1986). A great many amendments were introduced in 1980 (Decree-Law 100/1980) and later in 1982 (Law 1/1982), 1987 (Decree-Law 40/1987, which was rejected by the National Assembly, however, on 4 July 1995), 1994 (Law 44/1994), 1998 (Law 11/1998) and 2000 (Law 21/2000). An amendment to attribute Kuwaiti nationality to the children of Kuwaiti mothers and foreign fathers was proposed in January 2006 by Islamist parliamentarians,[11] but parliament was soon dissolved and new elections were held in the summer.

The British decision to disengage from the Gulf by the end of 1971 hastened the independence of the other emirates. Since the 1960s Bahrain and Qatar have had basic nationality legislation, while the United Arab Emirates drafted regulations on federal citizenship a year after independence. The 1963 Bahraini Nationality Law (Law 8/1963)[12] was amended only in 1981 (Decree-Law 10/1981 on the nationality of a foreign woman married to a Bahraini national) and 1989 (Decree-Law 12/1989 on the attribution and acquisition by naturalisation of the husband or the father), whereas the 1961 Qatari Nationality Law (Law 2/1961) was modified in 1963 (Law 19/1963 on restoration and on the nationality of a foreign woman married to a Qatari national), 1966 and 1969 (Decree-Laws 17/1966 and 3/1969 on naturalisation). In 2005 Qatari Law 38/2005 repealed Law 2/1961 and laid down stricter rules for Qatari nationality. The original provisions of the 1972 Federal UAE Nationality Law (Federal Law 17/1972) were sensibly tightened after the oil crisis in 1975 (Federal Law 10/1975).

The British withdrawal from the Gulf also affected Oman, even if the country had never technically been a British protectorate. The 1972 Omani Nationality Law (Law 1/1972) was already enacted after the bloodless coup of Sultan Qābūs but was later repealed by the Sultani Decree (*marsūm sultānī*) 3/1983. The 1983 legislation was extensively amended in 1986 (Sultani Decree 5/1986) and slightly in 1994 (Sultani Decree 95/1994) and 1999 (Sultani Decree 72/1999).

3.1.5.9 Yemen

North Yemen was the first dominion of the Ottoman Empire to become independent in 1918, whereas South Yemen was kept under British control. In 1962 a coup turned North Yemen (then the Mutawakkilite Kingdom of Yemen) into the Yemen Arab Republic (YAR), and marked the beginning of a civil war in which regional and international forces were actively engaged.

In late 1967 South Yemen became independent as the People's Republic of South Yemen (PRSY), and in 1968 the first PRSY Nationality legislation was enacted (Law 4/1968) and later amended in 1970 (Law 10/1970) and 1971 (Law 5/1971). North Yemen, on the other hand, passed a YAR Nationality Law only in 1975 (Law 2/1975). Both the southern and northern legislation, nonetheless, referred to a sole 'Yemeni nationality' (al-jinsīyah al-yamanīyah) with no further distinctions.

In 1990, after the country's reunification and the adoption by popular referendum of a new Constitution for the Republic of Yemen, a law on Yemeni nationality was approved (Law 6/1990). The 1990 Yemeni Nationality Law was amended in 2003 to allow a Yemeni woman married to a foreigner to regain her Yemeni nationality in case of divorce (talāq) or the absence, death or subsequent mental incapacity of the husband (Law 24/2003).

3.1.5.10 Sudan

Under Anglo-Egyptian rule, a piece of legislation defining who was to be considered Sudanese was enacted in 1948 (qānūn ta'rīf 'al-sudānī'). The 1948 Law assumed 31 December 1897, when Sudan was almost entirely under British control, as the watershed for nationality, thus leaving out entire bordering regions (like Dār Fūr) and kin groups (like the banū ʿĀmir and the banū Swirarāt), which would be subdued later. Once independence was attained in 1956, the Khartoum Parliament passed a Sudanese Nationality Law in 1957 (Law 22/1957), amended after ʿAbbūd's coup (laws 66/1959 and 40/1963 on loss of nationality), while the rules regarding naturalisation were modified after Numayrī's coup (laws 55/1970 and 26/1977).

3.1.5.11 Libya

The four Libyan provinces were officially annexed by Italy in 1939 by means of the Royal Decree-Law 70/1939. For Muslim Libyans the Decree established a 'special Italian citizenship' that did not require relinquishing Islamic personal status and inheritance law (art. 4). Granted by the Italian Governor General, the 'special' citizenship afforded more civil, political and military rights than the ones enjoyed by 'ordinary' Libyans (art. 6). Moreover, article 37 of the 1939 Decree repealed the provisions of Royal Decree-Law 2012/1934, which offered ordinary Italian citizenship but entailed loss of Muslim personal and inheritance status (art. 8).

Libya attained independence in 1952 as a kingdom under Idrīs al-Sanūsī, who signed the Libyan Nationality Law (Law 17/1954) in 1954, amended after the revolution in 1974 (Law 47/1974), 1976 (Law 48/1976) and 1979 (Law 3/1979, instituting the change of name to Great Socialist People's Libyan Arab Jamāhīrīyah).

A singular Law on Arab Citizenship was passed in 1980 (Law 18/1980) combining principles of pan-Arabism and Islam. Arab citizenship is the citizenship of the 'citizen' (*muwātin*) of the Jamāhīrīyah (art. 1) and of every Arab who enters (*yadkhul*) Libyan territory showing the desire of acquiring it (art. 2). The latter provision drew on the 1950 Israeli Law of Return but did not apply to Palestinian Arabs as a form of support for the 'anti-Zionist cause' (art. 3). No naturalisation was available to non-Arabs, whereas apostasy from Islam offered a valid legal basis for the deprivation of citizenship (art. 10(8)). Enforced in a context of need for a foreign workforce, the 1980 Arab Citizenship Law did not alter the effectiveness of the 1954 Libyan Nationality Law and was later suspended on grounds of only being a way to obtain travel documents.

3.1.5.12 Morocco

Moroccan territories did not recognise Ottoman suzerainty, but Moroccan nationality developed nonetheless in a context of capitulatory privileges and foreign presence. Foreign naturalisation violated the principle of perpetual allegiance, already deeply felt in the Sultanate and included in the Convention of Madrid of 1880 upon Moroccan request (art. 15). A turning point in the establishment of Moroccan nationality was the *affaire Abdel-Hakim*. In 1903 Tunisian-born counsellor of the Moroccan Court ʿAbd al-hakīm appeared before a French court to appeal the decision of the French plenipotentiary in Tangier banning him from re-entering Morocco. The appellant claimed that there was but one Islamic citizenship, and that residence in a territory had the legal value of French *domicile*. The court, however, ruled that Muslims under French protection (like Tunisians) could not escape French jurisdiction by the sheer change of residence and by resorting to the concept of 'Islamic citizenship', because Islamic citizenship no longer existed and many nationalities had been formed in the fold of Islam.[13]

Under the Protectorate, nationality regulations varied according to the zone of influence. In the Spanish zone, nationality was attributed according to local customs, and Spanish tribunals in Morocco would decide on the law applicable to dual nationals. As a general rule, Moroccan nationality was 'transmitted' by virtue of paternal *jus sanguinis* and no naturalisation was allowed. In the Tangier free zone, capitulations were abolished in 1923 by the Convention of Paris (art. 13), and the principle of perpetual allegiance of the 1880 Convention of Madrid was applied. In the French zone, the existence of a Moroccan nationality was never questioned but was never regulated either. It had been a matter of jurisprudence to delineate the rules of Moroccan nationality, which was attributed by *jus sanguinis* and *jus soli*, whereas French naturalisation was facilitated by the adoption of *législations parallèles* (the Moroccan *Zahīr* and the French *Décret* of 8 November 1921). A positive conflict of nationalities would arise in the not infrequ'nt case of mixed marriage. The child of a French mother and a Moroccan father would be considered a French national by the 1945 French Code, and a Moroccan by Moroccan law. In 1948 the issue was addressed by stipulating that children of Moroccan fathers and French mothers could not take advantage of their French nationality in Morocco without the Sultan's consent.

After attaining independence in 1956, a Moroccan Nationality Code (*qānūn al-jinsīyah al-maghribīyah*) modelled on the 1945 French *Code de la nationalité* was drafted by an ad-hoc commission that included several French jurists, like Decroux. The commission completed its work in two years, and the results were enshrined in the *Zahīr sharīf* 250-58-1 of 6 September 1958, which drew also on the nationality legislation of other Arab and non-Arab Muslim countries. Perpetual allegiance is upheld, while Moroccan courts keep filling the gaps in the 1958 Royal Decree and reaffirming the pre-eminence of Moroccan nationality over every other nationality. The 1958 Moroccan Nationality Code was amended in 2007 (*Zahīr sharīf* 80-07-1 of 23 March 2007) to allow for the attribution of Moroccan nationality by maternal *jus sanguinis* (art. 6) and the acquisition by operation of law of Moroccan nationality by a child born abroad of unknown parents who is in the custody (*kafālah*) of a Moroccan national (art. 9). The 2007 Decree also withheld naturalisation from persons who committed terrorist acts (art. 11(1)(4)) and prescribed the revocation of Moroccan nationality if the terrorist acts were committed after naturalisation (art. 22).

3.1.5.13 Tunisia

Following the establishment of the French Protectorate, many Europeans settled in Tunisia. In a move to abolish foreign capitulations, France adopted in Tunisia the same system of the *législations parallèles* as for Morocco. On 8 November 1921 the French President issued a *Décret* granting French nationality to every child born in Tunisia of a father who was himself born in Tunisia and was under French jurisdiction, while simultaneously the Bey of Tunis issued a *marsūm* imposing Tunisian nationality on every child born in Tunisia of a father who was himself born in Tunisia. French Tunisians were judged by French courts according to metropolitan law. They were thus considered apostates, and state authorities had to build special graveyards for them.

Shortly before independence, the Tunisian Nationality Law of 1956 (Order 2/1956) regulated only the cases where French nationality was not involved (art. 10-12). After the promulgation of the Republican Constitution of 1959, rules on Tunisian nationality were laid down by Decree-Law 6/1963. This would later be converted into Law 7/1963, known as the Tunisian Nationality Code (*majallat al-jinsīyah al-tūnisīyah*). The 1963 Code was amended to make loss of nationality effective only after foreign naturalisation (Law 79/1975) or for public or military foreign service (Law 81/1984). Provisions regarding maternal *jus sanguinis* were modified in 1993 to allow the child born abroad of a Tunisian mother to acquire Tunisian nationality by operation of law when coming of age or upon joint request of the parents (Law 62/1993), and amended again in 2002 to stipulate that the mother's request is sufficient in case of death, absence or legal incapacity of the father (Law 4/2002).

3.1.5.14 *Algeria*
Algeria had a unique colonial status that influenced the development of Algerian nationality (Mahiou 2005). Since the passing of the 1848 French Constitution, Algeria had been a French territory (art. 109), but Algerians were not French nationals. The *Senatus Consultum* of 14 July 1865 stipulated that the Muslim (art. 1) and Jewish (art. 2) Algerian natives were French citizens subject to their own religious laws. Algerian natives were not full-fledged citizens and were governed by a special *Code de l'Indigénat* applied by administrative, not judicial, authorities. Nationality and citizenship were thus divided. On the one hand, French people living in Algeria who were French nationals and citizens (*nationaux et citoyens français*), while on the other hand Algerian natives who were French nationals but subjects (*nationaux et sujets français*) without civil and political rights if not naturalised. Algerian Jews were collectively granted French citizenship by the *Décret Crémieux* of 24 October 1870, which subjected them to metropolitan law, not Mosaic law. Algerian Muslims had to wait until the interbellum to see the *Loi Jonnart* of 4 February 1919 open the way to naturalisation, especially for veterans and elites. Naturalisation, however, involved the loss of Muslim personal status, an act that entailed apostasy according to the famous 1937 *fatwà* of sheikh Ben Badis, leader of the Association of Muslim Algerian Ulema.[14]

After the Second World War, equality of rights and duties was proclaimed by the *Ordonnance* of 7 March 1944 and later confirmed by the *Loi Lamine Guèye* of 7 May 1946 (which granted French citizenship to all the subjects of France's territories and overseas departments) and the 1946 Constitution. The Law of 20 September 1946 granted French citizenship to all Algerian subjects, who were not required, however, to renounce their Muslim personal status. Equality did not affect the electoral legislation, though, which continued to provide for a separate and unequal system of representation both to the Algerian Assembly and to the French Parliament for *Pieds-noirs* (population of European descent of Algeria) and 'Muslim French' (those who were first *indigènes*, then *sujets français*, were eventually identified as *musulmans français*).

Only with the Algerian War and the coming of the French Fifth Republic were full equality and the 'integration policy' laid out under the Law of 4 October 1958. During the Algerian War of Independence, *Pieds-noirs* were invited to choose Algerian nationality and forsake French citizenship, or otherwise be considered as foreigners. The Evian agreements that ended the Algerian War allowed for the option for either of the two nationalities, and the right of option had to be exercised within three years by 1965. In 1962 most *Pieds-noirs* and a large number of *Harkis* (Muslim Algerians serving as auxiliaries with the French Army) left Algeria for France.

After independence, an Algerian Nationality Code was passed on 27 March 1963. After a sharp confrontation, the solution adopted by the Code was the attribution of Algerian nationality by filiation of an Algerian father, who had to have at least two ascendants in the paternal line born in Algeria and subject to Islamic law (art. 34). As a result, all *Pieds-noirs* (both those of European descent and the Jews) were deprived of Algerian nationality.

In 1970 the 1963 Code was repealed and substituted by Order (*amr*) 86/1970. The 1970 Algerian Nationality Code maintained the pre-eminence of (paternal) *jus sanguinis*, the requirement of strong assimilation for naturalisation and strict control to avoid cases of dual nationality. In 2005 the Code was amended by the Order 1/2005 to allow for the attribution of Algerian nationality by maternal *jus sanguinis* and the acquisition of Algerian nationality by marriage.

3.2 Nationality (*jinsīyah*) in the Arab world

In the Arab world, nationality (*jinsīyah*) is not considered a matter of public law but rather of private international law (conflict of laws), as it is in France. Some Arab scholars, however, have recently started to underline its constitutional relevance. Among these is al-Bustānī, who lately published a comparative study of Arab nationality laws for which he adopted general categories meant to overpass national definitory discrepancies and embrace the different local expressions (al-Bustānī 2003). The study contains heavy ideological overtones, however, that colour the exposition and need to be taken into account, even if its comparative value should not be underestimated. Arab works are quite modestly comparative by and large, as they take on a predominant model or opt for regional comparisons (the Gulf, the Arab East or the Arab West). Shaped according to the French model, and at the same time attentive to national lexical peculiarities, al-Bustānī's categories are adopted here as a framework for a systematic comparison of Arab legislation on nationality; a synopsis of the rules of attribution, acquisition, loss and reintegration of nationality in the Arab world. This choice is also motivated by the desire to present the non-Arab reader with the point of view of Arab scholars by means of their own systematisation of nationality regulations.

In this section, references to national legislation are given in the abbreviated form of the main piece of legislation regulating nationality in each country. Egypt's Nationality Law 26/1975 is thus indicated as (1975 EgNL), Iraq's Nationality Law 43/1963 as (1963 IqNL), Jordan's Nationality Law 6/1954 as (1954 JoNL), Lebanon's Nationality Decision 15/S of 1925 as (1925 LbND), Syria's Nationality Legislative Decree 276/1969 as (1969 SyNLD), Saudi Arabia's Nationality Regulations of 19 October 1954 as (1954 SaNR), Kuwait's Nationality Emiri Decree 15/1959 as (1959 KwNED), Bahrain's Nationality Law 8/1963 (1963 BhNL), Qatar's Nationality Law 38/2005 as (2005 QaNL), the United Arab Emirates' Federal Nationality Law 17/1972 as (1972 AeFNL), Oman's Nationality Sultani Decree 3/1983 as (1983 OmNSD), Yemen's Nationality Law 6/1990 as (1990 YeNL), Sudan's Nationality Law 22/1957 as (1957 SdNL), Libya's Nationality Law 17/1954 as (1954 LyNL), Morocco's Nationality Code of 6 September 1958 as (1958 MaNC), Tunisia's Nationality Code of 22 April 1963 as (1963 TnNC) and Algeria's Nationality Code of 15 December 1970 as (1970 DzNC). Amendments are indicated in parentheses after the abbreviated law, e.g. art. 1 of the Egyptian Nationality Law 26/1975 as amended by Law 154/2004 to allow for the attribution of Egyptian nationality by maternal *jus sanguinis* will be shortened as: '1975 EgNL(2004), art. 1'.

3.2.1   Acquisition of nationality
(Ahkām iktisāb al-jinsīyah)

A brief introduction to Arab studies on nationality is invariably devoted to 'Islamic nationality', or rather the 'Islamic concept of nationality' (al-mafhūm al-islāmī li-l-jinsīyah). Arab scholars argue that Islamic nationality dominated until the end of the 19th century and was later replaced by a host of local nationalities as a result of the Treaty of Lausanne of 1923.

In the historic development of local nationalities, then, a line is drawn between the 'founding nationality' (*jinsīyat al-ta'sīs*), derived from the Ottoman dismemberment, and the 'populating nationality' (*jinsīyat al-ta°mīr*), created by national legislation after independence. The latter is commonly referred to simply as 'nationality' (*jinsīyah*).

In the discussion of how nationality is acquired, national legislation and legal literature both make a distinction between 'original nationality' (*al-jinsīyah al-aslīyah* or *jinsīyat al-asl*) and 'acquired nationality' (*al-jinsīyah al-muktasabah*), the former being attributed at birth and the second acquired after it.

Original nationality is acquired at birth and from birth and is therefore identified also as 'nationality of birth' (*jinsīyat al-mīlād*). Other scholars, by contrast, emphasise the role of the state and label this nationality as 'granted nationality' (*al-jinsīyah al-mamnūhah*) or 'imposed nationality' (*al-jinsīyah al-mafrūdah*). Birth is technically the key event in the acquisition of original nationality, so much so that if original nationality is established after birth, it is applied back from the moment of birth.

Acquired nationality is the other major access gate to nationality. It is obtained through an event taking place after birth and gains effect only from the moment of that event. A wide lexicon is used to account for the differences between acquired and original nationality, the former being 'subsequent' (*lāhiqah*) while the latter attributed at birth, 'foreign' (*tāri'ah*) or 'secondary' (*thānawīyah*) instead of the 'normal' or 'first' nationality attributed to the person or – lastly – 'elective' (*mukhtārah*) to mark the person's role in the process of acquisition.

3.2.1.1 Attribution of nationality of origin (Iktisāb al-jinsīyah al-aslīyah)

In the nationality legislation of Arab countries, the basic principle for the establishment (*thubūt*) or acquisition (*iktisāb*, but also *kasb*) of the nationality of origin is *jus sanguinis* (*haqq al-dam*), while *jus soli* (*haqq al-iqlīm*) is relegated to a secondary, or exceptional role (*istithnā'ī*). A particular combination of *jus sanguinis* and *jus soli*, usually known as double *jus soli*, is seen by Arab jurists as '*jus sanguinis* strengthened by *jus soli*' (*haqq al-dam mu°azzaz bi-haqq al-iqlīm*).

3.2.1.1.1 Jus sanguinis (Asās haqq al-dam wahdah)

Jus sanguinis (*haqq al-dam*) is based on legitimate filiation (*al-bunūwah al-shar°īyah*), i.e. birth within wedlock, and entails 'entering the nationality of the state to which the father belongs' (*yadkhul fī jinsīyat al-dawlah al-latī yantamī ilayhā abūh*) by virtue of mere birth. Nationality attributed by *jus sanguinis* is then labelled as 'nationality by descent' (*jinsīyat al-nasab*), since it descends from a national source (*intisāb ilà asl watanī*). 'Filiation' and 'descent' share here the same root *n.s.b.* Paternal *jus sanguinis (haqq al-dam al-abawī)* – bond (*irtibāt*) or descent by paternal filiation (*inhidār bi-l-nasab min al-ab*) – is the main way nationality is attributed by Arab legislation, even if there are minor differences.

Maternal *jus sanguinis (haqq al-dam al-umūmī* or *al-ummī*), on the contrary, comes into play only in exceptional (*istithnā'ī*) cases (Bakhīt 2001; Khālid 2006), as when the child is born out of wedlock (*al-walad ghayr al-sharʿī*, or illegitimate filiation) or the father is of unknown nationality (*majhūl al-jinsīyah*) or stateless (*al-ab ʿadīm al-jinsīyah*). Maternal descent is therefore a secondary form of *jus sanguinis (al-sūrah al-thānawīyah li-haqq al-dam*), preventive (*haqq al-dam al-wiqāʾī*) or precautionary (*al-ihtiyātī*), and Arab nationality laws impose other requirements to attribute the mother's nationality to the child.

Some Arab countries recently amended their legislation to conform to the UN Convention on the Elimination of All Forms of Discrimination against Women (CEDAW, art. 9(2)) by guaranteeing gender equality in the attribution of nationality to children. Ever since 1963, the Tunisian Nationality Code has attributed the mother's Tunisian nationality to the child born in Tunisia, but in 1993 an amendment allowed also for the acquisition of Tunisian nationality by operation of law to the child of a Tunisian mother born out of the country (Law 62/1993). Attribution by maternal *jus sanguinis*, by contrast, was introduced in Egypt by Law 154/2004 (1975 EgNL(2004), art. 2(1)(1)), in Algeria by Order 1/2005 (1970 DzNC(2005), art. 6), and in Morocco by Decree 80/2007 (1958 MaNC(2007), art. 6). A broad campaign, known as 'Claiming Equal Citizenship: The Campaign for Arab Women's Right to Nationality', vigorously calls for amending the other Arab laws, and the issue is under discussion in Lebanon, Jordan, Bahrain and Kuwait.

Some legislation stipulates that nationality is attributed to the child of a national father born within or out of the boundaries of the state (1963 IqNL, art. 4(1)(1); 1969 SyNLD, art. 3(1)(a); 1954 SaNR, art. 7; 1959 KwNED, art. 2; 1963 BhNL(1989), art. 4(1)(a); 2005 QaNL, art. 1 (1)(4); 1972 AeFNL(1975), art. 2(1)(b); 1983 OmNSD(1986), art. 1(1)), whereas the place of birth is not even mentioned in other texts (1975 EgNL, art. 2(1)(1); 1954 JoNL(1963), art. 3(1)(3); 1925 LbND, art. 1(1)(1); 1990 YeNL, art. 3(1)(a); 1957 SdNL, art. 5(2);[15] 1958 MaNC(2007), art. 6 (1)(1); 1963 TnNC, art. 6(1)(1); 1970 DzNC(2005), art. 6(1)). Cases of dual nationality can arise if the child is given another nationality by maternal *jus sanguinis* or by *jus soli.*

Nationality is attributed by birth if the father is a national at the child's birth. If the father loses his nationality before the child is born, his nationality will not be attributed to the child. Conversely, if the father acquires nationality before the child's birth, his nationality will be attributed to the child.

In order to be attributed nationality, the child has to be born within wedlock. Religion is not explicitly named, but religious rules on legitimate filiation implicitly apply, and as far as Islamic *sharīʿah* is involved, adoption and legal recognition of the child are key issues that affect nationality regulations. Adoption (*tabannī*) and child custody (*kafālah*), for instance, may lead to the acquisition of nationality by operation of law in Tunisia and Morocco respectively.

Maternal *jus sanguinis* plays a role only if the nationality of the father is unknown (*jahālat al-jinsīyah*) or he is stateless (*inʿidām al-jinsīyah*)[16] for most Arab legislation. Gulf laws also include the case of unknown paternity or illegitimate filiation (the child *majhūl al-ab aw lam tuthabbit nisbatuhu li-abīhi qānūn*[an]; 1959 KwNED(1980), art. 3(1); 1963 BhNL (1989), art. 4(1)(b); 1972 AeFNL(1975), art. 2(c-d); 1983 OmNSD(1994), art. 1(2)).

3.2.1.1.2 *Jus sanguinis strengthened by jus soli (Haqq al-dam muʿazzaz bi-haqq al-iqlīm)*

What Arab scholars call '*jus sanguinis* strengthened by *jus soli*' (*haqq al-dam muʿazzaz bi-haqq al-iqlīm*) concerns two different cases. Namely, when birth on the territory is required to reinforce the weak maternal *jus sanguinis*, and when birth of the father or the grandfather on the territory is required to the child born abroad.

On the one hand, when nationality cannot be attributed by paternal descent, maternal descent is taken into account, even if its weakness needs to be supported by birth on the territory of the state (1975 EgNL, art. 2(1); 1963 IqNL, art. 4(1)(2); 1954 JoNL(1963), art. 3(1)(4); 1969 SyNLD, art. 3(1)(b); 1954 SaNR (1985), art. 8;[17] 1990 YeNL, art. 3(1)(b-c); 1963 TnNC, art. 6(1)(3)).

On the other hand, the attribution of the father's nationality to the child born out of the territory only if the father or the grandfather was born within the boundaries of the state was a controversial provision of the 1963 Bahraini Nationality Law later repealed by Decree-Law 12/ 1989 (al-Bustānī 2003: 137ff). The Bahraini solution, however, had the positive effect of limiting the 'transmission' of Bahraini nationality through generations that no longer had any attachment to the country. By repealing the original provision, Bahrain joined the ranks of other Arab countries claiming perpetual nationality of their offspring.

3.2.1.1.3 *Jus soli (Asās haqq al-iqlīm aw makān al-wilādah)*

With the exception of Lebanon, Syria and Libya, the attribution of nationality by *jus soli* (*haqq al-iqlīm*) is quite limited in the Arab world, and even in these three countries *jus soli* is thought of as a means to reduce cases of statelessness. According to Lebanese, Syrian and Libyan laws, nationality can be attributed by virtue of birth on the country's soil only if it is not possible to attribute any other nationality to the person (1925 LbND, art. 1(1)(2); 1969 SyNLD, art. 3(1)(d);[18] 1954 LyNL (1976), art. 4(1)(a)).

Elsewhere, nationality can be attributed by *jus soli* only if both parents are unknown (*majhūlayn*) or of unknown nationality (*majhūlay 'l-jinsīyah*) (1975 EgNL, art. 2(1)(4); 1963 IqNL, art. 4(1)(3); 1954 JoNL (1963), art. 3(1)(5); 1954 SaNR(1960), art. 8; 1959 KwNED, art. 3(2); 1963 BhNL(1989), art. 5; 1972 AeFNL(1975), art. 2(e); 1983 OmNSD (1986), art. 1(3); 1990 YeNL, art. 3(1)(d); 1957 SdNL, art. 6; 1958 MaNC (2007), art. 7(1)(2); 1963 TnNC, art. 9-10; 1970 DzNC(2005), art. 7(1) (1)). The 2005 Qatari Nationality Law is the only piece of Arab legislation that allows only for the acquisition of 'naturalisation nationality' to the foundling (2005 QaNL, art. 2(2)).

Double *jus soli* (*haqq al-iqlīm mudā^{c}af^{an}*) – i.e. the attribution of nationality to the child born in the country to an alien father, or grandfather, born himself within the boundaries of the state – is a recessive model on the whole at present. Introduced in France in 1851, it was later adopted by the 1869 Ottoman Nationality Law and by some Arab legislation. An example is the Egyptian Decree-Law 29/1929, which required the father to be either an Arabic speaker or a Muslim (art. 6). Currently double *jus soli*, or 'double birth' (*al-mīlād al-mudā^{c}af*) or 'recurring birth' (*al-wilādah al-mutakarrirah*), leads to acquisition by operation of law of nationality in just a few pieces of legislation (1963 IqNL (1964), art. 6; 1958 MaNC(2007), art. 9(1)(1)).

For the attribution of nationality by *jus soli*, further requirements than mere birth on the territory are usually set out. Besides the child's birth (*shart al-wilādah bi-l-nisbah li-l-tifl*), the parents need to be habitually resident in the country (*iqāmah li-darajat al-tawattun bi-l-nisbah li-l-wālidayn*), and both or either one of them needs to be stateless (*in^{c}i-dām jinsīyatihimā aw jinsīyat ahadihimā*).

3.2.1.2   Acquisition of foreign nationality
(Iktisāb al-jinsīyah al-tāri'ah – al-jinsīyah al-muktasabah)
Acquisition of nationality has special features in the Arab world, where an intermediate category between the national and the foreigner is commonly outlined: the Arab. Some scholars even set apart rules of acquisition that apply to Arabs and foreigners alike (*shurūt mushtarakah*), and those 'added or extended' (*shurūt munfasilah, ayy al-latī tatāl*) imposed on foreigners alone. Among shared requirements are (1) legal capacity, (2) absence of illnesses or other health conditions prohibiting work, (3) good behaviour and (4) absence of criminal conviction for an infamous crime, whereas further conditions for foreigners are (5) pro-

longed residency, (6) knowledge of Arabic, (7) qualification and competence and (8) residence at the submission of the application form
(al-Bustānī 2003: 152ff).

Even if being Arab (and Muslim) may play a major role in the acquisition process in the Arab world – sometimes on and sometimes off
the record – there is no legal reason to explain the rules of acquisition
in two different sections (one for Arabs and one for non-Arabs). Most
Arab scholars organise them in a single section.

The traditional distinction between acquisition by operation of law
and by decision of the authority seems to be fading, since acquisition
by operation of law is ordinarily subject to administrative discretionary
power. The Arab West, more susceptible to French influence, maintains sections dedicated to acquisition *par le bienfait de la loi* (*iktisāb
bi-fadl al-qānūn* or *bi-hukm al-qānūn*) for cases of combination of *jus
sanguinis* and *jus soli* (1958 MaNC(2007), art. 9(1)(1); 1963 TnNC, art. 12;
1970 DzNC, art. 9), marriage (1958 MaNC(2007), art. 10; 1963 TnNC,
art. 13-14; 1970 DzNC(2005), art. 9-*bis*) and adoption (*tabannī*; 1963
TnNC, art. 18) or child custody (*kafālah*; 1958 MaNC(2007), art. 9(1)
(2)).

3.2.1.2.1   Naturalisation (al-Tajannus)

Naturalisation (*tajannus*) is by far the main form of acquisition of a foreign nationality in the Arab world, even if it arouses evident legislative
hostility. Not uniquely, naturalisation is generally subject to conditions
pertaining to the person's assimilation in the political community. In
this context, Arab legislation clearly favours the acquisition of nationality by other Arabs, who belong to the same socio-political entity that
transcends national borders.

Requirements for ordinary naturalisation (Shurūt al-tajannus al-ᶜādī)
Among the conditions commonly set for ordinary naturalisation by
Arab legislation are legal capacity (or full capacity: *kamāl al-ahlīyah*), absence of health conditions that hinder any ability to work (*khilwuhu
min al-amrād al-sārīyah wa-l-ᶜāhāt wa-l-ᶜilal al-latī tumnaᶜuhu min muzā-
walat ayy ᶜamal*), good behaviour (*husn al-sulūk wa-l-sīrah al-mahmūdah*)
and absence of criminal conviction for infamous crimes (ᶜ*adam
al-hukm ᶜalayhi bi-ᶜuqūbah jinā'īyah aw bi-ᶜuqūbah muqayyidat al-hurrīyah fī jarīmah shā'inah*). The indetermination of these conditions sagaciously extends the scope of discretionary powers.

Residency is assumed as the main indicator of the attachment to the
state of the alien applying for naturalisation. Long or prolonged residency (*al-iqāmah al-tawīlah*, or *al-madīdah*) is required by all nationality
laws, even if there are considerable differences in the determination of
the length. Gulf legislation is undoubtedly the strictest, demanding le-

gal and uninterrupted residence of twenty years (1959 KwNED(1980), art. 4(1)(1); 1983 OmNSD(1986), art. 2(3)) twenty-five years (1963 BhNL, art. 6(1); 2005 QaNL, art. 2(1)(1)), or thirty years (1972 AefNL, art. 8). Other national laws vary from fifteen years (1963 IqNL(1964), art. 8(4)(a)) to ten years (1975 EgNL, art. 4(5); 1954 SaNR(2004), art. 9 (1)(a); 1957 SdNL(1970), art. 8(1)(b)), seven years (1970 DzNC, art. 10 (1)(1)), five years (1925 LbND, art. 3(1)(1); 1969 SyNLD, art. 4(1)(b); 1958 MaNC(2007), art. 11(1)(1); 1963 TnNC, art. 20), or four years (1954 JoNL, art. 12(1)(1)). Libya and Yemen have special provisions. In the former only Arabs can apply for ordinary naturalisation, after having fulfilled residency requirements of five years (1954 LyNL(1979), art. 5(1)(b)), or four if married to a Libyan woman (1954 LyNL(1979), art. 5(1)(a)), while in the latter only Muslims can apply after ten years of residence (1990 YeNL, art. 5(1)(2)). In order to favour the naturalisation of Arabs, Syria eliminated the residency requirement (*ilghā' al-muddah*; 1969 SyNLD, art. 6(1)),[19] whereas Iraq and other Gulf countries shortened its length (*takhfīf al-muddah*), in Iraq from fifteen to ten years (1963 IqNL(1964), art. 8(1)(c)), in Kuwait from twenty to fifteen years (1959 KwNED(1980), art. 4(1)(1)), in Bahrain from 25 to fifteen years (1963 BhNL, art. 6(1)) and in the UAE from 30 to seven (1972 AefNL(1975), art. 6).[20] The determination of who is to be considered an 'Arab', however, is not unambiguous. The Syrian Legislative Decree 276/1969 attempted an *a contrario* definition of the 'Arab' by identifying the 'foreigner' (*ajnabī*) as the person who possesses neither Syrian nationality nor the nationality of any other Arab country (*kull man lā yatamatta[c] bi-jinsīyat al-jumhūrīyah al-[c]arabīyah al-sūrīyah aw jinsīyat ayy balad [c]arabī 'ākhar*, 1969 SyNLD, art. (1)(c)). Nothing is said, though, of the Arab 'by origin or descent' (*[c]arabī al-asl*).

With the exception of Lebanon and Algeria,[21] all other Arab countries require a certain degree of knowledge of Arabic in order to be naturalised. A few nationality laws demand that one be knowledgeable of the language, with good speaking, reading and writing abilities (*an yujayyid al-lughah al-[c]arabīyah tahadduth[an] wa-qirā'a[tan] wa-kitāba[tan]*; 1954 SaNR(2004), art. 9(1)(6); 1954 JoNL(1963), art. 12(1)(4)), most sheer knowledge (*ilmām bi-l-lughah*; 1975 EgNL, art. 4(4-5); 1969 SyNLD, art. 4(1)(f); 1972 AefNL, art. 7-8; 1983 OmNSD, art. 2(1); 1990 YeNL, art. 5(1)(5); 1957 SdNL, art. 8(1)(c)[22]), and others require only sufficient knowledge (*ma[c]rifah kāfīah*; 1959 KwNED(1980), art. 4(1)(3)[23]; 1963 BhNL, art. 6(1)(c); 2005 QaNL, art. 2(1)(4); 1958 MaNC(2007), art. 11(1) (5); 1963 TnNC, art. 23(1)(2)[24]).

The person applying for naturalisation must prove to be in good 'economic condition' (*al-hālah al-māddīyah*; 1975 EgNL, art. 4(4)(4); 1963 IqNL(1964), art. 8(1)(e) and (4)(d); 1954 JoNL(1963), art. 12(1)(7); 1969 SyNLD, art. 4(e); 1954 SaNR(2004), art. 9(1)(e); 1959 KwNED

(1980), art. 4(1)(2); 2005 QaNL, art. 2(1)(2); 1972 AeFNL, art. 8; 1983 OmNSD, art. 2(4); 1990 YeNL, art. 5(1)(4); 1954 LyNL(1979), art. 5(2) (e); 1958 MaNC(2007), art. 11(1)(6); 1970 DzNC, art. 10(1)(5)). Noteworthy exceptions are Lebanon, Sudan and Tunisia, whereas the Bahraini Nationality Law stipulates that candidates need to have real property in the country registered in their name (1963 BhNL, art. 6(1)(d)), and the Syrian Legislative Decree lifts the requirement for the Arab (1969 SyNLD, art. 6).

Being a Muslim is an explicit requirement under Kuwaiti and Yemeni nationality laws, whereas it is implicitly so in Saudi Arabia. In Kuwait, a special piece of legislation (Law 1/1982) was passed to bar naturalisation to non-Muslims. If the candidate is not a Muslim, conversion to Islam must take place five years before applying for Kuwaiti nationality, and if, once naturalised, the convert commits apostasy, the naturalisation decree shall be declared null and void (1959 KwNED (1982), art. 4(1)(5)). Yemeni nationality is open only to Muslims, but no prior time limit is set for conversion to Islam (1990 YeNL, art. 5). In Saudi Arabia, on the contrary, being a Muslim has not been openly required by law since the regulations on Hejazi and Nejdi nationality of 1930 (art. 6-7) were introduced, but legal scholars agree that it is an implicit clause (*shart al-islām*, al-Munīfī 1974: 120, al-Qāsim 1977: 76 and ʿAshshūsh 1991: 194f). The executive regulations of Royal Decree 54/M of 2004 demand that good behaviour, stipulated by 1954 SaNR (2004), art. 9(1)(c), be proved by a certificate signed by the imam of the mosque of the neighbourhood where the candidate lives (Ministerial Decree 74/WZ of 2005, art. 14(1)(1)).

Good behaviour generally consists of lack of criminal conviction for infamous crimes or crimes against state security, but is framed differently in every piece of legislation (1975 EgNL, art. 4(4)(2); 1963 IqNL (1964), art. 8(1)(d) and (4)(c); 1954 JoNL, art. 12(1)(5); 1969 SyNLD, art. 4(d); 1954 SaNR(2004), art. 9(1)(c); 1959 KwNED(1980), art. 4(1) (2); 1963 BhNL, art. 6(1)(b); 2005 QaNL, art. 2(1)(3); 1972 AeFNL, art. 8; 1983 OmNSD, art. 2(3); 1990 YeNL, art. 5(1)(3); 1957 SdNL, art. 8(1)(d); 1954 LyNL(1979), art. 5(2)(b); 1958 MaNC(2007), art. 11(1)(4); 1963 TnNC, art. 23(1)(5); 1970 DzNC, art. 10(1)(4)). In 2007, Morocco introduced terrorist crimes (*jarīmah irhābīyah*), along with other breaches of criminal law, as a legitimate reason to deny naturalisation (1958 MaNC (2007), art. 11(1)(4)).

Some legislation subordinates naturalisation to the loss of the previous nationality, in order to avoid cases of dual nationality. In Jordan, authorities do not deliver certificates of naturalisation unless the loss of the previous nationality is proved (1954 JoNL, art. 13(3)), while in the Gulf a term after naturalisation is assigned for relinquishing previous nationality (1954 SaNR(2004), art. 9(2); 1959 KwNED(1980), art. 11-*bis*;

1972 AeFNL, art. 11; 1983 OmNSD, art. 2(5)). Dual nationality (*jam*^{c} *bayna jinsīyatayn*) of Arab nationals was regulated by the Convention of the Arab League of 5 April 1954. Under this regulation, the Arab national of a signatory state (Jordan, Syria, Iraq, Saudi Arabia, Lebanon, and Yemen) would lose his nationality when being granted the nationality of another signatory state upon consent (*bi-muwāfaqah*) of the former (art. 6), but the Convention never came into force for lack of ratifications.

Requirements for extraordinary naturalisation (Shurūt al-tajannus al-khāss)
Besides ordinary naturalisation, Arab nationality laws lay down rules for extraordinary, or exceptional naturalisation (*al-tajannus al-khāss* or *al-istithnā'ī*), in order to grant nationality to the alien who has offered special service to the country.

Foreign nationals can be awarded nationality (*mukāfa'at al-jinsīyah*) for meritorious service. Service can be qualified as 'important' (*khidmāt dhāt sha'n*; 1925 LbND, art. 3(1)(3)), 'exceptional' (*khidmāt istithnā'īyah*; 1958 MaNC(2007), art. 12) or 'outstanding' (*khidmāt jalīlah*; 1975 EgNL, art. 5; 1954 SaNR, art. 29; 1959 KwNED(1980), art. 5(1); 1963 BhNL, art. 6(2); 2005 QaNL, art. 6; 1972 AeFNL, art. 9), and usually needs to have been rendered to the country, but in Syria it can also be provided to the *ummah*, i.e. the Arab nation in the jargon of the Syrian Nationality legislation (1969 SyNLD, art. 6(1)(b))[25]. Other legislation confers full discretionary authority to state departments to legally bestow nationality (1954 JoNL(1956), art. 13(2); 1963 BhNL, art. 6(2); 1983 OmNSD, art. 3).

Extraordinary naturalisation can also be granted to Levantine nationals who left their country. The Lebanese and Jordanian laws use a 'local' definition of expatriate (*al-mughtarib al-watanī*), namely a Lebanese or Jordanian expatriate (LbLaw 31 January 1946, art. 2;[26] 1954 JoNL, art. 2(d)[27]), whereas the Syrian legislation refers to a wider concept of 'national' expatriate (*al-mughtarib al-qawmī*), viz. the individual of Arab origin who possesses a non-Arab nationality (1969 SyNLD, art. 1(6))[28].

Effects of naturalisation ('Āthār al-tajannus)
Naturalisation has individual and familial effects. Arab nationality laws, however, sensibly differ on the magnitude and significance of such effects.

With regard to the 'individual' or 'special' effects of naturalisation (*al-'āthār al-fardīyah* or *al-khāssah*), nationality legislation generally requires a certain amount of time (from five to ten years) after naturalisation before bestowing equal rights and duties on the naturalised. Restrictions to the civil and political rights of the naturalised may be set out either in nationality laws or in laws regulating other sectors, such as electoral or civil service legislation. On one end of the spectrum is the perpetual exclusion (*hirmān mutbiq mu'abbad*) of political rights in Qatar and the UAE (2005 QaNL, art. 16(2); 1972 AeFNL, art. 13[29]),[30] which have even established a policy of hereditary naturalisation status (*tajannus bi-l-wirāthah*). An extended exclusion (*hirmān muwaqqat madīd*) is set down by legislation in other Gulf states like Kuwait (30 years for political rights; 1959 KwNED(1986), art. 6), whereas most laws stipulate a short exclusion period (*hirmān muwaqqat qasīr*), such as fifteen years for the non-Arab Muslim naturalised in Yemen (1990 YeNL, art. 23), ten years in Lebanon, Bahrain and Qatar for being employed in the civil service (*al-wazā'if al-ʿāmmah*; Law 7 June 1937, art. 1; 1963 BhNL, art. 6(3);[31] 2005 QaNL, art. 16(1)) and five years in Egypt, Jordan, Morocco, Tunisia and Algeria (1975 EgNL, art. 9; 1954 JoNL (1987), art. 14; 1958 MaNC, art. 17; 1963 TnNC, art. 26; 1970 DzNC, art. 16).

In the Arab West aliens are allowed to change their names upon naturalisation (*taghyīr al-ism*). The French model and the Islamic tradition of acquiring an Islamic name upon conversion intertwine in the laws of the Maghreb (1958 MaNC, art. 13(2); 1970 DzNC(2005), art. 12(2)).

'General' or 'familial' effects of naturalisation (*al-'āthār al-ʿāmmah* or *al-ʿā'ilīyah*) are commonly imposed on minor children and on wives of the naturalised. In some cases the father's naturalisation can result in the naturalisation of children who have already come of age.[32] Like wives, adult children have to express their intention to acquire Lebanese nationality in the father's application for naturalisation, even if they are not resident in Lebanon (1925 LbND, art. 4). Syrian legislation, however, requires a short residency of two years (1969 SyNLD, art. 7).

The father's naturalisation entails the naturalisation of his minor children, with no further requirement (*dūn shurūt*; 1954 JoNL, art. 9; 1925 LbND, art. 4; 1959 KwNED, (1980), art. 7; 1963 BhNL(1989), art. 6(4); 1972 AeFNL, art. 10; 1983 OmNSD(1986), art. 4; 1957 SdNL, art. 8(4); 1958 MaNC(2007), art. 18; 1963 TnNC, art. 25; 1970 DzNC (2005), art. 17(1)),[33] upon express request in the father's application as exemplified in Libya (1954 LyNL, art. 6) or under condition of residency (*shart iqāmah mawsūfah*; 1975 EgNL, art. 6(2); 1969 SyNLD (1972), art. 8(2); 1954 SaNR(2004), art. 14(1)(b); 2005 QaNL, art. 4; 1990 YeNL, art. 9). Most legislation, however, allows the minor children of the naturalised to opt back to their previous nationality when they come of age (1975 EgNL, art. 6(2); 1925 LbND, art. 4; 1969 SyNLD, art. 8(3); 1954 SaNR(2004), art. 14(1)(b); 1959 KwNED(1980), art. 7; 1963 BhNL(1989), art. 6(4); 2005 QaNL, art. 4; 1972 AeFNL, art. 10; 1983 OmNSD(1986), art. 4; 1990 YeNL, art. 9; 1954 LyNL, art. 6; 1958 MaNC(2007), art. 18(3);[34] 1970 DzNC(2005), art. 17(2)).

The principle of unity of nationality within the family (*mabda' wahdat al-jinsīyah fī 'l-ʿā'ilah*) is broadly applied in Arab nationality laws, and thus the naturalisation of the husband generally results in the naturalisation of the wife or wives.

3.2.1.2.2   Acquisition by marriage – mixed marriages
(Iktisāb bi-fiʿl al-zawāj – al-Zawāj al-mukhtalit)

Acquisition of nationality by marriage must be distinguished from the wife's acquisition of nationality due to her husband's naturalisation, even if both are applications of the principle of unity of nationality within the family. In the former case, the wife 'follows' the husband's nationality status by acquiring his nationality, whereas in the latter case, the wife 'follows' the husband's change of nationality status. However, restrictions are often imposed on mixed marriages in the Arab world.

In only a few Arab countries does a foreign husband acquire domestic nationality by marriage. Nationality is granted at once upon residence in Tunisia (1963 TnNC, art. 21(2)), after one year of residence in Lebanon (1925 LbND, art. 3), two in Algeria (1970 DzNC(2005), art. 9-*bis*)[35] and ten in Oman (1983 OmNSD(1986), art. 2(2)).

Most legislation, however, rules that only the foreign wife can acquire the domestic nationality of the husband, even if with notable differences (ʿAbd al-rahmān 1991; al-Bāz 2001). The drastic imposition of the husband's nationality was progressively abandoned, especially after the UN Convention on the Nationality of Married Women came into force on 29 January 1957. A vestige of the previous orientation is the Tunisian provision that confers nationality to the foreign wife deprived of her original nationality by her national law because of her marriage to a foreigner (1963 TnNC, art. 13).

In order to respect the wife's will, Arab nationality laws demand an application for the acquisition of the husband's nationality. Other than that, some dispose the acquisition by operation of law (*binā*^{an} *ʿalà talab al-zawjah wa-bi-quwwat al-qānūn*), while others subject the grant of nationality to the state's consent (*binā*^{an} *ʿalà talab al-zawjah wa-muwāfaqat al-dawlah*). But in both cases further requirements (such as residency, lasting marriage, etc.) are generally set down. Acquisition by operation of the law is clearly set down only in the UAE Law (1972 AeFNL, art. 3), because other legislation allows the intervention of state authorities to bar the conferment of nationality (*bi-hirmān al-zawjah min haqq al-dukhūl fī 'l-jinsīyah*; 1975 EgNL, art. 7; 1959 KwNED(1980), art. 8; 1963 BhNL(1981), art. 7; 2005 QaNL, art. 8; 1990 YeNL, art. 11). On the other hand, state consent is explicitly required by other Arab nationality laws (1963 IqNL, art. 12(1)(a); 1954 JoNL(1987), art. 8; 1925 LbND(1960), art. 5; 1969 SyNLD, art. 8, 9, and 19; 1954 SaNR(2004), art. 16; 1983 OmNSD(1986), art. 5; 1957 SdNL(1970 and 1977), art. 9; 1954 LyNL, art. 7; 1958 MaNC(2007), art. 10; 1963 TnNC, art. 14; 1970 DzNC(2005), art. 9-bis).

For some Arab nationality laws the wife's acquisition of the husband's nationality depends on continued familial life. If the marriage ends and the wife remarries or acquires another nationality, she is stripped of her former husband's nationality (1969 SyNLD(1972), art. 13; 1954 SaNR(2004), art. 16; 1963 BhNL, art. 7(2); 2005 QaNL, art. 9; 1972 AeFNL, art. 4; 1954 LyNL, art. 7(2)).

On the other hand, the national woman who marries a foreigner is usually allowed to keep her nationality, if her husband's national law allows her to do so (1975 EgNL, art. 12; 1963 IqNL, art. 12(2); 1954 JoNL (1987), art. 8(2); 1925 LbND(1960), art. 6; 1969 SyNLD, art. 12; 1954 SaNR(2004), art. 17; 1959 KwNED(1980), art. 10; 1963 BhNL(1981), art. 7(1); 2005 QaNL, art. 10; 1972 AeFNL(1975), art. 14; 1983 OmNSD (1986), art. 11; 1990 YeNL, art. 10; 1957 SdNL, art. 12(1)(a); 1954 LyNL, art. 8). In the Maghreb the issue is framed in terms of allowing the woman to relinquish her previous nationality when marrying a foreigner (1958 MaNC(2007), art. 19(1)(3); 1963 TnNC, art. 30; 1970 DzNC (2005), art. 18(3))

The issue of the effects of the acquisition of the husband's nationality on the wife's earlier children is not addressed by Arab legislation and literature. The lack of interest is grounded more on sociological than legal reasons, and only Lebanese scholars debate the possible extension of the provision of 1925 LbND, art. 4, to this case (al-Bustānī 2003: 271ff).

3.2.2   Loss of nationality and its restoration
(Faqd al-jinsīyah wa-istirdāduhā)

Legal literature uses a broad variety of terms to identify nationality's various states of pathology, such as extinction (zawāl al-jinsīyah), loss (khasārat al-jinsīyah), deprivation (isqāt al-jinsīyah) and renunciation (al-takhallī ᶜan al-jinsīyah). But legislation commonly resorts to the all-embracing faqd (or fiqdān) al-jinsīyah, loss and sudden withdrawal, and then distinguishes between voluntary and involuntary loss. Scholars also employ different concepts with regard to the restoration of nationality according to the distinct systematisation adopted in the nationality laws. Some cover restoration before loss as a form of facilitated naturalisation (ᶜAbbūd 1986: 83ff; ᶜAbd al-ᶜāl 2001: 201ff), whereas others after loss and in connection with the causes of the loss (al-Rāwī 1984;

Riyād 1988; ʿAshshūsh & Bākhashab 1990; Dīb 1999; Sādiq & al-Haddād 2001).

3.2.2.1 Loss due to change (al-Faqd bi-l-taghyīr)

Freedom to change nationality and perpetual allegiance[36] are competing principles on which Arab legislation has variously drawn. If the freedom to change nationality prevails, foreign naturalisation automatically entails loss of nationality, whereas if perpetual allegiance proves stronger, loss of nationality for foreign naturalisation is subject to state consent, in the absence of which the national who acquires a foreign nationality will still be considered a national. Some laws infer from foreign naturalisation a lack of loyalty to the country and thus strip those who became naturalised of their nationality as a form of punishment (ʿiqābī deprivation), while other laws refuse to consider the national as a foreigner and surreptitiously allow for dual nationality. The latter approach is typical of countries with high migration figures that want to keep their nationals linked to the home country by hook or by crook.

Requiring permission to relinquish present nationality and acquire foreign nationality seems to serve the double purpose of ensuring that nationals forsaking their nationality have fully complied with all their duties, and somehow of discouraging them. Authorisation (tarkhīs) or permission (idhn) are issued by decree of the head of state, the council of ministers or a single minister, according to the different provisions, but all agree that without such decree the foreign naturalised must be treated as a national (1975 EgNL, art. 10; 1954 JoNL(1987), art. 15, and 17(a); 1925 LbND, art. 8(1)(1), and Law of 31 December 1946, art. 1; 1969 SyNLD, art. 10; 1954 SaNR, art. 11; 1990 YeNL, art. 22; 1958 MaNC(2007), art. 19; 1963 TnNC, art. 30; 1970 DzNC(2005), art. 18).[37] If the nationality law under which the person intends to naturalise prescribes loss of previous nationality to complete the procedure, the naturalisation inevitably aborts.

The punitive deprivation of nationality for having acquired foreign nationality without state permission is the main orientation of Gulf legislation (1963 IqNL(1980), art. 11; 1959 KwNED(1980), art. 11; 1963 BhNL, art. 9(1)(a); 2005 QaNL, art. 11(1)(5); 1972 AeFNL(1975), art. 15 (c); 1983 OmNSD, art. 9; 1957 SdNL, art. 12(1)(a); 1954 LyNL(1976), art. 9(1)). In order to conform to the provisions of the 1954 Arab League Convention on the limitation of cases of dual nationality among signatory states (art. 6), Jordan stipulated automatic loss of nationality for the Jordanian who acquires the nationality of another Arab country (1954 JoNL, art. 16).

3.2.2.2 Loss due to deprivation (al-Faqd bi-l-tajrīd)

When the loyalty (walā') of the national to the country fades away, the individual is stripped of his nationality (tajrīd). While al-faqd bi-l-taghyīr is aimed at avoiding cases of dual nationality, al-faqd bi-l-tajrīd is by far the most common cause of statelessness.

For the deprivation of nationality (al-faqd bi-l-tajrīd), a distinction is made between the national by descent and the naturalised. Only for the latter is nationality withdrawn (sahb al-jinsīyah) for reasons related both to the naturalisation process and to acts following naturalisation. A second set of causes of loss also applies to the national by descent and includes acts contrary to the loyalty due to the country. In order to translate the French déchéance Arab authors employ the term isqāt (loss), which can be optional (jawāzī) or mandatory (wujūbī).

Naturalisation can be revoked if it was obtained mendaciously (bi-aq-wāl kādhibah), by fraud or error (bi-tarīq al-ghashsh aw al-khata'), forgery or falsification (tazwīr aw tazyīf) of documents, evidence or testimony (1975 EgNL, art. 15(1); 1954 JoNL, art. 19(1)(2); 1969 SyNLD, art. 20; 1954 SaNR, art. 22; 1959 KwNED, art. 13(1); 1963 BhNL, art. 8(1); 2005 QaNL, art. 12(1)(1); 1972 AeFNL(1975), art. 16(1)(3); 1983 OmNSD, art. 13(1); 1990 YeNL, art. 18(1)(c); 1957 SdNL(1959), art. 13(1)(a); 1954 LyNL(1979), art. 10(1)(a); 1958 MaNC, art. 14(2); 1963 TnNC, art. 37; 1970 DzNC(2005), art. 13). No time limit is set for revoking naturalisation in the abovementioned cases,[38] while the naturalised can be stripped of nationality within a number of years (usually five or ten) after naturalisation if convicted for crimes – generally crimes against public morality (jarā'im khulqīyah) or infamous crimes (jarā'im al-shar-af) – or for having endangered public order or the security of the state (1975 EgNL, art. 15(2)(1-2); 1963 IqNL, art. 19; 1954 JoNL, art. 19(1)(1); LbLaw 31 January 1946(1962), art. 2(2)(1); 1954 SaNR(2004), art. 21(1) (b); 1959 KwNED(1980), art. 13(2); 1963 BhNL(1981), art. 8(2); 2005 QaNL, art. 12(1)(2); 1972 AeFNL(1975), art. 16(1)(1); 1983 OmNSD, art. 13(5); 1990 YeNL, art. 18(1)(a); 1957 SdNL(1959), art. 13(1)(c); 1954 LyNL(1979), art. 10(1)(b); 1958 MaNC(2007), art. 22(1)(1); 1963 TnNC, art. 33; 1970 DzNC(2005), art. 22(1)(1)). In Lebanon, the UAE, Egypt and Qatar naturalised citizens can be deprived of nationality if they leave the country for more than five, four, two or one consecutive years respectively (LbLaw 31 January 1946, art. 3; 1972 AeFNL(1975), art. 16 (1)(4); 1975 EgNL, art. 15(2)(3); 2005 QaNL, art. 12(1)(4)). In Kuwait the naturalised can be deprived of nationality if they abandon Islam or be-have in a way that shows their intention to apostatise (bi-irtidādihi ʿan al-islām aw-sulūkihi maslakᵃⁿ yaqtaʿ bi-nīyatihi fī dhālika; 1959 KwNED (1982), art. 4(1)(5)), and in Oman if they profess atheism (1983 OmNSD, art. 13(2)).

The main reason for stripping nationals – whether by origin or naturalisation – of their nationality (*isqāt al-jinsīyah*) is their connection to another state (*al-irtibāt bi-dawlah ajnabīyah*; 1975 EgNL, art. 16; 1963 IqNL, art. 20; 1954 JoNL, art. 18; 1925 LbND, art. 8, and LbLaw 31 January 1946, art. 1; 1969 SyNLD, art. 21; 1954 SaNR, art. 13; 1959 KwNED, art. 14; 1963 BhNL, art. 10; 2005 QaNL, art. 11; 1972 AeFNL, art. 15; 1983 OmNSD, art. 13; 1957 SdNL, art. 12; 1954 LyNL(1979), art. 10(2); 1958 MaNC(2007), art. 19, 20, and 22; 1963 TnNC, art. 32; 1970 DzNC(2005), art. 22).[39] The connection is generally inferred from serving in the government or military of another country without the consent of the national's own government. Nationals are deprived of their nationality after refusing to obey the government's order to leave the office (1975 EgNL, art. 16(1)(4); 1963 IqNL, art. 20(1)(2); 1954 JoNL, art. 18(1-2); 1925 LbND, art. 8(2), and LbLaw 31 January 1946, art. 1(1)(2-4); 1969 SyNLD, art. 21(1)(c); 1954 SaNR, art. 13(1)(d); 1959 KwNED, art. 14(1)(1); 1963 BhNL, art. 10(1)(a); 2005 QaNL, art. 11(1)(1); 1972 AeFNL, art. 15(1)(a); 1983 OmNSD, art. 13(3); 1957 SdNL(1959), art. 13(2); 1954 LyNL(1979), art. 10(2)(k); 1958 MaNC, art. 23(3); 1963 TnNC, art. 32; 1970 DzNC, art. 23). Zionism is a cause for deprivation under Egyptian law (*idhā ĭttasaf bi-ayy waqt min al-awqāt bi-l-sahyūnīyah*; 1975 EgNL, art. 16(1)(7)). Supporting Zionism or merely visiting Israel is a cause for deprivation under Libyan law (1954 LyNL(1979), art. 10(2)(c))[40]. Under Libyan law, the national can also be stripped of Libyan nationality for apostasy from Islam (1954 LyNL(1979), art. 10(2)(h)). The spectrum of discretionary powers concerning deprivation is quite broad: either they are unlimited (1954 SaNR, art. 29) or they are ruled out completely (1990 YeNL, art. 17).

3.2.2.3 Restoration (Istirdād al-jinsīyah)
Restoration of nationality can reverse the effects of loss due to change or deprivation. In the former case, the resumption is usually requested by the former national (*istirjāʿ* or *istiʿādah*), whereas in the latter case, the return is undertaken by state authorities (*radd* or *iʿādah*). Restoration is strongly affected by the consideration of the voluntary or involuntary causes of the loss.

Resumption of nationality (*istirjāʿ* or *istiʿādah*) after the *al-faqd bi-l-taghyīr* varies according to the position of the former national. Adults who freely decided to forsake their nationality are treated differently from children or spouses who merely 'followed' their fathers' or husbands' status. Different treatment is also accorded to nationals by origin or naturalisation, or to situations where the causes of the loss still persist or have vanished. Nationals who acquired a foreign nationality and want to reverse their decision usually need only to apply for resumption (1975 EgNL, art. 18; 1954 JoNL(1987), art. 17(1)(b); LbLaw 31

January 1946, art. 2; 1969 SyNLD, art. 24; 1963 BhNL, art. 11; 1972 AeFNL(1975), art. 17; 1983 OmNSD(1986), art. 12(b); 1990 YeNL, art. 15; 1958 MaNC, art. 15), while some legislation requires residency or marriage (1963 IqNL(1964), art. 11(2); 1959 KwNED(1980), art. 11 (2); 2005 QaNL, art. 7;[41] 1970 DzNC, art. 14;) and others simply do not provide for resumption and impose the naturalisation process.

The woman who has lost her nationality to acquire her husband's can resume it when the marriage comes to an end (1975 EgNL, art. 13; 1963 IqNL(1972), art. 12(2); 1954 JoNL(1987), art. 8(2); 1925 LbND (1960), art. 7; 1969 SyNLD, art. 14; 1954 SaNR, art. 18; 1959 KwNED (1980), art. 12; 1963 BhNL(1981), art. 7(1); 2005 QaNL, art. 10; 1972 AeFNL(1975), art. 17; 1983 OmNSD(1986), art. 11; 1990 YeNL, art. 14; 1954 LyNL, art. 8(2)). During marriage, the wife's resumption of her previous nationality may be allowed either by an explicit provision (1975 EgNL, art. 13(1)) or by the vagueness of the text (1959 KwNED (1980), art. 12; 2005 QaNL, art. 10).

Under all Arab nationality laws, minors who acquired a foreign nationality by virtue of their father's naturalisation can claim their original nationality when they come of age, but only few laws devote special provisions to the case (a case in point is 1983 OmNSD, art. 9), and general rules for restoration need to be applied.

Resumption applies only to nationals by origin in the UAE, where the Federal Law states that nationality is granted only once (1972 AeFNL, art. 12). Moreover, the son of a naturalised citizen is also considered naturalised, not only in the UAE but also in some other Gulf countries like Bahrain and Qatar (hereditary naturalisation, or *tajannus bi-l-wirāthah*; 1963 BhNL(1989), art. 6(4); 2005 QaNL, art. 2(2); 1972 AeFNL(1975), art. 17).[42]

Return of nationality after deprivation (*radd* or *iᶜādah*) is not set down in many nationality laws, and nationals stripped of their nationality need to apply for naturalisation if they want to regain their nationality status. In other cases, state authorities have extensive discretionary powers to return nationality to former nationals, but laws generally stipulate the act that needs to be adopted (1969 SyNLD, art. 24; 1959 KwNED, art. 15; 1963 BhNL, art. 11; 2005 QaNL, art. 11(2); 1972 AeFNL, art. 20; 1990 YeNL, art. 16) and sometimes expressly require that the causes that had brought about the deprivation must have been removed (1983 OmNSD, art. 14). Only in Egypt does the law require that at least five years have to elapse from loss to restoration (1975 EgNL, art. 18(1)).

3.3   Nationality (*jinsīyah*) in the Islamic perspective

The emergence of the nation-state and nationality represented a challenge for Islam, which refuses to accept any form of membership that goes beyond or cuts across confessional lines. Conversely, the long-standing kin relations – subsumed rather than superseded by the Islamic order – discreetly adapted to the new secular membership, the rules of which in many ways coincided with principles of kin affiliation.

The existence of an 'Islamic citizenship' has been – and still is in many respects – a highly divisive and controversial issue. The debate started in the late 19th century, kindled by the pan-Islamist thinker al-Afghānī (d. 1897), who examined the problematic relations between Islam and nationality in an article titled *al-Jinsīyah wa-l-diyānah al-islāmīyah* (Nationality and the Islamic Religion). The article was published in *al-ʿUrwah al-wuthqà* (The Firmest Bond), a journal al-Afghānī founded in Paris in 1884 with his foremost Arab disciple, the Egyptian reformist ʿAbduh (d. 1905).

Since for many Arab constitutions Islam is proclaimed the official religion of the state, and Islamic law (*al-sharīʿah al-islāmīyah*) serves as a source of its positive law, Islamic citizenship cannot be discarded as a matter of mere historical interest but rather must be considered in its actual and potential implications. Some provisions of Arab nationality laws, for instance, openly breach Islamic rules when allowing for the naturalisation of non-Muslims who are not even People of the Book (*ahl al-kitāb*), or when stripping the nationality of a Muslim for reasons other than apostasy. On the other hand, these secular laws can be regarded as irrespective of Islamic law when they do not provide for discrimination based on religious affiliation or for the deprivation of nationality of the Muslim who commits apostasy.

Some Islamic scholars reject the idea of an 'Islamic citizenship', which would conflict with Islam's universalism and would, conversely, vehiculate notions of secular affiliation unrelated to Islam (al-Jaddāwī 1983: 84ff; Sultān 1986: 155ff).[43] Others advocate the existence of an 'Islamic citizenship', even if they disagree on its basis: Islam or Islamic law (Salāmah 1989: 63ff). The distinction is not irrelevant. If Islamic citizenship is based only on Islam, conversion to Islam is then the only way to become a member of the polity, and *dhimmī*s are thus excluded (Madkūr 1983: 98ff; Sultān 1986: 220ff). A more recent orientation places the cornerstone of Islamic citizenship (Shaltūt 1985) in the law (*sharīʿah*) rather than in the creed (*ʿaqīdah*). *Dhimmī*s are thus allowed to be residents (*rābitat al-mawtin*) but not citizens (*rābitat al-jinsīyah*; al-Sanūsī 1957). If Muslims and *dhimmī*s are awarded the same Islamic citizenship, it all comes down to residence rights, not citizenship rights (Jamāl al-dīn 2001 and 2004).

A brief overview of rules and terms of secular nationality and Islamic citizenship in the Arab world helps cast some light on the points of friction and agreement between the two forms of membership, on the different ways of legitimation and on the efforts to read the secular regulations of modern nationality from an Islamic point of view.

3.3.1 Attribution

The attribution of nationality by paternal descent (paternal *jus sanguinis*) is fully compliant with Islamic thought, both for the Muslim by virtue of faith (*īmān*), and for the non-Muslim by virtue of the safe-conduct (*amān*). The determination of nationality (*thubūt al-jinsīyah*) is derived from the determination of filiation (*thubūt al-nasab*). The principle of *jus soli*, on the other hand, applies almost exclusively to the foundling (*laqīt*) in Arab nationality laws, and here again is in full accordance with Islamic law: if a foundling is found in an area inhabited mainly by Muslims it is considered a Muslim, whereas if it is found in an area inhabited mainly by non-Muslims it is considered a non-Muslim (ibn Qayyim al-Jawzīyah, *Ahkām ahl al-dhimmah*).

3.3.2 Acquisition

Acquisition of nationality is traced back to the shift from short-term safe-conduct (*amān mu'aqqat*) to perpetual safe-conduct (*amān mu'abbad* or *ʿahd al-dhimmah*). Under classical Islamic law, the Muslim who takes up residence in the *dār al-islām* becomes *ipso facto* a Muslim citizen, while the non-Muslim belonging to the *ahl al-kitāb* can reside for one year on safe-conduct as a *musta'min*. If he stays longer, he can be 'naturalised' as a *dhimmī*, and from that moment on he will be subject to the rules of *dhimmah*. This 'naturalisation' is discretionary and can be granted even if the non-Muslim never resided on Islamic territory, unlike the secular rules that require longer or shorter residency.

Acquisition by marriage is inspired by the principle of unity of nationality within the family (*mabda' wahdat al-jinsīyah fī 'l-ʿā'ilah*). The classical doctrine of mixed marriages teaches that if a foreign non-Muslim woman resident in the *dār al-islām* (*musta'minah*) marries a Muslim or a *dhimmī*, she becomes a *dhimmīyah* by marriage, whereas the foreign non-Muslim man resident in the *dār al-islām* (*musta'min*) who marries a *dhimmīyah* does not become a *dhimmī* by marriage (al-Sarakhsī, *al-Siyar al-kabīr*). Acquisition of Islamic citizenship by marriage depends therefore on the religious and gender-related status of the spouses and their residence.

The effects of what can be described as 'Islamic naturalisation' are direct and immediate. Muslims enjoy the citizen status upon their entry into the *dār al-islām*, and non-Muslims upon their 'naturalisation', having to abide by the *dhimmah* rules from that same moment. As for familial effects of naturalisation, the non-Muslim wife of the Muslim who enters the *dār al-islām*, or of the non-Muslim who becomes a *dhimmī*, becomes herself a *dhimmīyah*. Likewise, the minor children of the former or of the latter follow the status of their father.[44]

3.3.3   Loss

Perpetual allegiance, a principle retained by most Arab nationality laws, is one of the most shared and common elements and survived the decline of the model in Europe. Muslims do not lose their nationality when leaving the *dār al-islām*, nor do *dhimmī*s, unless the latter intend not to return to the Islamic territory.[45]

Causes of loss are different for Muslim citizens and *dhimmī*s. A Muslim can be stripped of Islamic citizenship only for apostasy, whereas *dhimmī*s can voluntary or involuntary be deprived of their Islamic denizenship. The classical breaches of the *dhimmah* are reorganised in these two categories. *Dhimmī*s can forsake their status by (1) converting to Islam and becoming full-fledged Islamic citizens,[46] or by (2) relocating to the *dār al-harb* and taking up residence there (*lihāq al-dhimmī bi-dār al-harb fa-yasīr min ahlihā*). By contrast, they can be involuntarily deprived of denizenship if they (3) refuse to pay the *jizyah*,[47] (4) fight against Muslims, (5) attack a Muslim trying to kill him or turn him away from his religion, (6) commit adultery with a Muslim woman, (7) spy or harbour a spy working against Muslims, (8) utter blasphemy against God, His Book, His religion or His prophet or (9) practice brigandage.

The effects of the loss of Islamic citizenship are invariably personal, both in the case of the Muslim abandoning Islam and of the *dhimmī* breaching the conditions of protection (*dhimmah*) in any of the abovementioned ways. Neither the wife nor minor children are required to follow the father's loss of citizenship.

4 Citizenship and the three levels of membership

After a general outline of the three main levels of membership in the Arab world, this closing chapter is devoted to the interplay of these levels in the determination of the sphere of individual rights. Every level has a different take on the individual, the rights and duties that should be attached to him – or her – and the extent of the exercise of the former or compliance to the latter.

Citizenship (*muwātanah*) in the Arab world is essentially defined by the individual's membership in a kin group, in a religious community and in a nation-state. Arab intellectuals and activists who are engaged in the struggle for equality and full citizenship rights condemn the current system and call for the eradication of all forms of discrimination between citizens based on any voluntary or involuntary membership (al-Jābirī 1990; Ben Achour 1993).

Membership is generally established by birth, thus involuntarily. From the *banū Fulān* ('the sons of Tom', i.e. the members of the kin group) down to the *abnā' al-balad* ('the sons of the homeland', i.e. the citizens of the nation-state), descent is the key device of membership. Both *banūn* and *abnā'* are plural variants of the singular *ibn* (son), showing the importance of *jus sanguinis* in the logic of Arab membership.

Interesting analogies and contrasts can be drawn with the Roman system of status (*status libertātis*, *familiæ* and *civitātis*, all relevant for full legal capacity). The *status libertātis* lost its relevance with the abolition of slavery, but the *status familiæ* would still be applicable (even if some adjustment would be required, since the Roman kin system was much more rigid than the Arab, where a *status gentis* would be more appropriate), a *status religiōnis* should be added (for its bearing on the determination of applicable law) and the *status civitātis* would maintain its importance as a condition for the enjoyment of civil, political and social rights of the modern Arab state.

4.1 Citizenship and the kin group (*status gentis*)

The kin system affects both nationality (*jinsīyah*) and citizenship (*mu-wātanah*). In other words, the *status gentis* contributes to the definition of both the individuals' relations with the state and their sphere of rights. Kin affiliation is a resilient and vital feature of Arab society, in spite of all the endeavours of the religious communities, and later the nation-states, to do away with it. Kin membership does not play the same role throughout the region. It presents different local features, and urbanisation certainly tends to weaken the kin system by discon-necting the individual from stricter control by the kin group. The kin organisation's intrinsic ability to adjust to new conditions, however, grants it continuity.

Limitations of certain kin groups' rights are usually carried out by com-munal denial or deprivation of nationality (*jinsīyah*), even disregarding national legislation. A case in point is the denial of Kuwaiti nationality to some nomadic kin groups known as *bidūn* (literally: 'without', from the phrase: *bidūn jinsīyah*, 'without nationality'). *Bidūn*s used to live across the borders between Kuwait and Saudi Arabia, but in the 1960s they settled in Kuwait. They did not register with the Kuwaiti authori-ties, who seized the chance to keep a stateless and rightless population on their territory. Grants of nationality were repeatedly postponed, and most *bidūn*s are still stateless, excluded even from the strict rules of Kuwaiti naturalisation.

A case of communal deprivation is that of the al-Ghufrān in Qatar. Six thousand members of this branch of the al-Murrah tribe were stripped of their Qatari nationality in March 2005 for lack of loyalty to the Emir. The al-Ghufrān allegedly remained loyal to the former ruler, sheikh Khalīfah Āl Thānī – deposed by his son Hamad in 1995 – and were accused of having backed a failed coup to restore Khalīfah's rule over Qatar in 1996. In order to force the al-Ghufrān out of the country, they were denied access to state schools and hospitals, were served with eviction notices, fired from public offices and deprived of water and en-ergy.[1] Qatari authorities, however, claimed that they were acting legally against cases of dual nationality (namely Qatari and Saudi), which is forbidden under the provisions of the new Qatari Nationality Law 38/2005 (art. 18). In February 2006 restoration of Qatari citizenship was announced for those who had 'regularised' their position (*man sahhahū awdā'ahum*).[2]

Conversely, in Bahrain nationality is granted to counterbalance the overwhelming demographic majority of Bahraini Shias. Bahraini authorities have naturalised many members of a kin group, the Āl al-Dawsarī or al-Dawāsir, who had migrated to mainland Saudi Arabia in the 1920s. The Āl al-Dawsarī are Sunnis from the Nejd region who settled in Bahrain with the Āl Khalīfah (Bahrain's ruling family) in 1783, but left the country in 1923 due to conflicts with the British forces. After the promulgation of the 2002 Bahraini constitution, large groups of the Āl al-Dawsarī were naturalised in order to be enfranchised and vote in Bahraini elections. Such 'political naturalisation' (al-tajannus al-siyāsī) has been repeatedly censured by opposition societies,[3] mainly Shias, whose electoral force is not adequately mirrored in elected bodies, partly due to heavy sectarian gerrymandering, naturalisation of Sunni expatriate workers[4] and extension of voting rights in local elections to nationals of other Gulf Cooperation Council member states.

Membership in a certain kin group affects attribution, acquisition or loss of nationality not only in the Gulf, where it is undoubtedly easier to detect, but also in other countries, as is the case with the attribution of Jordanian nationality to nomadic tribes of northern Jordan,[5] or Lebanese nationality to the groups of the Wādī Khālid or the 'Seven Towns' (al-qurà al-sabʿ).[6]

Kin groups also played a significant role in the creation or the configuration of nation-states, and still represent one of the main political channels in the Middle East. Group solidarity (ʿasabīyah), in particular, is a raw nerve in contemporary Arab society, even if at times concealed (Sharābī 1990, al-Jābirī 1995). The 2004 Arab Human Development Report considers it the 'major and more dangerous challenge facing the spirit of citizenship' (rūh al-muwātanah).[7]

Public institutions are often permeated by influential kin groups, which usually hold and control both lower and higher state positions (Khoury & Kostiner 1990, Bonte, Conte & Dresch 2001). Here again, intensity varies. In the Gulf the state (dawlah) and the ruling family (al-usrah al-hākimah) are but a hendiadys,[8] whereas in other areas the influence is not as plain but is nonetheless not irrelevant (Abdul-Jabar & Dawod 2003).[9] For instance, major kin groups tend to have representatives in the elected bodies thanks to internal campaigning (candidates are generally selected by and within the group's notables), and electoral constituencies can be drawn according to the group's needs.[10] Even parties and kin groups sometimes overlap, as in Yemen, where the phenomenon is known as 'tribality of the party' (qabalīyat al-hizb) or 'partification of the tribe' (tahzīb al-qabīlah). In the case of the Berbers of Kabylie, protests against the modern Algerian state were organised through kin channels (ʿarsh, plur: ʿarūsh; Basagana & Sayad 1974), and in the spring of 2001 the movement adopted the eloquent name of 'citizens of the ʿarūsh' (Salhi 2003).

Some features of traditional kin justice can still be found in the folds of contemporary judicial systems. On the one hand, rules and procedures of customary law may survive in an informal setting (abū Hassān 1987), and on the other hand they may be incorporated into state legislation if the state wants to control them. In Jordan, the Ministry of Justice has been undertaking a project to bring traditional tort settlement (*sulh* or *musālahah*) under judicial control as a 'criminal mediation' (*al-wisātah al-jinā'īyah*).

Kin order links up with the ethnic dimension, a problematic and unresolved issue throughout the Middle East, from the Kurds in the Arab East to the Berbers in the Arab West, while Arabs experience similar hardships in Iran in the Arab-majority region of Khawzastān.[11] Migrations complicate the situation even more: high migration flows within the Arab world, from Arab to non-Arab countries (especially from North African Arab countries) and from non-Arab to Arab countries (especially to Gulf countries) are recorded. The issue of ethnicity in the Arab world has been addressed by all the main political currents of the 20th century (pan-Arabism (Sātiᶜ al-Husrī and ᶜAflaq), pan-Islamism (Khalaf allāh, but also al-ᶜAbbūd, al-ᶜAnānī, al-Najīb) and Regionalism (al-Sayyid)), but is yet unsettled.

4.2   Citizenship and the religious community (*status religiōnis*)

Relations among religious communities (*tā'ifah* or *millah*) are regulated along the lines of the Ottoman *millet* system. At the top of the ladder is the Islamic community (*millet-i hākime*, or ruling *millet* under the Ottomans), and individual rights are modulated according to religious affiliation.[12] Relations among different Islamic denominations escape this systematisation but are nonetheless quite relevant for the political life of the Muslim.[13]

The prominence of the Islamic community leads to an almost impenetrable political system that excludes non-Muslims, even if non-Muslims have held important ministerial positions (especially in the past, and mainly in the Levant). All through the 20th century, non-Muslims (chiefly Christians) contributed to the Arab renaissance (*al-nahdah* or *al-yaqzah al-ᶜarabīyah*) more than their low demographic figures might suggest, and played an active role in the organisation of new nation-states, notably at middle and top administrative levels. The status of non-Muslims greatly depends on the relations they establish with the authority. They therefore live in a state of subjection to these authorities, and any change in the power structure affects them directly and immediately. This dependence on the authority earned non-Muslim Arabs the reputation of being particularly loyal to the state. Non-Muslims' insecurity, however, is at the root of the large migrations of Eastern Christians, the Lebanese diaspora and the hardships of Palestinian Christians of Israel and the Occupied Territories.

The constitutions of almost all Arab countries stipulate that the president has to be Muslim.[14] On the other hand, the oath 'in the name of God, Most Gracious, Most Merciful' (bi-sm^i ăllāh al-rahmān al-rahīm), which is required for some key state positions, can also be pronounced by non-Muslims, although it is a very Islamic-oriented invocation. Remarkably, some local 'Islams' have supported the formation of national communities (al-ummah al-watanīyah) by projecting onto them what Islam declared as constitutive of the Islamic community (al-ummah al-islāmīyah), and have presented the centralisation of power of the nation-state as fully compliant with the classical Islamic doctrine of the wilāyah. Such a stance is now questioned on many sides. On the one hand, radical Islamists believe that the nation-state openly challenges the unity of the Islamic ummah, and on the other hand, ethnic and religious minorities condemn an Islam that denies their traditional peculiarities. Supranational Islamic movements still need to overcome serious obstacles in order to take root, but processes of political and administrative decentralisation, conversely, are quickly developing and may even breathe some new life into the kin organisation.

In a complex set of jurisdictions and legislative frameworks, Islamic law and the Islamic judge maintain a privileged position in all the Arab systems (except Lebanon; Gannagé 1983). In spite of its confessional nature and the ensuing personal character, Islamic law operates as a reference system, applying even to non-Muslims in certain cases. Both legislation and case law ensure the maximum extension of Islamic law and the broadest jurisdiction to the Islamic judge through a particular adaptation of the conflict of laws rules (Aldeeb 1979; Charfi 1987; Deprez 1988; Aluffi Beck-Peccoz 1993), viz. by invoking public policy (réserve d'ordre public).

Islamic law applies to the non-Muslim not only when the opposing party is Muslim, but also when non-Muslim parties belong to different communities (tā'ifah). In Egypt, for instance, state tribunals – which have replaced confessional jurisdictions since 1955 (el-Geddawi 2001) – apply Islamic law according to the Hanafi rite to non-Muslims as well if the parties are affiliated to different religions (diyānah), denominations (millah) or communities (tā'ifah).[15] The Egyptian solution raises some questions: can the Christian husband of a Christian wife belonging to a tā'ifah or millah other than his own take one or more wives? Or can he divorce his wife according to the rules of talāq? Egyptian courts apply Islamic law not only for the prerogative of religion but also for the prerogative of citizenship, as in the case of the non-Muslim Egyptian married to a non-Muslim foreign woman of another *tā'ifah*.[16]

An even trickier question is: what law applies to the personal status of a foreign Muslim? According to conflict of laws rules, the national law of the subject should be applicable, but some courts (most notably the Egyptian Court of Cassation[17] and the Moroccan Supreme Court[18]) invoke public policy and resort to Islamic law as a *lex fori*. This policy has a curious outcome: Islamic law becomes applicable to foreign Muslims whose national law may not abide by Islamic principles, as it does to those whose national law does abide by Islamic principles. Therefore, *lex fori* is treated as the only applicable Islamic law, regardless of all other interpretations. On the other hand, the principle of unity of the Islamic community, irrespective of national borders or distinctions, proves its enduring legal strength.

Matters of personal status are regulated throughout the Arab world on religious bases. If there are no local minorities in the country with special rules on personal status, the court will apply Islamic law as *lex fori*. The Moroccan Nationality Code of 1958 used to expressly provide for it, but since the 2007 amendment the text only refers to the 2004 Moroccan Family Code.

Religious affiliation affects the citizenship of the individual in many ways, even if it is rarely delineated in legislation. Special provisions involving religion can be found in the 1954 Libyan Nationality Law (1979), which strips citizens of their Libyan nationality for committing apostasy (art. 10(2)(h)); in the 1959 Kuwaiti Nationality Law (1982), which requires conversion to Islam in order to naturalise (art. 4(1)(5)); in the 1990 Yemeni Nationality Law, which does not allow for the naturalisation of non-Muslims (art. 5-6); and in the 1983 Omani Nationality Law, which deprives nationality to whoever upholds non-religious (*lā dīnīyah*) beliefs (art. 13(2)). The doors of nationality can thus be closed to non-Muslims, and forsaking Islam can be a reason to end the relation between the individual and the state.

Even where apostasy has no effect on nationality status, apostasy elicits such a general condemnation in society that the individual charged of being a renegade is often forced to relocate or abandon the country. In such circumstances, nationality is of little help, even if the person is not stripped of it. A remarkable case in point is that of Hussayn ᶜAlī Qambar, since it took place in a country – Kuwait – where a clear position on *status religiōnis* had been adopted (Law 1/1982). In May 1996 a Kuwaiti Shia Court declared Qambar's apostasy and called for his execution, but state authorities unexpectedly showed a conciliatory attitude and issued him a passport with which he left the country (Longva 2002).

In most Arab countries, apostasy is no longer punished by death, but it still carries serious legal and social consequences (Peters & De Vries 1976-1977). Accusing someone of being an apostate is also a means of political coercion, especially in the actual historical phase of re-Islamisation, or Islamic awakening (*al-sahwah al-islāmīyah*). The death penalty for apostasy has been a matter for contentious dispute throughout Islamic history, especially in the 19th and 20th century. Drawing on the Qur'ān and the Sunnah, reformers like ʿAbduh or Ridā championed the idea that apostasy was not sufficient for the death penalty. The renegade also had to pose a real threat to the Islamic state. Most ʿulamā', however, follow the traditional rule, advocating the execution of the renegade, who – in their view – is a threat to the Islamic state by the sole act of apostasy (ʿAwdah 1981: I, 536; al-Ghazzālī 1963: 101f; Bilmen 1949-1952: III, 483ff).[19] Since contemporary legislation does not prescribe the death penalty for apostasy, an Egyptian Islamist like ʿAwdah maintains that it is upon every Muslim to kill the apostate, and the killer will not be liable because the Egyptian Penal Code states that no one can be punished for acts rendered *bona fide* on the basis of a right established by Islamic law (art. 60; ʿAwdah 1981: I, 535-538). Besides the death penalty, apostasy has other severe civil consequences in personal status and inheritance law, where Islamic law has a firmer grip. For instance, marriage can be nullified for the apostasy of one of the spouses. This is the most common legal action against an alleged apostate, and Islamist activists usually file suits in state courts to pronounce the separation of the couple (*tafrīq*).[20]

Accusations of apostasy (*takfīr*) have been used throughout Islamic history as a means of political struggle (ever since the Kharijite schism, in the early days of Islam), but recently *takfīr* has turned into a political strategy that takes the name of *takfīrīyah*. While in the past the accusation was addressed to rival political groups of militant Islam (namely, Arab communists), it is now directed towards the entire ruling system, accused of being corrupt and disposed to the infidel West (Ramadān 1995).

Members of religious minorities endure limitations of citizenship rights. Even in a formally secular state like Lebanon (although based on communitarianism: *al-tā'ifīyah*), the political, social and demographic equilibrium is so delicate that religious-related aspects of nationality and citizenship stir great political animosity. Every naturalisation decree turns into a battlefield, especially on the repartition of naturalisation candidates by community (Maktabi 2000). Lebanese religious authorities intervene, as was the case with Decree 5274/1994 of 20 June 1994, which was contested by the Maronite League (*al-Rābitah al-mārūnīyah*) in the Lebanese Council of State. The Decree was sent back for reconsideration, and competent state authorities (namely, the president of the Lebanese Republic and the Interior Ministry) regularly reported to the Maronite Patriarch on how the work was advancing.

The condition of Jews became more critical after the foundation of the state of Israel in 1948 due to unrelenting Arab hostility. Many Jews moved to Israel and others migrated to other countries, thus leaving Jewish Mizrahi communities in the Arab world close to extinction. In Morocco, the members of one of the largest Jewish (Sephardi) communities left in the region are at times considered 'foreigners' by state authorities, even if scholars censure such a practice (al-Hussayn 2000). In the state of Israel, conversely, non-Ashkenazi Jewish and Arab non-Jewish citizens alike endure discriminatory practices. Among the many facets of the conflict in the Middle East is the case of the members of the South Lebanon Army, who were granted Israeli denizenship (and later full citizenship) because they had to flee Lebanon due to their role in the war.

4.3   Citizenship and the nation-state (status civitatis)

Nationality regulations are obliged to comply with some international and constitutional provisions. At the international level, the 1948 Universal Declaration of Human Rights and the 1966 UN Covenants have set a general framework for nationality legislation, along with more specific conventions such as the 1958 Convention on the Nationality of Married Women, the 1961 Convention on the Reduction of Statelessness, the 1966 Convention on the Elimination of All Forms of Racial Discrimination, the 1979 Convention on the Elimination of All Forms of Discrimination Against Women and the 1989 Convention on the Rights of the Child. These conventions have generally been signed and ratified by Arab countries but rarely implemented.

At a regional level, the most relevant international document is the 1945 Charter of the Arab League, which stipulates that one of the statutory purposes of the League is the close cooperation of member-states on nationality matters (jinsīyah; art. 2(d)). Accordingly, an agreement on nationality was signed in 1945 but never ratified. Its implementation thus became the free choice of its signatory parties. Some reference to nationality can be found in regional declarations of human rights, but only one of them recently entered into force. Arab charters do carry some reference to nationality, however, thanks to the emphasis placed on Arab nationalism (al-qawmīyah al-ʿarabīyah) that allows them to embrace all Arab citizens, Muslims and non-Muslims alike.[21] A right to nationality is recognised by the 1994 Arab Charter of Human Rights (and its 2004 update). The original version provided that none could be either arbitrarily deprived of his original (*asliyah*) nationality or prevented from acquiring another nationality (art. 24). But the 2004 update broadened the 1994 formulation by stipulating that every person has a right to nationality and cannot be arbitrarily or illegally stripped of it (art. 29).[22] The update (*Tahdīth al-mīthāq al-ʿarabī li-huqūq al-insān*) entered into force in early 2008 (having been ratified by Jordan, Bahrain, Libya, Algeria, the UAE, Palestine and Yemen).

Arab constitutions usually prescribe that nationality be regulated by law[23] and that nationals cannot be arbitrarily deprived of it.[24] Particular political conditions may require further, specific provisions. Such is the case with Bahrain, where the practice of exiling citizens by simply barring them from re-entering the country was outlawed by the 2002 Constitution (art. 17(b)). The 2005 Iraqi Constitution, on the other hand, expressly proscribed the depriving of nationality to 'Iraqis by birth' and recognised the right of all those who had been illegally stripped of their Iraqi nationality to be reintegrated into the citizen's status (art. 18(3)(a)). The agreement on a date by which reconsideration of arbitrary deprivations had to start could not be reached, and indication of the date was left out of the final draft submitted to popular referendum.

Several questions on the definition of nationality and citizenship in the Arab world are still open, due to major, thorny issues of international law and regional politics. The paramount problem is probably Palestinian citizenship, i.e. citizenship of the Palestinians of the Occupied Territories, of Israel, of the refugee camps in neighbouring countries and of the diasporic communities. The solution is further complicated by the unclear international personality of the Palestinian National Authority. In the Arab West, the definition of the status of Western Sahara is also still pending and affects the citizenship status of Sahrawis. Even the UN referendum on self-determination[25] has not yet taken place because an agreement on who is entitled to participate in it could not be reached. In the regional plan, 'Gulf citizenship' (or the Gulf Cooperation Council citizenship) can be regarded as an interesting experiment in the area and seems oriented towards the European model of integration. Even a radical reform of the Arab League – widely and repeatedly announced over the last decades – would positively affect the determination and the coordination of state disciplines of nationality, since it is one of the League's main statutory purposes.

The theoretical debate on citizenship emerged in the Arab world at the turn of the 20th century, along with the discourse on the nation-state. The dispute soon focused on the status of non-Muslims in the Islamic world. Instead of looking into the concept of citizenship and defining its contents (viz. the position of the individual *vis-à-vis* the state and the bundle of rights attached to citizenship), intellectuals and reformers engaged in arguments over the equality of Muslims and non-Muslims in an Arab-Islamic state. All the major trends of modern and contemporary Arab-Islamic thought – Islamic Reformism, Arab Nationalism, the Muslim Left and anti-Western Modernism – took a stand on the issue.

The dominant position was the one championed by intellectuals like al-Mawdūdī, who maintained that non-Muslims could enjoy only limited political rights (namely, they could not serve as heads of states or representatives; al-Mawdūdī 1978). For others, like Zaydān, the state was free to grant citizenship to *dhimmī*s if they respected Islamic principles and served the public good (Zaydān 1963). Western scholars thus defined the status of non-Muslims in the new nation-states of the region as a 'second-class citizenship' or 'non-citizenship' (MacDonald 1913; Khadduri 1955). Occupying an isolated position is the Egyptian thinker and journalist Huwaydī, who advocated full citizenship rights (*huqūq al-muwātanah al-kāmilah*) for non-Muslims, rejecting the category of *dhimmah*, which he considered a pre-Islamic practice included in non-binding *hadīth*s (Huwaydī 1985). Other – more conventional – authors tried to accommodate the status of non-Muslims living under Muslim authority (*wilāyah*) with the notion of citizenship, but only achieved modest results. The Tunisian Islamist al-Ghannūshī, for instance, proposed a distinction between a 'general or public citizenship' (*al-muwātanah al-ᶜāmmah*) for Muslims, and a 'special or private citizenship' (*al-muwātanah al-khāssah*) for non-Muslims, justifying the discrimination on grounds of the non-Muslims' free choice (al-Ghannūshī 1993). Likewise, the Iraqi intellectual al-ᶜAlwānī dismissed citizenship as a byproduct of Western secularism incompatible with Islam, and asserted that 'religious separatism' would favour non-Muslim minorities anyhow (al-ᶜAlwānī 1993). Some Islamist thinkers like the Egyptian ᶜAmārah or the Sudanese Nādir argued that citizenship was not an un-Islamic concept but in fact was an originally Islamic idea developed during the first Medinese years of Muhammad (ᶜAmārah 1989; Nādir 1999).

The ongoing debate is still quite heated in Egypt, where Christian Copts make up the largest non-Muslim religious community of the Arab world. Faced with the rise of political Islam, Coptic religious authorities promote dialogue and public awareness on citizenship within Egyptian society. Ever since the early 1990s, both Muslim and Christian intellectuals, jurists, politicians and scholars have been called to contribute to the discussion, and their contributions have been systematically published and circulated.

Since the end of the 20th century the debate on citizenship has gained renewed impetus and interest, mainly as a result of external pressure on the status of women in the Arab-Islamic context. The risk, however, is to fall into the same circularity as in the past. Intellectuals discuss the possibility of a woman enjoying citizenship rights equal to those of a man, but do not address the core issue of what citizenship is about, in the Arab world as a whole or in each individual Arab country.[26] Even the term *muwātin* (citizen) still does not appear n Arab works on Islamic or constitutional law, with some rare exceptions (Ghalyūn 1996; Karcic 2005).

Lately, Arab politicians and media are increasingly bringing citizenship into the public discourse. The greater recurrence of the terms 'citizen' and 'citizenship' does not by itself guarantee the achievement of a corresponding advancement. Thus, the witty question raised by the Coptic Egyptian intellectual Rizq in a conference on democratisation and modernisation in Egypt sounds even more thought-provoking: 'Are we subjects or citizens?'[27]

It was precisely in Egypt in March 2007 that a controversial constitutional reform introduced 'citizenship' (*muwātanah*) in the 1971 Egyptian constitution. For the first time in world history, a constitution established a 'democratic system based on citizenship' (*nizāmuhā dīmuqrātī yaqūm ʿalà asās al-muwātanah*; art. 1).[28] The choice, however, was but a means to serve other, more pressing ends of regime stability.[29]

4.4 Contrasting citizenships: the role of migrations

Migrations are a major testing ground for citizenship, for the East and the West alike. International migration phenomena are quite diversified throughout the Arab world. Large human flows reach oil-rich Gulf countries from the Far East, sub-Saharan Africa or other Arab countries (i.e. 'inter-Arab migration'), other groups of skilled workers leave the Levant for Europe, the Americas or Oceania, while movements of mostly unskilled workers from North Africa head for the nearby shores of southern Europe.

In the Gulf, the numbers of expatriate communities make the few Gulf citizens a true elite, living separately from the mass of foreign workers. In Europe, Arab migrants are but a small group among the immigrant communities, but in the public eye they represent the 'immigrant' *par excellence* due to their strongly defined and affirmed identity.

The doors of Gulf nationality are closed to Arab and non-Arab migrants. After the oil crisis, Gulf countries introduced even stricter regulations for naturalisation and extended the period after naturalisation in which political rights are suspended. The broad discretionary powers of state authorities in repatriating migrants (usually reconsideration cannot be filed due to laxity of legislation or lack of judicial remedies against administrative decisions for foreigners; ᶜAshshūsh 1991: 57-75), together with the massive amount of foreign workers waiting beyond the borders, make the 'privileged' residence in the Gulf a precarious and arbitrarily revocable condition (al-Fayfī 1994; al-Mūsà & ᶜAzīz 1981; al-Sabāh 1987).

In Europe, conversely, the acquisition of nationality, or its attribution by *jus soli*, is more accessible to foreign migrants, and fundamental civil rights are generally enjoyed even by foreigners. As for Arab migrants, their membership in the kin group is often quiescent but can be reactivated – habitually in the country of origin – during key phases of human life – according to the Arab mentality – such as marriage. Membership in the religious community, on the contrary, remains vibrant as a basic component of the migrant's identity. The differences in the concepts of religious freedom that prevail in the migrant's original and recipient legal and social environments, however, often lead to friction between the local society and the Arab Muslim migrant communities. Islamic law, for instance, is a fundamental element of Islam. Accordingly, 'Islamic religious freedom' includes the right for non-Muslims to be judged according to their confessional law, and by judges of their own community. Conversely, however, Muslims who acquire a European nationality are subject to the positive, secular law of that country, like all the other citizens. Here, membership in the nation-state clashes with religious affiliation. Acquiring a foreign, non-Islamic nationality for many Muslim intellectuals meant apostasy, and some courts have upheld the view, especially in the colonial years. A leaflet with the revealing titling 'Change of Nationality is Apostasy and Treason'[30] has been recently re-published in Paris, with all the *fatwà*s and articles on the effect of foreign naturalisation (al-Jazā'irī 1993). Muslim migrants who did not naturalise, on the other hand, can be judged on Islamic law as formulated in their own countries of origin, thanks to the rules of conflict of laws (if public policy is not invoked; Mezghani 2003). Nationality – originally seen as an evil innovation against the unity of the Islamic *ummah* – can now serve as a means for Muslim migrants to abide by Islamic law (as framed in their own countries of origin). At present Arab Muslims who migrated to Europe in the 1990s are not eligible for nationality in most cases, but more and more will soon meet the residency requirements. What will be the stance of sending and receiving countries on the naturalisation of Muslims? On the European side, no country has a system of Islamic courts for its Muslim citizens except Greece, but the Greek exception is limited to the historic

Muslim communities of Thrace, and newly settled Muslim expatriate communities cannot file their suits in these special courts (Tsitselikis 2004). On the Arab side, some countries – like Morocco – spelled out in their legislation that rules of personal status will be applied to their nationals even if in possession of another nationality.[31] The conflict between territorial and personal law, i.e. national versus religious affiliation, was an issue that was raised in the colonial age both for France in the Muslim West and for Italy in Libya, but migration fluxes helped to renew the interest on the topic.

4.5   Patterns of citizenship in the Arab world

By intertwining and overlapping, the three levels of membership determine the actual extension of individual citizenship (muwātanah) and affect the local regulations on nationality (jinsīyah). Analysing the rules governing the jinsīyah, some specific characteristics of the muwātanah can be detected, but the latter's distinctive peculiarities usually lay beneath the folds of each country's legal system. With this caveat, some patterns can be reconstructed, and some strain on conflicting fields presented.

A general, preliminary remark regards the form: nationality is regulated throughout the Arab world by state legislation (even in countries more ideologically opposed to positive law). This should not come as a surprise, since nationality surfaced with the modern nation-state and its determination is considered one of the bastions of state sovereignty. Membership in the kin group and the religious community, on the other hand, has remained within the traditional domain of customary and confessional law but nonetheless has played quite a relevant role in the state's legal system.

Responses to the actual content of nationality regulations, conversely, follow the rules of model circulation in comparative law. Some regulations matching Arab mentality have been fully implemented and some were rejected by the legal environment, while other local rules even prevailed on the foreign model.

Attribution of nationality by jus sanguinis can undoubtedly be included among the principles that were fully implemented due to their conformity with the local legal environment. Descent is the main source of affiliation in the Arab world: paternal descent for membership in the kin group, the religious community and also the nation-state. Maternal descent, by contrast, is still an open issue in many Arab countries. Even if no religious obstacle stands in the way of its introduction or implementation, the strong appeal of paternal descent and the firm opposition to dual nationality somehow hinder it.

If not attributed by paternal descent, nationality in the Arab world is essentially closed. *Jus soli* plays a very limited role in the attribution of nationality, while its acquisition by naturalisation is not only cautiously restricted by legislation but also severely circumscribed by the discretionary powers granted to state authorities by international law and internal legislation. The degree of openness of nationality legislation fluctuates between more liberal sending countries like Egypt or Lebanon and traditionally more conservative receiving countries like the Gulf Cooperation Council member states.

Acquisition of nationality is generally easier for those who present some ethnic or religious affinity with the country. Most Arab legislation provides for special naturalisation rules for nationals of other Arab countries (co-ethnic preference) and a few also for foreign Muslims (co-religious preference). Such preferences, however, chiefly operate under the silent mechanisations of legislation, especially when internal ethnic or religious balances are unstable (such as in Iraq, Bahrain or Lebanon), while some ethnic, religious or national categories can be excluded for sheer political reasons (namely, the taboo stabilisation (*tawtīn*) of Palestinians).

The most strident and enduring rejections, however, are to be found outside the province of the rules on attribution, acquisition or loss of nationality (adjusted but somehow internalised by all Arab countries). Rather, they concern citizenship as a vehicle for the principles of equality and territoriality. Personal status regulations provide an interesting case in point: how can citizenship be incorporated in a system that applies different laws to its citizens and the same law to a citizen and a foreigner? When the first nationality law to be applied in the Arab world was introduced by the Porte in 1869, the intent was precisely to subject all Ottoman nationals to the same law. Even then, reality fell short of expectations nevertheless, and personal status was left out and maintained under the traditional confessional system.

Predominance of the form and the formal territoriality of positive law (*qānūn*), however, should not overshadow the resilience and vitality of the personality of confessional laws (*sharī͑ah*). Thanks to conflict of laws rules, even nationality grants confessional laws an unintentional and unexpected renewed vigour. For instance, Arab migrants (Muslims and non-Muslims alike) are subject to their confessional law as their national law, even abroad.

On the other hand, a special feature of the late 19th century European model of citizenship, i.e. perpetual allegiance, was acquired by Arab systems and is preserved, even if it has been abandoned in the European systems where the model originated. Major Arab sending countries rather tend to strengthen the principle of perpetual allegiance, and reinvigorate the patriotic sentiments of their expatriate communities towards the home country in order to take advantage of these national communities abroad.

Some later mutations of the European model (viz. after its first circulation in the Arab world), however, have been accepted and introduced in some Arab countries as well. Such is the case with the extension of the principle of non-discrimination between man and woman in the domain of nationality rules. European pieces of legislation were amended to allow for the attribution of nationality by maternal descent on equal footing. Likewise, some Arab countries – especially in North Africa – are introducing in their legislation the attribution by maternal *jus sanguinis* alongside with the dominant paternal regulation. These reforms of the nationality laws are adopted in a context of fervent debate on the full citizenship of women.

Notes

Introduction

1. Elements of pre-Islamic poetry suggest – according to some scholars – that some form of contact was established, albeit limited to the needs of commerce.
2. The most famous controversy was the one sparked by al-Ghazzālī (d. 1111 AD), who openly criticised Avicenna (Ibn Sinā', d. 1037 AD) and al-Fārābī (d. 950 AD) in *The Incoherence of the Philosophers* (*Tahāfut al-falāsifah*). Almost a century later, Ibn Rushd (d. 1198 AD) refuted al-Ghazzālī's arguments in *The Incoherence of the Incoherence* (*Tahāfut al-Tahāfut*).
3. It has been told that Muhammad said, 'Beware. Every one of you is a shepherd and every one is answerable with regard to his flock. The caliph is a shepherd over the people and shall be questioned about his subjects (as to how he conducted their affairs). A man is a guardian over the members of his family and shall be questioned about them (as to how he looked after their physical and moral well-being). A woman is a guardian over the household of her husband and his children and shall be questioned about them (as to how she managed the household and brought up the children). A slave is a guardian over the property of his master and shall be questioned about it (as to how he safeguarded his trust). Beware, every one of you is a guardian and every one of you shall be questioned with regard to his trust.' See *kullukum rā*^{cin} *wa-kullukum mas'ūl* ^{c}*an ra*^{c}*īyatih, fa-l-imām rā*^{cin} *wa-huwa mas'ūl* ^{c}*an ra*^{c}*īyatih, wa-l-rajul rā*^{cin} ^{c}*alà ahlihi wa-huwa mas'ūl* ^{c}*an ra*^{c}*īyatih, wa-l-mar'ah rā*^{c}*īyah* ^{c}*alà bayt zawjihā wa-hiya mas'ūlah* ^{c}*an ra*^{c}*īyatihā, wa-l-*^{c}*abd rā*^{cin} ^{c}*alà māl sayyidihi wa-huwa mas'ūl* ^{c}*an ra*^{c}*īyatih, a-lā fa-kullukum rā*^{cin} *wa-kullukum mas'ūl* ^{c}*an ra*^{c}*īyatih*, in al-Bukhārī, *jum*^{c}*ah*, 11, *janā'iz*, 32, *istiqrād*, 20, *wasāyā*, 9, ^{c}*itq*, 17, 19, *nikāh*, 81, 90, *ahkām*, 1; Muslim, *imārah*, 20; abū Dāwūd, *imārah*, 1, 13; al-Tirmidhī, *jihād*, 27; ibn Hanbal, 2 (5, 54, 55, 108, 111, 121).
4. Similarly: in Turkish, *vatandaş* and, in Persian, *hamvatan*.
5. Reference is to the *Affaire Abdel-Hakim*, ruled by the *Tribunal civil de la Seine* on 2 May 1903. See *Dalloz jurisprudence générale*, 1908, II, 123, commented on by de Boeck. For further details on the case, see Chapter Three.

Chapter 1

1. When referring to the 'subject', and later to the 'citizen', it was clearly understood that the reference was solely to the *paterfamilias*, the male head of the household. This has been the case long since the abandonment of political Aristotelianism.
2. Sharing the same social structure did not entail 'social union', however (Tyan 1954: 3f).

3   According to Saʿīd, even Mecca's centrality in pre-Islamic studies is due only to the city's being the cradle of Islam (Saʿīd 2006).

4   E.g. the ʿĀds, the Thamūds, the Irams, the Jurhums, the Tasms and the Jadīses.

5   According to Genesis, Joktan is son of Eber (Hebrew: ʿĒber, Arabic: ʿĀbir), son of Selach (Hebrew: Shālah, Arabic: Shālakh), son of Arpacsad (Hebrew: 'Arpakhshadh, Arabic: Arfakhshadh), son of Sem (Hebrew: Shēm, Arabic: Sām) son of Noah (Hebrew: Nōakh, Arabic: Nūh). Gen. 10:1-25.

6   For the tōlʿdōth of Ishmael (Hebrew: Yishmāʿēl, Arabic: Ismāʿīl) see Gen. 25:12-18.

7   Especially under the reign of the Caliph Marwān ibn al-Hakīm (64-65 AH/684-685 AD) (al-Kaʿbī 2005, ʿAlī 1951-1960). A Jewish convert to Islam, the Palmyrene abū Yaʿqūb is believed to be the one who provided fictitious genealogies that linked Arabs with Biblical figures (Goldziher 1889, I: 178).

8   In 1412 al-Qalqashandī (d. 1418 AD) published his most renowned work, the Subh al-aʿshà fī sināʿat al-inshā' (Dawn of the Blind in the Art of Composition). In the Subh al-aʿshà, al-Qalqashandī devoted a section to genealogies, deeming its knowledge to be necessary for the good secretary, who had to properly identify the recipients and suitably address them. Later on, al-Qalqashandī dedicated an entire work to genealogies, the Nihāyat al-arab fī maʿrifat ansāb al-ʿarab (The Ultimate Goal in the Knowledge of the Lineages of the Arabs), and its 1416 rectification (istidrāk), the Qalā'id al-jumān fī 'l-taʿrīf bi-qabā'il ʿarab al-zamān (The Necklaces of Pearls in the Identification of the Tribes of the Arabs of the Past).

9   The role of social and political relations in determining kin relationships is also starting to be acknowledged in the Arab world. See the recent work by Muhammad Saʿīd and his theory on the origins and formation of familiar alliances, i.e. the īlāfs (Saʿīd 2006).

10 After the birth of the first child, the name of the parent is preceded by the kunyah: composition of abū ('father of') or umm ('mother of') and the name of the firstborn.

11 According to Robertson Smith one of the typical characters of 'tribal religions' is their particularism; the individual is responsible to the deity for all damage caused to another member of the group but can freely deceive, plunder or kill any 'stranger'. See in particular Robertson Smith's first two Lectures on the Religion of Semites (Robertson Smith 1923).

12 Robertson Smith deems it an application of the Arab proverb 'the child [belongs] to the bed' (al-walad li-l-firāsh; Robertson Smith 1885: 142). Muslim scholars consider it a prophetic tradition (hadīth), and include it in traditional collections. According to Goldziher, correspondence with the Latin maxim 'the father is the one established by the wedding' (pater est quem nuptiæ demonstrant) would confirm some influence of Roman law (Goldziher 1889: I, 184). Schacht, on the other hand, argues that such a rule never played any 'effective role' in Islamic law (Schacht 1950: 182). Not so for Linant de Bellefonds (Linant de Bellefonds 1973: 26f).

13 The prophetic tradition is related in the form 'the child [belongs] to the bed, and to the fornicator [belongs] the stone' (al-walad li-l-firāsh wa-li-l-ʿāhir al-hajar), as reported in al-Bukhārī, wasāyā, 4, buyūʿ, 3, 100, maghāzī, 53, farā'id, 18, 28, hudūd, 23, ahkām, 29; Muslim, ridāʿ, 36, 38; abū Dāwūd, talāq, 34; al-Tirmidhī, ridāʿ, 8, wasāyā, 5; al-Nasā'ī, talāq, 48; ibn Mājah, nikāh, 59, wasāyā, 6; al-Dārimī, nikāh, 41, farā'id, 35; (Mālik) al-Muwatta', aqdiyah, 20; ibn Hanbal, 1 (59, 65, 104), 4 (186, 187, 238, 239), 5 (267, 326), 6 (129, 200, 237, 247).

14 The contrast with the principle of exogamy induces anthropologists to speak of a 'Middle Eastern anomaly' (Fabietti 2002: 58f).

15 Ibn Saʿd reports that walā' was contracted at a specific time of year (on the tenth day of dhū 'l-hijjah), and a particular way of shaking hands sealed the agreement, as in a

completed sale. In Mecca it was contracted in the Ka'bah, thus assuming a clear religious connotation (*Tabaqāt*: VI, 77 and V, 41ff).

16   Al-Nawawī (d. 1278 AD) even accounts for the principle *mawlà al-qawm min anfusihim* ('the client of the group is a full member', literally: 'one of their own [by nature]'); the expression *min anfusihim* was precisely used to make the distinction between the full, original member and the client (al-Nawawī, *Tahdhīb*: I, 14, cit. in Tyan 1954: 26f). This principle is related in many variants as a prophetic tradition (al-Bukhārī, *manāqib*, 14, *farā'id*, 24; abū Dāwūd, *zakāh*, 29; al-Tirmidhī, *zakāh*, 25; al-Nasā'ī, *zakāh*, 97; al-Dārimī, *siyar*, 82; ibn Hanbal, 2 (448), 4 (35, 340), 6 (8, 10, 390)).

17   Reported by al-Nawawī, and also transposed in a prophetic tradition (al-Tirmidhī, *farā'id*, 53).

18   This is a breach of the principle of unconditional assistance condensed in the Arab maxim: 'help your brother, be he the wrongdoer or the wronged' (*unsur akhāk zālim^{an} kān aw mazlūm^{an}*). The maxim was later transposed in a prophetic tradition (al-Bukhārī, *mazālim*, 4).

19   The Arab proverb 'noble blood is the vengeance granting peace' (*al-dam al-karīm huwa al-tha'r al-munīm*) shows the lack of the principle of personal responsibility and proportionality with the offence; noble blood is the blood of one of the notables of the offender's group and not necessarily the offender's, while the vengeance granting peace is a clear reference to the physical and moral satisfaction that comes with vengeance.

20   The religious character of the duty was first noticed by Goldziher (1889: I, 23), and later fully analysed by Lammens (1924b: 181ff). See Tyan as well (1926).

21   See Nallino's 'Sulla costituzione delle tribù arabe prima dell'islamismo' (1939-1948: III, 64ff).

22   If the *sayyid* could not pay the blood money, he could be delivered into the hands of the lawful avengers (al-Qālī, *Dhayl al-amālī*: 22).

23   The commander is recognised the right to one fourth of the booty, the *mirbā'*, hence the title *rābi'* o *sayyid al-mirbā'*. But see, *contra*, Caetani (1905-1926: IV, 368f).

24   With some exceptions, as in the case of Hārith ibn 'Abbād (Cheikho 1890-1891: 271).

25   *Hilm* is at once gentleness, clemency, mildness, forbearance, patience, insight, discernment and reason.

26   In the case of *mala'*, the term preferred in Qur'ān (66:24, 34, and 48; 69:29, and 32), the use in the sense of 'assembly of notables' is confirmed by commentators (ibn Hishām, *al-Sīrah al-nabawīyah*: II, 232f).

Chapter 2

1   Authenticity admitted by scholars like Caetani or Lammens, known for their cautiousness towards the Islamic tradition. Wensinck believes, though, that the document dates from the days of the rupture of relations with the Jews (Wensinck (ed. Behn) 1975: 70f).

2   See Guillaume's translation: *The Life of Muhammad* (Oxford 1955). The text of the Charter is not included in the works of al-Wāqidī, al-Balādhurī and al-Tabarī. According to Rubin, Ibn Ishāq (d. 761) himself had to adapt some parts of the Charter (like art. 25) to the later deteriorated relations with the Jews (Rubin 1985: 19f).

3   The division into articles was introduced by Wellhausen (1884-1889: IV) and is still followed by most scholars, except for Serjeant (1964 and 1978).

4   *Ummah* in the sense of 'group of people' or 'community' could be related to the Hebrew *ummā*, the Aramaic *umetha*, or the Accadic *ummatu* (Denny 1975: 34-70).

5   Submission was stipulated in early pacts between Muhammad and the Christian po-
    pulation of Najrān (Ibn Sa^{c}d, *Tabaqāt*: I, 21 and 85, Ibn al-Athīr, *al-Kāmil*: II, 122,
    and al-Maqrīzī, *Imtā^c*: I, 502. On the pact, see Armand Abel, *La Convention de Nedj-
    rân et le développement du «droit de gens» dans l'islam classique*, Brussels, 1945), or Ta-
    bālah and Jurash (al-Balādhurī, *Futūh al-buldān*: 70 and 79f).

6   Similarity with Saint Augustine's concept of the *anĭma naturalĭter christiāna* (*De Civi-
    tate Dei*, XV) is pointed out by Kerber, who transforms the formula in: *anima natura-
    liter muslimica* (1991: 86ff).

7   See also Q. 42:13, 44:8 and 98:5.

8   Tradition passed down in different versions. See *kull insān taliduhu ummuhu ^{c}alà 'l-fi-
    trah*, in Muslim, *qadar*, 25, or: *kull mawlūd yūlad, wulida ^{c}alà 'l-fitrah; kull nasamah tū-
    lad ^{c}alà 'l-fitrah*, in al-Bukhārī, *janā'iz*, 92; abū Dāwūd, *sunnah*, 17; al-Tirmidhī, *qudar*,
    5; (Mālik) *al-Muwatta'*, *janā'iz*, 52, ibn Hanbal, 2 (233, 275, 393, 410, 481), 3 (252).

9   The sacrifice is grounded in *hadīth*s. See *ma^{c}a al-ghulām ^{c}aqīqah, fa-ahrīqū ^{c}anhu da-
    man wa-amītū ^{c}anhu al-adhà*, in al-Bukhārī, *^{c}aqīqah*, 2; abū Dāwūd, *adāhī*, 20; al-Tir-
    midhī, *adāhī*, 16; al-Nasā'ī, *^{c}aqīqah*, 2; ibn Mājah, *dhabā'ih*, 1; ibn Hanbal, 4 (17, 18,
    214, 215), 5 (12). The different amount of livestock for a boy or a girl is also grounded
    in *hadīth*s. See *^{c}an al-ghulām shātān, wa-^{c}an al-jārīyah shāh*, in abū Dāwūd, *adāhī*, 20;
    al-Tirmidhī, *adāhī*, 16; al-Nasā'ī, *^{c}aqīqah*, 1-4; ibn Mājah, *dhabā'ih*, 1; al-Dārimī, *adāhī*,
    9; ibn Hanbal, 2 (183, 185, 194), 6 (31, 158, 251, 381, 422, 456).

10 See *wa-tafarraqu ummatī ^{c}alà thalāth wa-sab^{c}īn firqah*, in abū Dāwūd, *sunnah*, 1;
    al-Dārimī, *siyar*, 74.

11 In another of his works, *Faysal al-tafriqah bayna al-islām wa-l-zandaqah* (The Decisive
    Criterion of Distinction between Islam and Masked Infidelity), al-Ghazzālī identified
    Muhammad as the sole infallible master. The righteous path for the Muslim is to ac-
    cept Muhammad's preaching by faith.

12 See *lā nubūwah ba^{c}dī*, in Muslim, *fadā'il al-sahābah*, 30-32; ibn Hanbal, 5 (454) or the
    more renowned *wa-anā khātim al-nabīyīn*, in al-Bukhārī, *manāqib*, 18, *tafsīr sūrah
    XVII*, 5; Muslim, *īmān*, 327; abū Dāwūd, *fitan*, 1; al-Tirmidhī, *qiyāmah*, 10; al-Dārimī,
    muqaddimah, 8; ibn Hanbal, 1 (296), 2 (398, 436), 4 (127, 128), 5 (278), and similarly
    also in ibn Mājah, *iqāmah*, 25.

13 See *al-muslim akhū 'l-muslim*, in al-Bukhārī, *mazālim*, 3; Muslim, *birr*, 32; abū Dāwūd,
    adab, 38; al-Tirmidhī, *hudūd*, 3, *birr*, 18, *tafsīr sūrah IX*, 2; ibn Hanbal, 2 (9, 68), 5
    (24, 71).

14 Translation by Hourani from the collection: abū 'l-^{c}Abbās Ahmad ibn ^{c}Abd al-halīm
    ibn Taymīyah, *Majmū^{c}at al-rasā'il al-kubrà*, Cairo, 1905, I, 307-309 (Hourani 1991:
    180).

15 *Narantakath v. Parakkal*, 45 Indian Law Reports (Madras) 986 (1922). The Madras
    ruling has been interpreted as an effort to eliminate religious discrimination, typical
    of Anglo-Mohammedan Law (Fyzee 1965: 57-67). For an earlier rule in the same
    sense see *Hakim Khalil Ahmad v. Malik Israfi*, 37 Indian Law Reports (Patna) 302
    (1917).

16 See art. 260(3)(a) and (b). Subsection (a) reads: '"Muslim" means a person who be-
    lieves in the unity and oneness of Almighty Allah, in the absolute and unqualified
    Prophethood of Muhammad (PBUH), the last of the prophets, and does not believe,
    or recognize as a prophet or religious reformer, any person who claimed or claims to
    be a prophet, in any sense of the word or any description whatsoever, after Muham-
    mad (PBUH).' Subsection (b) reads: '"Non Muslim" means a person who is not a
    Muslim and includes a person belonging to the Christians, Hindus, Sikh, Buddhist
    or Parsi community, a person of the Qadiani Group or Lahori Group (who call them-
    selves "Ahmadis" or by any other name) or a Baha'i, and a person belonging to any
    of the scheduled castes.'

17 The 1974 Declaration, adopted at the annual conference of the Muslim World League held in Mecca with the participation of over 140 delegations of Muslim countries and organisations, read: 'A subversive movement against Islam and the Muslim world, which falsely and deceitfully claims to be an Islamic sect; which under the guise of Islam and for the sake of mundane interests contrives and plans to damage the very foundations of Islam'.

18 The six recommendations read: '(1) All the Muslim organisations in the world must keep a vigilant eye on all the activities of Qadianis in their respective countries, to confine them all strictly to their schools, institutions and orphanages only. Moreover the Muslims of the world must be shown the true picture of Qadianism and be briefed of their various tactics so that the Muslims of the world are saved from their designs; (2) They must be declared non-Muslims and ousted from the fold of Islam. And must be barred from entering the Holy lands; (3) There must be no dealings with the Qadianis. They must be boycotted socially, economically and culturally. Nor may they be married with or to. Nor may they be allowed to be buried in the Muslims' graveyards. And they must be treated like other non-Muslims; (4) All the Muslim countries must impose restrictions on the activities of the claimant of Prophethood Mirza Ghulam Ahmed Qadiani's followers, must declare them a non-Muslim minority must not entrust them with any post of responsibility in any Muslim country; (5) The alterations effected by them in the Holy Quran must be made public and the people be briefed on them and all these be prohibited for further publication; (6) All such groups as are deviators from Islam must be treated at par with the Qadianis'.

19 The Law was challenged in March 1975, but the High Court rejected the challenge.

20 The Egyptian government itself appealed the ruling of the Court of Administrative Litigations of Cairo, after the heated questions of 3 May 2006 in Parliament. See *al-Hayāh*, 4 May 2006.

21 Only a few scholars hold the opposite view. Among them, the Kūfah jurist al-Nakha^{c}ī (d. 713), the 'Prince of believers' for the Sunnah (*amīr al-mu'minīn li-l-hadīth*) al-Thawrī (d. 772), and some Andalusi scholars. Against the latter, ibn Hazm (d. 1064) devotes a section of his *Kitāb al-Muhallà* to confute their arguments.

22 See *man baddala dīnahu fa-ŭqtulūh*, in al-Bukhārī, *jihād*, 149, *istitābah*, 2, *i^{c}tisām*, 28; abū Dāwūd, *hudūd*, 1; al-Tirmidhī, *hudūd*, 25; al-Nasā'ī, *tahrīm*, 14; ibn Mājah, *hudūd*, 2; ibn Hanbal, 1 (217, 283, 323), 5 (231).

23 See *lā yahill dam imri' muslim yashhad an lā ilāh illā allāh wa-annī rasūl allāh illā biihdà thalāth: al-nafs bi-l-nafs, al-thayyib al-zānī, wa-l-māriq min al-dīn al-tārik li-l-jamā-^{c}ah*, in al-Bukhārī, *diyāt*, 6; Muslim, *qasāmah*, 25, 26; abū Dāwūd, *hudūd*, 1; al-Tirmidhī, *hudūd*, 15; al-Nasā'ī, *tahrīm*, 5, 11, 14; al-Dārimī, *siyar*, 11; ibn Hanbal, 1 (61, 63, 65, 70, 163, 382, 428, 444, 465), 2 (181, 214).

24 Different compilations are strongly influenced by the scholar's background and environment. A good case in point is the *Majma^c al-anhur* of the Hanafi jurist Shaykhzādeh (d. 1667 AD); it was clearly conceived in a Persian milieu.

25 See *mā kānat hādhihi tuqātil fī-man yuqātil*, in abū Dāwūd, *jihād*, 111; ibn Mājah, *jihād*, 30; ibn Hanbal, 2 (115), 3 (488), 4 (178).

26 See *anna ^{c}Alīy^{an} harraqa qawm^{an} irtaddū ^{c}an al-islām*, in al-Tirmidhī, *hudūd*, 25; al-Bukhārī, *jihād*, 149, *istitābah*, 2; al-Nasā'ī, *tahrīm*, 14; ibn Hanbal, 1 (217, 282, 322).

27 See *lā ta^{c}adhdhibū bi-^{c}adhāb allāh* in al-Bukhārī, *istitābah*, 2; abū Dāwūd, *hudūd*, 1; al-Tirmidhī, *hudūd*, 25; al-Nasā'ī, *tahrīm*, 14; ibn Hanbal, 1 (217, 220, 282).

28 See *man kharaja muhāriban li-llāh wa-rasūlihi yuqtal aw yuslab aw yunfà min al-ard*, in al-Nasā'ī, *tahrīm*, 11, *qasāmah*, 14; abū Dāwūd, *hudūd*, 1.

29 Capital punishment is also prescribed for the prophet or the dreamer of dreams who entices apostasy (Deu. 13:2-6, NJB), but stoning to death is specified only for the common Jew (Deu. 13:7-12, NJB).

30 See *l^e-haddîh^akā min-had-derekh* (Deu. 13:6, MT), and *l^e-haddîh^akā mē-^cal 'Adōnāi* (Deu. 13:11, MT).

31 See *'îsh 'ô-'ishshâ ^asher ya^{ca}śe 'eth-hā-ra^c b^{ec}ênê 'Adōnāi-^elōhekhā la-^{ca}bhōr b^erîthô way-yēlekh way-ya^{ca}bhōdh ^elōhîm ^ahērîm way-yishtahû lāhem* (Deu. 17:2-3, MT).

32 Stoning to death is the common punishment for apostasy or idolatry (properly the service to foreign gods: ^{ca}bhōdhāh zārâh, one of the Talmudic treatises), except for the men of the city that apostatised, who must be put to the sword.

33 The casuistic approach of Islamic scholars as applied to jurisdiction proves highly un-economical. A detailed but concise overview can be found in Ahmad ^cAbd al-karīm Salāmah, *Mabādi' al-qānūn al-duwalī al-khāss al-islāmī al-muqārin* (Cairo, 1989) 139-168.

34 Only if the law infringes a fixed Islamic rule (*qat^cī* not just *ijtihādī*) according to Ridā (1970: IV, 1309ff) or Shaltūt (1969: 37ff), in all cases according to stricter scholars like ^cAwdah (1981: II, 708ff).

35 Some scholars encourage the foundation of a new theoretical model to handle inter-national relations on a peaceful basis (Salāmah 1989: 24; and al-Zuhaylī 1983: 130ff).

36 The phrase in Arabic sounds fairly baroque: *lahum mā li-l-muslimīn wa-^calayhim mā ^calā 'l-muslimīn* (literally: 'to them [is] what is to Muslims and upon them what is upon Muslims'; al-Qaradāwī 1977 and al-Mawdūdī 1978).

37 A covenant (*^cahd*) differs from international treatises (*mu^cāhadah*) and common con-tracts (*^caqd*) (al-Buhūtī, *Kashshāf al-qinā^c ^can matn al-iqnā^c*).

38 The control over *dhimmīs* was generally vested in the *muhtasib* (Tyan 1938: 642f). Ibn Hanbal listed nine violations of the covenant: (1) non-payment of the *jizyah* (^cadam badhl al-jizyah); (2) refusing to abide by Islamic rules (*ibā' iltizām ahkām al-islām*); (3) fighting against Muslims (*qitāl al-muslimīn*); (4) entering the *dār al-harb* and establishing his residence there (*lihāq bi-dār al-harb muqīm^{an}*); (5) committing adultery with a Muslim woman or raping her (*al-zinā bi-muslimah aw yusībuhā bi-sm al-nikāh*); (6) brigandage (*qat^c al-tarīq*); (7) uttering blasphemy against God, His Book, His religion or His prophet (*dhikr allāh aw kitābihi aw dīnihi aw rasūlihi bi-sū' wa-nah-wih*); (8) spying or harbouring a spy (*tajassus aw īwā' jāsūs*); (9) attacking a Muslim to kill him or turn him away from his religion (*al-ta^caddī ^calā muslim bi-qatl aw fitnatihi ^can dīnih*). See al-Hujāwī al-Maqdisī (d. 1560 AD), *al-Iqnā^c fī fiqh al-imām Ahmad Ibn Hanbal* (Beirut, s.d.) II, 54f.

39 Santillana opened his treatise on Islamic law with the rather sharp statement that Is-lam maintained the kin group in its substantial features, and only substituted the bond of blood (social and political basis of the Arab tribe) with the bond of the com-mon faith, quoting Q. 9:3 (1926: I, 1). From another perspective, the anthropologist and psychoanalyst Chebel explored the elements of continuity of pre-Islamic Arab characteristics in Islam in the work *Le sujet en islam* (Paris 2002). Of particular inter-est here is chapter five, tellingly entitled: '*Individu/Ummah, ou le triomphe de l'am-bivalence*' (Chebel 2002: 148-191).

40 The permanence of the Arab traditional mentality even in the celebrated Islamic *aurea ætas* is portrayed in a work by al-Maqrīzī (d. 1442) on the conflict between the two main branches of the Quraish, the banū Umayyah and the banū Hāshim: *al-Nizā^c wa-l-takhāsum fī-mā bayna banī Umayyah wa-banī Hāshim* (Leiden, 1888).

41 See *innamā 'l-mu'minīna ikhwa^{tun} fa-aslihū bayna akhawaykum wa-ittaqū āllāh^a la^calla-kum turhamūna* (Q. 49:10); but also Q. 3:103; 9:11; 59:9-10 and the *hadīth* 'The Mus-lim is a brother to the Muslim, he should not oppress him, neither hand him over [to an oppressor]' – *al-muslim akhū 'l-muslim, lā yazlimuhu wa-lā yuslimuh*, in

al-Bukhārī, *mazālim*, 3; *ikrāh*, 7; Muslim, *birr*, 58; abū Dāwūd, *adab*, 38; al-Tirmidhī, *hudūd*, 3; ibn Hanbal, 2 (91), 4 (104).

42 In Baghdad the unit term *qatā'i^c* was preferred to *khitat*.

43 The latter being the case of the Jews of Yathrib (Wellhausen 1884-1889: IV, 7ff).

44 See *man aslama ^calà yad ghayrihi fa-huwa mawlāh*, reported by al-San^cānī (d. 827), al-^cAsqalānī (d. 1449), ibn Manzūr (d. 1312), ibn al-Athīr (d. 1210), al-Sarakhsī (d. 1090) and ibn al-Jawzī (d. 1201), but not included in any of the six major collections of *hadīths*, which, however, recount the tradition of Tamīm al-Dārī asking Muhammad: 'What is the Sunnah about a man who accepted Islam by advice and persuasion of a Muslim?' and Muhammad's reply: 'He is the nearest to him in life and in death' (*huwa awlà al-nās bi-mahyāhu wa-mamātih*), in al-Bukhārī, *farā'id*, 22; abū Dāwūd, *farā'id*, 13; al-Tirmidhī, *farā'id*, 20; ibn Mājah, *farā'id*, 18; al-Dārimī, *farā'id*, 34; ibn Hanbal, 4 (102, 103). The verb *awlà* comes from the same root (*w.l.y*) of *walā'*.

45 Traditionally expressed in the form: *lahum mā lanā wa-^calayhim mā ^calaynā*.

46 The adage: 'Clientage is a tie like a kin tie' (*al-walā' luhmah ka-luhmat al-nasab*) is often quoted (al-Nawawī, *Tahdhīb al-asmā' wa-l-lughāt*), and it is also reported as a *hadīth* in al-Tirmidhī, *farā'id*, 53.

47 Equality was backed by many traditions, the most renowned probably being the one on Bilāl, Muhammad's Ethiopian muezzin. Some Western scholars advance doubts on the authenticity of these traditions, especially the one on Bilāl, and present other narratives of opposite significance (Lewis 1971).

48 See *isma^cū wa-atī^cū wa-in istu^cmila ^calaykum ^cabd^{un} habashīy^{un} ka'anna ra'sahu zabībah*, in al-Bukhārī, *ahkām*, 4; Muslim, *imārah*, 26, 27; abū Dāwūd, *sunnah*, 5; al-Tirmidhī, *jihād*, 28, ^c*ilm*, 16; al-Nasā'ī, *bay^cah*, 26; ibn Mājah, *jihād*, 39; ibn Hanbal, 4 (69, 70), 5 (381), 6 (402, 403).

49 See *inna hādhā 'l-amr fī Quraysh*, in al-Bukhārī, *ahkām*, 2; al-Dārimī, *siyar*, 77; Muslim, *imārah*, 4, 8; ibn Hanbal, 6 (94). Al-Māwardī also quoted: 'Princes are from the Quraish'. See *al-umarā' min Quraysh*, in al-Bukhārī, *ahkām*, 2; al-Dārimī, *siyar*, 77; ibn Hanbal, 3 (129, 183), 4 (421, 424).

50 See *nahnu al-umarā' wa-antum al-wuzarā'*, in al-Bukhārī, *fadā'il ashāb al-nabī*, 5; ibn Hanbal, 1 (5).

51 See *lan tanfa^cakum arhāmukum wa-lā awlādukum yawm^a al-qiyāma^{ti} yafsilu baynakum wa-ăllāh^u bi-mā ta^cmalūna basīr^{un}* (Q. 60:3).

52 See *ya ayyuhā 'l-nās^u innā khalaqnākum min dhakarⁱⁿ wa-unthà wa-ja^calnākum shu^cūb^{an} wa-qabā'il^a li-ta^cārafū inna akramakum ^cinda ăllāhⁱ atqākum inna ăllāh^a ^calīm^{un} khabīr^{un}*.

53 Although the sole example of non-Persian *Shu^cūbīyah* literature is *al-Filāhah al-nabatīyah* (Nabatean Agriculture) by ibn Wahshīyah (d. 951).

54 See ibn al-Athīr, *al-Kāmil fī 'l-tārīkh*, Tornberg's edition (Leiden 1851: IX, 228-293).

Chapter 3

1 See Msgr. al-Homsī's witty remark: '*Les Turcs excellaient dans l'art d'assouplir, suivant les circonstances, les rigeurs des exigences coraniques*' (Homsy 1956: 19).

2 An 1856 Anglo-Moroccan Treaty expressly provided for the same treatment of Muslim and non-Muslim British subjects *vis-à-vis* Moroccan authorities (Belkeziz 1963: 8).

3 In 1788 the French ambassador Choiseul-Gouffier even stated that the Ottoman Empire was: '*une des plus riches colonies de la France*' (Masson 1911: 279).

4   Figures are clear: in Aleppo in 1793 there were as many as 1,500 dragomans, but only six of them actually acted as professional interpreters. The phenomenon was so widespread that the term *berātlı* was coined for the *dhimmī* holding a patent (*berāt*).

5   Egypt is a good case in point for indigenous nationality, which is believed to have been theorised for the first time there (Badawi Pacha 1926).

6   A strong connection between the Nationality Law of 26 June 1889 and the Conscription Law of 15 July 1889 is usually drawn (Niboyet 1947: I, 128).

7   Former Ottoman subjects, having opted for a foreign nationality and having been ordered to leave Egypt, could be ousted under the 1929 provisions, while earlier they were considered Egyptian nationals (*Journal of Mixed Courts*, 25-26 March 1929).

8   Law 42/1924 was repeatedly amended in 1928 (Law 3/1928), 1932 (Law 16/1932), 1933 (Decree 62/1933), 1941 (Law 6/1941), 1950 (Law 1/1950), 1951 (Law 12/1951) and 1954 (Law 17/1954).

9   Palestinians refugees are those recognised by the United Nations Relief and Work Agency. The UNRWA for Palestine Refugees in the Near East was established by Resolution 302(IV) of the UN General Assembly on 8 December 1949.

10 *Jus soli* also played a role in the 1937 Bahraini Nationality Law, issued when the country was under British protection.

11 *al-Ra'y*, 8 January 2006.

12 Integrated by the Law 11/1963 of 12 October 1963.

13 Decision of the *Tribunal Civil de la Seine* of 2 May 1903 (*Dalloz jurisprudence générale* 1908: II, 123).

14 The *fatwà* was issued in Constantine (Algeria) on 10 Jumādà al-thānī 1356 AH, first published on the Algerian *al-Basā'ir* (III: 95) of 14 January 1938 and recently republished in Paris in 1993 (al-Jazā'irī 1993). A French translation read: 'l'action d'acquérir une nationalité non musulmane (*jinsīyah ghayr islāmīyah*) implique l'abandon de la législation mahométane (*al-sharīᶜah al-islāmīyah*). Même la renonciation à un seul précepte du Coran entraîne, selon la doctrine admise par tous les oulémas de l'islam (*bi-l-ijmāᶜ*), l'apostasie. Le naturalisé est un renégat' (Collot & Henry 1978: 126).

15 Only if the father is a Sudani by birth (Law 55/1970).

16 The case, originally provided for by 1959 KwNED, art. 3(1), was later repealed to prevent children of Kuwait's *bidūn*s from acquiring Kuwaiti nationality (Decree-Law 100/1980).

17 Even if the case is listed in the section of attribution of nationality, it really is a form of facilitated naturalisation (ᶜAshshūsh 1991: 216-221).

18 The original provision of Decision 16/S of 19 January 1925 was later reproduced in the Legislative Decrees 21/1953, and 276/1969.

19 The sixth section of Legislative Decree 276/1969 is titled 'Special rules for the sons of the Arab lands' (*ahkām khāssah bi-abnā' al-bilād al-ᶜarabīyah*). 'Sons' is a literal translation, but *abnā'* can also be translated as 'nationals' or 'citizens'.

20 A further reduction to three years is granted to nationals of Oman, Qatar and Bahrain (1972 AeFNL(1975), art. 5(1)(a)), and to members of the Arab tribes that moved to the UAE from neighbouring countries (1972 AeFNL(1975), art. 5(1)(b)).

21 In Algeria, however, knowledge of Arabic can be considered a proof of the assimilation required by 1970 DzNC, art. 10(1)(7). Technically, the Libyan and Iraqi laws do not require knowledge of Arabic. In Libya, however, non-Arabs cannot even be naturalised, and in Iraq naturalisation of non-Arabs is a form of extraordinary naturalisation granted by the Council of Ministers according to 1963 IqNL, art. 8(2).

22 Otherwise the Sudanese Nationality Law doubles the residency requirement to twenty years.

23 The provision, however, tends to be interpreted in a stricter sense (ᶜAshshūsh & Bākhashab 1990: 244).

24 The Tunisian Nationality Code requires a knowledge of Arabic commensurate with the person's social status.

25 The Egyptian Nationality Law of 1958 laid down extraordinary naturalisation for aliens who rendered special service to Egypt, Arab nationalism (li-l-qawmīyah al-ʿarabīyah) or the Arab nation (li-l-ummah al-ʿarabīyah; Law 82/1958, art. 11(2)).

26 Once the Lebanese expatriate returns to Lebanon, the Council of Ministers issues a decree to make of him a Lebanese national.

27 Including the 'illegally occupied territories' (maghsūb) of Palestine.

28 The broad definition of 'national expatriate' was adopted also by the Iraqi Law 5/1975 (art. 17, soon repealed by Law 49/1975), and the Egyptian Law 82/1958 (art. 31(1)(c), repealed by Law 25/1975).

29 If original nationals of Oman, Qatar or Bahrain, the naturalised are granted full rights seven years after naturalisation.

30 It is not clear whether the 1983 Omani Nationality Law, which stipulates that the naturalised enjoys 'civil rights' (al-huqūq al-madanīyah) upon naturalisation, excludes political rights or includes them (1983 OmNSD, art. 7).

31 As well as for standing for legislative councils (tarshīh li-l-majālis al-niyābīyah).

32 In Oman adult children of the naturalised have – nonetheless – to fulfil all the requirements for naturalisation (1983 OmNSD(1986), art. 4).

33 In the Moroccan and Tunisian codes, however, the minor child is not naturalised if married.

34 Only if the children where at least sixteen years old at the father's naturalisation.

35 Only after three years of marriage, and proving good behaviour and adequate economic conditions.

36 Perpetual allegiance was a well-known concept even in Medieval Europe, both in Britain and on the continent (Lombardi 1967). Blackstone defined perpetual allegiance as 'the tie or "ligamen" [that] binds the subject to the King, in return for that protection which the King affords the subject' (Commentaries on the Laws of England: I, 366).

37 In Algeria and Morocco, however, loss of nationality is allowed only if foreign naturalisation takes place outside the country and with state permission. Even with state permission, therefore, a Moroccan or an Algerian national cannot acquire foreign nationality within national boundaries.

38 An exception is the Egyptian legislation that sets a time limit of ten years (1975 EgNL, art. 15(1)).

39 Only Yemeni nationals by naturalisation can be stripped of nationality (1990 YeNL, art. 19).

40 The similar Qatari provision contained in the 1961 Law, art. 15(1)(4), was not retained in the new Qatari Nationality Law 38/2005.

41 Political rights are suspended for ten years for any national who has resumed Qatari nationality (2005 QaNL, art. 15).

42 In Kuwait, Law 44/1994 added a paragraph (2) to the Kuwaiti Nationality Law, art. 7, laying down that the child born after the naturalisation of the father is a national by origin or descent (1959 KwNED(1994), art. 7(2)).

43 Authors of this orientation usually quote the ruling of the Egyptian Administrative Court (Mahkamat al-qadā' al-idārī) of 1 February 1951. See Majmūʿat ahkām al-qadā' al-idārī (v, 549).

44 The effects of the mother's conversion to Islam on minor children are debated (al-Dasūqī, Hāshīyah ʿalā 'l-sharh al-kabīr: VII, 200).

45 Loss of citizenship is thus properly conceivable only for non-Muslims (Jamāl al-dīn 1998: 148f).

46 The conversion of the *dhimmī* to Islam (*islām al-dhimmī*) is framed as a change of loyalty (*walā'*).

47 Since the *jizyah* was imposed on non-Muslims who did not serve in the Islamic army, a non-Muslim can be relieved of it if he serves in the army (ᶜĀmir 1979: 189).

Chapter 4

1   *al-Hayāh*, 1 April 2005.

2   *al-Hayāh*, 2 February 2006.

3   *al-Ayyām*, September 2003, and *al-Wasat*, August-November 2006.

4   Naturalisation of Sunni expatriate workers – especially those working in the military – was going on even before the Āl al-Dawsarī's case (Dazi-Héni 2001: 56).

5   See the addendum to the Jordanian Nationality Law 6/1954 (Provisional Law (*qānūn muᶜaqqat*) 18/1969 made permanent (*qānūn dā'imī*) in 1971).

6   The groups of the Wādī Khālid were excluded until 1993 because they had refused to register in the 1932 census, whereas those of the *al-qurà al-sabᶜ* had to wait until 2004 due to territorial disputes with Israel and their status of Palestinian refugees (even if they were listed in the 1921 census).

7   UNDP, *Taqrīr al-tanmiyah al-insānīyah al-ᶜarabīyah li-l-ᶜām 2004: Nahwa al-hurrīyah fī 'l-watan al-ᶜarabī*, 137ff

8   The original meaning of *dawlah* was actually 'dynasty'; only later was *dawlah* used to indicate by metonymy the 'state'.

9   See also the 1995 special issue '*Tribus, tribalisme et Etats au Moyen-Orient*' of *Monde arabe Maghreb-Machreq*, and, for Lebanon, Favre's work in the *Annuaire de l'Afrique du Nord* (Favres 2003).

10 Riots in Tafīlah and Naᶜūr (Jordan) followed the 2003 Jordanian general elections because candidates of some kin groups failed to win 'their' seats (*al-Dustūr*, 18-19 June 2003).

11 *al-Hayāh*, 18-19 April 2005.

12 Santillana wrote that only the Muslim is a full citizen (*cittadino* optimo iure) under Islamic law (Santillana 1926: I, 98).

13 Recently renewed tensions between Sunnis and Shias confirm it. Conversions from Sunni to Shia Islam (*tashyīᶜ* or *tashayyuᶜ*) is a taboo subject in the Arab world (especially in countries like Palestine or Yemen).

14 With the obvious exception of Lebanon.

15 In a case of family law involving an Armenian Catholic woman and a Maronite (Catholic) man, the Egyptian judge applied Islamic law. The Egyptian judge, however, has no religious legal education; the rule 'iura novit curia' does not apply, and it is thus upon the parties to argue the law (el-Geddawi 2001).

16 Egyptian Court of Cassation, 17 November 1960 (*Ahkām Mahkamat al-Naqd*, XI, 583ff) (el-Geddawi 1971).

17 Egyptian Court of Cassation, 31 January 1968 (*Ahkām Mahkamat al-Naqd*, XIX, 179ff) and 14 January 1970 (*Ahkām Mahkamat al-Naqd*, XXI, 96ff).

18 Moroccan Supreme Court, 24 November 1964 (*Journal de Droit international privé*, XCIII (1966), 389) and 5 July 1974 (*Journal de Droit international privé*, CV (1978), 681ff).

19 A scholar like al-Mawdūdī even asserts that death is to be preferred to exile or a life deprived of 'citizenship rights' (Peters & De Vries 1976-1977:16).

20 On the Abū Zayd case, see the protagonist's own recollection (Abu Zaid 2004).

21 Only a 1981 draft of the Charter of Human Rights in Islam (by the Organisation of the Islamic Conference) carried reference to nationality (art. 7), but such reference

was not included in the final version of the 1990 Cairo Declaration (*I'lān al-Qāhirah*). For the French texts see Aldeeb (1994).

22 *Li-kull shakhs al-haqq fī 'l-tamattu' bi-jinsīya^{tin}, wa-lā yajūz isqātuhā 'an ayy shakhs bi-shakl ta'assufī aw ghayr qānūnī.* Moreover, art. 29 is included in the list of the rights that cannot in any way be infringed (art. 4(b)).

23 So in Egypt (art. 6), Jordan (art. 5), Lebanon (art. 6), Sudan (art. 22), Algeria (art. 29) and Saudi Arabia (art. 35).

24 So in Iraq (art. 18), Qatar (art. 4), Oman (art. 15), United Arab Emirates (art. 8), Kuwait (art. 27) and Yemen (art. 22).

25 UN Security Council Resolution n. 690 of 29 April 1991 (MINURSO Mission).

26 On gender and citizenship in the Middle East see Tétreault (2000b: 70-87f).

27 *Hal nahnu ra'āyā am muwātinūn?* Opening of the conference organised by the 'Hiwār al-thaqāfāt' Society (Dialogue of Cultures) in Cairo in May 2004 ('Ayyād 2005).

28 Before the 2007 reform, art. 1 read: 'socialist democratic system based on the alliance of the working forces of the people'.

29 See the debates on the Egyptian official daily *al-Ahrām* and the independent *al-Misrī al-Yawm* (February-March 2007).

30 *Tabdīl al-jinsīyah riddah wa-khiyānah* (al-Jazā'irī 1993).

31 For the 2004 Moroccan Family Code (*mudawwanat al-usrah*), see art. 2(1)(1) of the *Zahīr sharīf* 1-04-22 issued on 3 February 2004.

Glossary of Arabic legal terms

ᶜabd – slave
adhān – call to prayer
ᶜadīm al-jinsīyah – stateless
ᶜahd – pact, covenant
   ᶜahd al-dhimmah – protection covenant
ahl – people
   ahl al-bayt – household of Muhammad
   ahl al-dhimmah – non-Muslims living in the *dār al-islām*
   ahl al-kitāb – People of the Book, Abrahamic non-Muslims
ahlīyah – capacity
   ahlīyah kāmilah – full capacity
aᶜjam – non-Arab foreigner (originally Persian)
ajnabī – non-Arab foreigner
amān – safe-conduct
   amān mu'abbad – perpetual safe-conduct
   amān mu'aqqat – short-term, temporary safe-conduct
amn al-dawlah – state security
ᶜaqd – contract
   ᶜaqd al-khilāfah – caliphate contract
ᶜaqīdah – creed, faith, belief
ᶜāqil – sane
ᶜāqilah – patron's protection
ᶜaql – reason
aqwāl kādhibah – deceit, mendacious statements
ᶜār – shame, disgrace, dishonour
ᶜarab – Arabs
arsh – penalty for certain wounds
ᶜasabīyah – group solidarity
ᶜashīrah – tribe
asl (pl. *usūl*) – origin, root
   usūl al-fiqh – 'roots' of Islamic law
'āthār – effects
   'āthār ᶜā'ilīyah – familial effects (of naturalisation)
   'āthār ᶜāmmah – general effects (of naturalisation)
   'āthār fardīyah – individual effects (of naturalisation)
   'āthār khāssah – special effects (of naturalisation)

bāb – door
badw – nomad
baghī (plur. *bughāh*) – rebel
bāligh – of age
bātil – invalid, null and void
bayᶜah – oath, homage
bayyinah – evidence
bunūwah – filiation
   bunūwah sharᶜīyah – legitimate filiation

damān – liability
dār – home, territory
   dār al-harb – home of war, enemy territory
   dār al-islām – home of Islam, territory of the Islamic state
   dār al-riddah – home of apostasy, territory of apostasy
darībah – impost, tax
darūrah – necessity
dawlah – state
   dawlah wataniyah – nation-state
dhimmah – engagement, undertaking, care as a duty of conscience
dhimmī – non-Muslim protected by a treaty of surrender
dīn – religion
diyah – blood-money
diyānah – religion, conscience, *forum internum*
dūn shurūt – unconditional
dustūr – constitution

faqd (or *fiqdān*) *al-jinsīyah* – loss, withdrawal of nationality
   faqd bi-l-taghyīr – loss due to change
faqīh (plur. *fuqahā'*) – jurist, religious lawyer of Islam
farᶜ (plur. *furūᶜ*) – branch
   furūᶜ al-fiqh – 'branches' of Islamic law
fard – individual
fard – duty
   fard ᶜayn – individual duty
   fard kifāyah – communal duty
faskh – cancellation
fāsid – defective, voidable
fatwà (plur. *fatāwà*) – considered legal opinion of a *muftī*
fiqh – Islamic jurisprudence
fitrah – innate religion

ghanīmah – booty
ghashsh – fraud, deceit

ghayr lāzim – revocable (contract)
ghayr shar͑ī – illegitimate
ghazw – assault, raid, incursion

habr – non-Muslim religious authority
habs – imprisonment
hadar – not protected
hadar – settled population
hadd (plur. *hudūd*) – fixed punishment
hadīth (plur. *ahādīth*) – formal tradition deriving from Muhammad
hajīn – offspring of an Arab man and a foreign woman (*a͑jamīyah*)
hakam – arbitrator
halāl – not forbidden
hālah māddīyah – economic condition
haqq (plur. *huqūq*) – right, *jus*
   haqq al-dam – *jus sanguinis*
   haqq al-dam al-abawī – paternal *jus sanguinis*
   haqq al-dam al-umūmī or *al-ummī* – maternal *jus sanguinis*
   haqq al-dam mu͑azzaz bi-haqq al-iqlīm – *jus sanguinis* strengthened by
     jus soli
   haqq al-iqlīm – *jus soli*
   haqq al-iqlīm mudā͑afᵃⁿ – double *jus soli*
   huqūq al-insān – human rights
   huqūq al-muwātanah – citizenship rights
   huqūq siyāsīyah – political rights
haram – sacred area, sanctuary
harām – forbidden
harb – war
harbī – enemy alien
hijrah – migration (Hegira)
   hijrah ajnabīyah – foreign migration
hīlah (plur. *hiyal*) – legal device, evasion
hilf – alliance
hilm – gentleness, temperance, insight
hizb – party
hudnah – truce
hukm (plur. *ahkām*) – legal qualification
   al-ahkām al-khamsah – the five legal qualifications

i͑ādat al-jinsīyah – return of nationality
͑ibādāt – acts of devotion, religious observances
ibn (plur. *banūn* and *abnā'*) – son
idhn – permission
iftā' – deliverance of formal legal opinions

ijmā^c – consensus
ijtihād – effort
   ijtihād al-ra'y – use of individual reasoning
ikhtilāf – disagreement, difference
ikrāh – duress
iktisāb or *kasb* – acquisition
   iktisāb al-jinsīyah – acquisition of nationality
ilghā' al-muddah – elimination of residency requirement
^cilm – science
   ^cilm al-fiqh – legal science, jurisprudence
   ^cilm al-nasab – science of lineages, genealogy
ilmām bi-l-lughah – language knowledge
imām – leader
īmān – faith, belief
imtiyāzāt – capitulations
infisāl – secession
intiqāl ^carabī – inter-Arab migration
^ciqāb – punishment, penalty
iqāmah – residency
   iqāmah madīdah – prolonged residency
   iqāmah tawīlah – long residency
iqlīm – territory
iqrār – acknowledgement, confession
irtidād – apostasy
ism – given name
isnād – chain of transmitters of a *hadīth*
isqāt al-jinsīyah – relinquishment, deprivation, loss of nationality
   isqāt jawāzī – optional loss
   isqāt wujūbī – mandatory loss
isti^cādat al-jinsīyah – resumption of nationality
istirdād al-jinsīyah – vindication, restoration of nationality
istirjā^c al-jinsīyah – resumption of nationality
istitābah – call on the apostate to repent

jā'iz – allowed, unobjectable
jam^c – collection, combination
   jam^c bayna jinsīyatayn – dual nationality
jamā^cah – group
jamāhīrīyah – ochlocracy
jāmi^c – great, central mosque
jam^cīyah – association
jarīmah (plur. *jarā'im*) – crime
   jarā'im khulqīyah – crimes against public morality
   jarā'im al-sharaf – infamous crimes

jināyah – tort, delict
jinsīyah – nationality
   jinsīyat al-asl or *jinsīyah aslīyah* – original nationality
   jinsīyat al-mīlād – nationality of birth
   jinsīyat al-nasab – nationality by descent
   jinsīyat al-taᶜmīr – populating nationality
   jinsīyat al-ta'sīs – founding nationality
   jinsīyah lāhiqah – subsequent nationality
   jinsīyah mafrūdah – imposed nationality
   jinsīyah mamnūhah – granted nationality
   jinsīyah mukhtārah – elective nationality
   jinsīyah muktasabah – acquired nationality
   jinsīyah thānawīyah – secondary nationality
   jinsīyah tāri'ah – foreign nationality
jiwār – protection
jizyah – poll-tax
jumhūrīyah – republic

kafā'ah – wedding adequacy, equality by birth
kāfir – unbeliever
kāhin – soothsayer
khalᶜ – expulsion from the group
khalīᶜ – dismissed or expelled member of a group
kharāj – land-tax
khasārat al-jinsīyah – loss of nationality
khata' – mistake, error
khidmah (plur. *khidmāt*) – service
   khidmāt dhāt sha'n – important services
   khidmāt jalīlah – outstanding services
   khidmāt istithnā'īyah – exceptional services
khitān – circumcision
khiyānah – treason
kunyah – agnomen

lā'ihah tanfīdhīyah – executive regulations
laqab – surname
laqīt – foundling
lāzim – binding

madhhab – rite or school of religious law
madrasah – school
mahkamah – court, tribunal
   mahkamah dustūrīyah – constitutional court
   mahkamah ibtidā'īyah – court of first instance

mahkamah al-isti'nāf – court of appeal
mahkamat al-naqd – court of cassation (Egypt)
mahkamat al-tamyīz – court of cassation (Lebanon, Syria)
mahkamah ᶜulyā – supreme court
mahr – nuptial gift
makrūh – reprehensible, disapproved
majallah – lawbook, code
majhūl – unknown
   majhūl al-jinsīyah – of unknown nationality
majlis – gathering, council
   majlis al-aᶜyān – council of notables, senate
   majlis al-dawlah – council of state
   majlis dustūrī – constitutional council
   majlis al-shaᶜb – people's assembly
   majlis al-shūrà – consultative council
   majlis al-ummah – national assembly
   majlis watanī – national assembly
   majlis al-wuzarā' – council of ministers
majnūn – insane
mala' – tribal gathering of notables
maᶜlūm – known, certain
mandūb – recommended
manh – granting, bestowal
marsūm – decree
   marsūm amīrī – emiri decree (Kuwait)
   marsūm bi-qānūn – decree-law
   marsūm ishtirāᶜī – legislative decree (Lebanon)
   marsūm malikī – royal decree
   marsūm sultānī – sultani decree (Oman)
   marsūm tashrīᶜī – legislative decree (Syria)
masjid – mosque
maslahah – interest
   maslahah ᶜāmmah – public interest
matn – text (of a *hadīth*)
mawlà – client or patron
mawtūr – lawful avenger of blood
mīlād mudāᶜaf – double *jus soli*
millah – community
muᶜāhadah – (international) treaty
mu'ākhā – fictitious brotherhood
muᶜāmalāt – (pecuniary) transactions
mubāh – indifferent
muftī – specialist in religious law (*fiqh*) who gives an authoritative opinion (*fatwà*)

mughtarib – expatriate
mukāfa'at al-jinsīyah – awarding of nationality
mukallaf – charged, responsabile
mukhtār – free to choose, having the choice or option
mulk – rule, supreme authority
mumayyiz – intelligent, discriminating minor
murtadd – apostate
   murtadd fitrī – apostate (Muslim by birth)
   murtadd millī – apostate (Muslim convert)
mustahabb – recommended
musta'min – non-Muslim granted a safe-conduct (*amān*)
mutajannis – naturalised citizen
mutawallī – (*waqf*) administrator, person in charge
muwāfaqah – agreement, assent
muwātanah – citizenship
muwātin – citizen

nabī – prophet
nādī or *nadwah* – circle, tribal assembly
nahdah (*ᶜarabīyah*) – Arab renaissance
nā'ib – deputy
nasab – patronymic ('son of')
naskh – repeal
nizām – ordinance
nīyah – intention, intent

qabīlah – tribe
qādī – Islamic judge
qā'id – leader, commander
qāᶜidah (plur. *qawāᶜid*) – base, rule, maxim
qānūn – (secular) law, code
   qānūn al-jihād aw al-harb – Islamic law of war
   al-qānūn al-islāmī li-l-umam – Islamic law of nations
qarār – decision
   qarār wizārī – ministerial decision
qasd – aim, purpose
qawmīyah – nationalism
   al-qawmīyah al-ᶜarabīyah – Arab nationalism
qiblah – direction of ritual prayer
qīmah – value
qisās – retaliation
qiyās – analogy, parity of reasoning

rābitah – bond, tie, connection
   rābitat al-jinsīyah – bond of nationality
   rābitat al-mawtin – bond of residency
radā^c – fosterage
radd al-jinsīyah – return of nationality
rahn (plur. *ruhūn*) – hostage
rā^cī – shepherd
ra'īs – head, chief
ra^cīyah (plur. *ra^cāyā*) – subject, herd, flock
rashwah – bribery
rasūl – messenger, prophet
ra'y – opinion, individual reasoning
riddah – secession, apostasy
rukn (plur. *arkān*) – essential element

sadaqah – charitable gift
sahb al-jinsīyah – withdrawal of nationality
sahīh – valid, legally effective
sahwah (*islāmīyah*) – Islamic awakening, re-Islamisation
salāh – ritual prayer
sarīh – explicit (declaration)
sayyid – master, chieftain
shahādah – testimony, evidence of witnesses, certificate
sharaf – nobility, honour, glory
sharī^cah – sacred law
sharīf (plur. *ashrāf*) – eminent, notable, noble
shart (plur. *shurūt*) – prerequisite, condition
   shart al-mīlād al-mawsūf – condition of a particular birth
   shart al-wilādah marratayn – condition of double birth
shaykh (plur. *shuyūkh*) – elder, notable, chieftain
shibh – quasi-
shūrà – consultation
siyāsah – policy, politics, administrative justice
   siyāsah shar^cīyah – *siyāsah* within the boundaries of *sharī^cah*
sulh or *musālahah* – amicable settlement
sultān – authority, dominion, ruling power
sunnah – precedent, normative legal custom

tabannī – adoption
tābi^c (plur. *atbā^c*) – subject, dependent
tafrīq – dissolution of marriage
taghyīr al-ism – name change
tahdīth – modernisation

tahkīm – arbitration
tahqīq – verification
tā'ifah – group, denomination, community
tā'ifīyah – communitarianism, sectarianism
tajannus – naturalisation
   tajannus ᶜādī – ordinary naturalisation
   tajannus bi-l-wirāthah – hereditary naturalisation
   tajannus khāss – extraordinary naturalisation
   tajannus istithnā'ī – exceptional naturalisation
tajrīd – deprivation
takfīr – accusation of apostasy
takhallī ᶜan al-jinsīyah – renunciation of nationality
takhfīf al-muddah – shortening of residency requirement
takhtīt – laying out of settlements
talāq – repudiation
tamsīr – laying out of settlements
taqīyah – simulation
taqwà – piety
tard – expulsion
tarkhīs – permission, authorisation
tashrīᶜ – legislation
tasmiyah – naming, appellation
tawbah – repentance
taᶜzīr – discretionary punishment awarded by the *qādī*
tazwīr – forgery, falsification
tazyīf – falsification, counterfeiting
thā'ir – lawful avenger of blood
tha'r – vengeance
thiqah – trust
thubūt – determination
   thubūt al-jinsīyah – determination of nationality
   thubūt al-nasab – determination of descent

ᶜudūl (sing.: *ᶜadl*) – professional witness, notary
ujrah – hire, rent
ᶜulamā' (sing.: *ᶜālim*) – religious scholars (experts in legal and religious
   matters)
ummah – community (the Islamic community, par excellence)
   al-ummah al-ᶜarabīyah – Arab community
   al-ummah al-islāmīyah – Islamic community
   al-ummah al-watanīyah – national community
ᶜumrah – minor pilgrimage to Mecca
ᶜurf – custom
usrah – family

wafd (plur. *wufūd*) – delegation
wājib – obligatory, binding, due
wakīl – deputy, agent, proxy
walā' – loyalty
walā' or *walā' ᶜiqd* – clientage, relationship of client and patron
   walā' al-islām – conversion clientage
   walā' al-khidmah – service clientage
   walā' al-muwālāh – friendship clientage
   walā' al-tabāᶜah – dependency clientage
   walā' ᶜitq – manumission clientage
walad – offspring
   walad ghayr sharᶜī – illegitimate offspring
walī – legal guardian
   walī al-dam – lawful avenger of blood
waqf – pious foundation, mortmain
wasī – executor, guardian appointed by testament
wasīyah – testament, legacy
watan – homeland, nation
   al-watan al-ᶜarabī – the Arab nation
wathīqah – written document
wazā'if ᶜumūmīyah or *al-ᶜāmmah* – civil service
wilādah mutakarrirah – recurring birth
wilāyah – authority, competence, jurisdiction
   wilāyah mutaᶜaddīyah – 'transitive' authority
   wilāyat al-khalīfah – caliphal authority
wisātah jinā'īyah – criminal mediation
wuqūf – abeyance (of rights and legal effects)

yaqzah (ᶜarabīyah) – Arab renaissance

zahīr – decree (Morocco)
zakāh – alms-tax
zawāj – marriage
   zawāj mukhtalit – mixed marriage
zawāl al-jinsīyah – extinction of nationality
zindīq – freethinker, atheist

Bibliography

In Arabic

Classics

abū Tammām, Habīb ibn Aws (d. 842). *Dīwān al-Hamāsah* (Bonn, 1828-1851).
abū Yūsuf, (d. 798). *al-Kharāj* (Beirut, 1979).
Azdī, abū Zakarīyā Yazīd ibn Mūh ibn Iyās ibn al-Qāsim al- (d. 945). *Ta'rīkh al-Mawsil* (Cairo, 1967).

Bakrī, abū ᶜUbayd ᶜAbd allāh ibn ᶜAbd al-ᶜazīz al- (d. 1094). *Simt al-la'āli' fī sharh Amālī al-Qālī* (Cairo, 1936).
Balādhurī, Ahmad ibn Yahyà al- (d. 892). *Futūh al-buldān* (Cairo, 1932).
— *Ansāb al-ashrāf* (Beirut, 2001).
Buhūtī, Mansūr ibn Yūnus ibn Idrīs al- (d. 1641). *Kashshāf al-qināᶜ ᶜan matn al-iqnāᶜ* (Cairo, 1982).
— Sharh muntahà al-irādāt (Beirut, s.d.).
Bukhārī, Muhammad ibn Ismāᶜīl ibn Ibrāhīm ibn al-Mughīrah ibn Bardizbah al- (d. 870). *Sahīh* (Beirut, s.d.).

Dasūqī, Muhammad ibn Ahmad ibn ᶜArafah al- (d. 1815). *Hāshīyah ᶜalà 'l-sharh al-kabīr (li-abī al-Barakāt Ahmad al-Dardīr)* (Cairo, 1926).
dhū 'l-Rummah, Ghaylān ibn ᶜUqbah (d. 735). *Dīwān* (Cambridge, 1919).
Dīnawarī, abū Hanīfah Ahmad ibn Dāwūd al- (d. 903). *al-Akhbār al-tiwāl* (Leiden, 1912).
Durayd ibn al-Simmah (d. 630). *Dīwān* (Damascus, 1981).

Fārābī, abū Nasr Muhammad ibn Muhammad al- (d. 950). *Kitāb ārā' ahl al-madīnah al-fā-dilah* (Oxford, 1985).
Fasawī, abū Yūsuf Yaᶜqūb ibn Sufyān al- (d. 890). *al-Maᶜrifah wa-l-tārīkh* (Beirut, 1981).

Ghazzālī, abū Hamīd Muhammad al- (d. 1111). *Faysal al-tafriqah bayna al-islām wa-l-zanda-qah* (Cairo, 1961).
— *Tahāfut al-falāsifah* (Cairo, 1980).

Hamdānī, al-Hasan ibn Ahmad al- (d. 945). *Sifāt jazīrat al-ᶜarab* (Sanaa, 1983).
Hattāb, abū ᶜAbd allāh Muhammad ibn Muhammad ibn ᶜAbd al-rahmān known as al- (d. 1547). *Mawāhib al-jalīl li-sharh mukhtasar abī al-Diyā' Khalīl* (Cairo, 1910).
Hujāwī, abū al-Najā Sharf al-dīn Mūsà ibn Ahmad al- al-Maqdisī (d. 1560). *al-Iqnāᶜ fī fiqh al-imām Ahmad Ibn Hanbal* (Beirut, s.d.).

ibn ᶜAbd al-hakam, ᶜAbd allāh (d. 829). *Sīrat ᶜUmar ibn ᶜAbd al-ᶜazīz* (Beirut, 1967).
ibn ᶜAbd allāh, abū Muhammad al-Hasan known as al-ᶜAbbāsī (d. 1310). *Āthār al-uwal fī tartīb al-duwal* (Beirut, 1989, or Cairo, 1887).

ibn ʿAbd Rabbih, abū ʿUmar Ahmad ibn Muhammad known as al-Andalūsī (d. 940). *alʿ-Iqd al-farīd* (Cairo, 1876).

ibn ʿAbdūn, abū Muhammad ʿAbd al-majīd ibn ʿAbd allāh (d. 1134). *Thalāth rasāʾil andalusīyah fī ādāb al-hisbah wa-l-muhtasib* (Cairo, 1955).

ibn ʿĀbidīn, Muhammad Amīn ibn ʿUmar (d. 1836). *Radd al-mukhtār ʿalà 'l-Durr al-mukhtār* (Cairo, 1844).

ibn abī Yaʿlà, abū al-Husayn Muhammad ibn Muhammad (d. 1131). *Tabaqāt al-Hanābilah* (Cairo, 1952).

ibn al-Athīr, abū al-Hasan ʿIzz al-dīn ʿAlī ibn Muhammad (d. 1223). *Tārīkh al-kāmil* (ed. by Carl J. Tornberg, 1851, or Cairo, 1873).

— *al-Kāmil fī 'l-tārīkh* (Beirut, 1966).

ibn al-Athīr, abū al-Saʿādāt Majd al-dīn al-Mubārak (d. 1210). *al-Nihāyah fī gharīb al-hadīth* (Cairo, 1963-1965).

ibn al-Humām, Muhammad ibn ʿAbd al-wāhid ibn ʿAbd al-hamīd al-Suyūsī (d. 1459). *Fath al-qadīr ʿalà sharh al-hidāyah li-l-Marghīnānī (1388-1457)* (Cairo, 1898).

ibn al-Jawzī, abū al-Faraj ʿAbd al-rahmān ibn ʿAlī ibn Muhammad (d. 1201). *al-Mawdūʿāt* (Medina, 1966-1968).

ibn al-Kalbī, abū al-Mundhir Hishām ibn Muhammad (d. 819). *Jamharat al-nasab* (Leiden, 1966).

ibn al-Muqaffaʿ, ʿAbd allāh (d. 760). *al-Adab al-kabīr* (Beirut, 1956).

— *Rasāʾil al-Bulaghāʾ* (Beirut, 1956).

ibn al-Murtadà, Ahmad ibn Yahyà (d. 1437). *al-Bahr al-zakhkhār al-jāmiʿ li-madhāhib ʿulamāʾ al-amsār* (Cairo, 1948).

ibn Bassām, abū al-Hasan ʿAlī known as al-Shantarīnī (d. 1147). *Dhakhīrah* (Madrid manuscript).

ibn Fūdī, ʿUthmān ibn Muhammad (d. 1817). *Ihyāʾ al-sunnah wa-ikhmād al-bidaʿ* (s.l., s.d.).

— *Bayān wujūb al-hijrah ʿalà 'l-ʿibād wa-bayān nasb al-imām wa-iqāmat al-jihād* (s.l., s.d.).

ibn Habīb, abū Jaʿfar Muhammad (d. 860). *al-Muhabbar* (Haydarabad, 1942).

ibn Hajar, Ahmad ibn ʿAlī known as al-ʿAsqalānī (d. 1449). *al-Matālib al-ʿālyah* (Kuwait, 1973).

ibn Hazm, abū Muhammad ʿAlī ibn Ahmad known as al-Andalūsī (d. 1064). *Jamharat ansāb al-ʿarab* (Cairo, 1948).

ibn Hishām, abū Muhammad ʿAbd al-malik (d. 834). *Sīrat rasūl allāh* (Cairo, 1911).

ibn Kathīr, abū al-Fidāʾ Ismāʿīl ibn ʿUmar (d. 1373). *al-Bidāyah wa-l-nihāyah fī 'l-tārīkh* (Cairo, 1932-1939).

ibn Khaldūn, ʿAbd al-rahmān (d. 1406). *al-Muqaddimah* (Tunis, 1993).

ibn Khayyāt ʿUsfūrī, abū ʿAmrū Khalīfa (d. 854). *Taʾrīkh* (Damascus, 1967).

ibn Manzūr, abū al-Fadl Jamāl al-dīn Muhammad ibn Mukarram (d. 1312). *Lisān al-ʿarab* (Cairo, 1981).

ibn Nujaym, Zayd al-dīn ibn Ibrāhīm (d. 1563). *al-Ashbāh wa-l-nazāʾir ʿalà madhhab abī Hanīfah al-nuʿmān* (Constantinoples, 1873).

ibn Qayyim al-Jawzīyah, abū ʿAbd allāh Muhammad ibn abī Bakr (d. 1350). *Ahkām ahl al-dhimmah* (Beirut, 1995).

ibn Qudāmah, *Muwaffaq al-dīn* abū Muhammad ʿAbd allāh ibn Ahmad ibn Mahmūd (d. 1223). *al-Mughnī* (Beirut, 1982).

ibn Qudāmah, *Shams al-dīn* abū Muhammad ʿAbd al-rahmān ibn Muhammad known as al-Maqdisī (d. 1290). *al-Sharh al-kabīr ʿalà matn al-Muqniʿ* (Beirut-Cairo, 1983).

ibn Qutaybah, abū Muhammad ʿAbd allāh ibn Muslim (d. 889). *al-Maʿārif* (Cairo, 1934).

— 'Kitāb al-ʿarab', *Rasāʾil al-bulaghāʾ* (Cairo, 1946).

ibn Rushd (Averroes), abū al-Walīd Muhammad ibn Ahmad (d. 1198). *Commentarium magnum in Aristotelis de anima libros* (Cambridge, 1953).

— *Tahāfut al-Tahāfut* (Cairo, 1964).

ibn Saᶜd, abū ᶜAbd allāh Muhammad (d. 845). *al-Tabaqāt al-kabīr* (Leiden, 1905-1921).

ibn Sinā' (Avicenna), al-Husayn ibn ᶜAbd allāh (d. 1037). *al-Shifā'* (Cairo, 1952).

ibn Taymīyah, Ahmad ibn ᶜAbd al-halīm (d. 1328). *Majmūᶜat al-rasā'il al-kubrà* (Cairo, 1905).

— *al-ᶜIsyān al-musallah aw qitāl ahl al-baghī fī dawlat al-islām wa-mawqif al-hakīm minh* (Beirut, 1992).

ibn Thābit, Hassān (d. 674). *Dīwān* (Leiden-London, 1910).

ibn Wahshīyah, abū Bakr Ahmad ibn ᶜAlī ibn Qays (d. 951). *al-Filāhah al-nabatīyah* (Leiden manuscript).

Isfahānī, abū al-Faraj ᶜAlī ibn al-Hussayn al- (d. 967). *al-Aghānī* (Cairo, 1868).

Jāhiz, abū ᶜUthmān ᶜAmr ibn Bahr al-Qinānī known as al- (d. 869). *al-Bayān wa-l-tabyīn* (Cairo, 1960).

— 'Dhamm akhlāq al-kuttāb', *Majmūᶜ al-rasā'il* (Cairo, 1906).

— 'Fī madh al-tujjār wa-dhamm ᶜamal al-sultān', *Three Essays of Abū ᶜOthmān ibn Bahr al-Jāhiz* (Cairo, 1926).

— *Tria opuscula auctore Abu Othman Amr Ibn Bahr al-Djahiz Basrensi* (Leiden, 1903).

Jawharī, abū Nasr Ismaᶜīl ibn Hammād al- (d. 1003). *Tāj al-lughah wa-sihāh al-ᶜarabīyah* (Cairo, 1865).

Jundī, Khalīl ibn Ishāq al- (d. 1374). *Mukhtasar* (Milan, 1919).

Kāsānī, ᶜAlā' al-dīn abū Bakr ibn Masᶜūd al- (d. 1191). *Badā'iᶜ al-sanā'iᶜ fī tartīb al-sharā'iᶜ* (Cairo, 1908).

Kindī, abū Yūsuf Yaᶜqūb ibn Ishāq al- (d. 873). *Rasā'il al-Kindī al-falsafīyah* (Cairo, 1950-1953).

Maᶜarrī, abū al-ᶜAlā' Ahmad ibn ᶜAbd allāh al- (d. 1058). *Risālat al-ghufrān* (Beirut, 1984).

Maghīlī, Muhammad ibn al-Karīm al- (d. 1503). *As'ilat al-Asqiyā wa-ajwibat al-Maghīlī* (Algiers, 1974).

Mālik ibn Anas (d. 795). *al-Muwatta'* (Beirut, 1981).

Maqrīzī, Ahmad ibn ᶜAlī al- (d. 1442). *al-Nizāᶜ wa-l-takhāsum fī-mā bayna banī Umayyah wa-banī Hāshim* (Leiden, 1888).

— *Imtāᶜ al-asmāᶜ bi-mā li-l-rasūl min al-anba' wa-l-amwāl wa-l-hafadah wa-l-matāᶜ* (Cairo, 1941).

Masᶜūdī, abū al-Hasan ᶜAlī ibn al-Husayn al- (d. 957). *Murūj al-dhahab wa-maᶜādin al-jawhar* (Paris, 1962).

Māwardī, abū al-Hasan ᶜAlī ibn Muhammad al- (d. 1058). *al-Ahkām al-sultānīyah* (Paris, 1901, or Cairo, 1978).

— *Kitāb qitāl ahl al-baghī min al-Hāwī al-kabīr* (Cairo, 1987).

Mawwāq, abū ᶜAlī Muhammad ibn Yūsuf al- (d. 1491). *al-Tāj wa-l-iklīl li-Mukhtasar Khalīl* (Cairo, 1910).

Mubarrad, abū al-ᶜAbbās Muhammad ibn Yazīd al- (d. 898). *al-Kāmil fī 'l-lughah wa-l-adab wa-l-nahw wa-l-tasrīf* (Cairo, 1905).

Murtadà al-Zabīdī, Muhammad (d. 1791). *Tāj al-ᶜarūs* (Kuwait, 1965-2001).

Muttaqī, ᶜAlā' al-dīn ᶜAlī ibn ᶜAbd al-malik al- (d. 1567). *Kanz al-ᶜummāl fī sunan al-aqwāl wa-l-afᶜāl* (Haydarabad, 1894-1897).

Nābighah al-Dhubyānī, al- (d. 670). *Dīwān* (Rome, 1953).

Nawawī, abū Zakarīyā Yahyà ibn Sharaf al- (d. 1277). *Tahdhīb al-asmā' wa-l-lughāt* (Cairo, 1930).

Nuwayrī, abū al-ᶜAbbās Ahmad ibn ᶜAbd al-Wahhāb al- (d. 1332), *Nihāyat al-arab fī funūn al-adab* (Cairo, 1923-1925).

Qālī, abū ᶜAlī Ismāᶜīl ibn al-Qāsim al- (d. 967). *al-Amālī* (Cairo, 1926).
— *Dhayl al-Amālī* (Cairo, 1926).
Qalqashandī, abū al-ᶜAbbās Ahmad ibn ᶜAlī ibn Ahmad ibn ᶜAbdallāh al-Fazārī al-Shāfiᶜī known as al- (d. 1418). *Subh al-aᶜshà fī sināᶜat al-inshā'* (Cairo, 1913-1919).
— *Nihāyat al-arab fī maᶜrifat ansāb al-ᶜarab* (Cairo, 1958).
— *Qalā'id al-jumān fī 'l-taᶜrīf bi-qabā'il ᶜarab al-zamān* (Cairo-Beirut, 1982).

Sanᶜānī, abū Bakr ᶜAbd al-razzāq ibn Hammām ibn Nāfiᶜ al-Yamanī al-Himyarī known as al- (d. 827). *al-Musannaf* (Beirut, 1960-1962).
Sarakhsī, Muhammad ibn Ahmad al- (d. 1090). *Sharh kitāb al-siyar al-kabīr (li-Muham-mad ibn al-Hasan al-Shaybānī)* (Haydarabad, 1916).
— *al-Mabsūt* (Cairo, 1906-1913).
Shāfiᶜī, abū ᶜAbd allāh Muhammad ibn Idrīs al- (d. 820). *al-Umm* (Cairo, 1903-1907, or Beirut, 1980).
Shahrahstānī, abū al-Fath Muhammad ibn ᶜAbd al-karīm ibn Ahmad al- (d. 1153). *al-Milal wa-l-nihal* (London, 1842-1846).
Shaybānī, abū ᶜAbd allāh Muhammad ibn al-Hasan al- (d. 804). *al-Siyar, al-qānūn al-du-walī al-islāmī* (Beirut, 1975).
— *al-Asl* (Beirut, 1990).
Shaykh zādah, ᶜAbd al-rahmān ibn Muhammad (d. 1667). *Majmaᶜ al-anhur sharh multaqà al-abhur* (Constantinoples, 1910).
Suyūtī, Jalāl al-dīn abū al-Fadl ᶜAbd al-rahmān ibn abī Bakr al- (d. 1505). *Tārīkh al-khulafā' umarā' al-mu'minīn* (Cairo, 1887).

Tabarī, abū Jaᶜfar Muhammad ibn Jarīr al- (d. 923). *Mukhtasar Ta'rīkh al-rusul wa-l-mulūk wa-l-khulafā'* (Cairo, 1939).

Wāqidī, abū ᶜAbd allāh Muhammad ibn ᶜUmar al- (d. 823). *al-Tārīkh wa-l-maghāzī* (Bei-rut, 1984).

Yaᶜqūbī, Ahmad ibn abī Yaᶜqūb ibn Jaᶜfar al- (d. 897). *Tārīkh* (Leiden, 1883).

Modern and contemporary works

(2000) *al-Wasā'il al-ᶜamalīyah li-tatbīq al-faqrah 't' min al-dustūr al-lubnānī*, Beirut-Brux-elles: CEDROMA-Bruylant.

ᶜAbbūd, Mūsà. *Durūs fī 'l-qānūn al-duwalī al-khāss al-maghribī*, Rabat, 1986.
ᶜAbbūd, Salih ibn ᶜAbd allāh al-. *Fikrat al-qawmīyah al-ᶜarabīyah fī daw' al-islām*, Riyadh, 1982.
ᶜAbd al-ᶜāl, ᶜUkkāshah Muhammad. *al-Jinsīyah wa-markaz al-ajānib fī tashrīᶜāt al-duwal al-ᶜarabīyah*, Cairo, 1987.
— *Durūs fī 'l-jinsīyah al-lubnānīyah*, Beirut, 1988.
— *al-Ittijāhāt al-hadīthah fī mushkilat 'tanāzuᶜ' al-jinsīyāt. Dirāsah tahlīlīyah wa-ta'sīlīyah fī 'l-qānūn al-misrī wa-l-qānūn al-muqāran*, Beirut, 1991.
— *Ahkām al-jinsīyah al-misrīyah*, Cairo, 1993.
— *al-Qānūn al-duwalī al-khāss fī dawlat al-imārāt al-ᶜarabīyah al-muttahidah*, Dubai, 1997.

— *al-Wasīt fī 'l-jinsīyah al-lubnānīyah. Dirāsah muqārinah maʿa al-tashrīʿāt al-ʿarabīyah*, Beirut, 2001.

ʿAbdalāwī, Idrīss al-ʿAlawī al-. *al-Madkhal fī dirāsat al-qānūn*, Casablanca, s.d.

ʿAbd al-bāqī, Ibrāhīm. *al-Jinsīyah fī qawānīn duwal al-maghrib al-ʿarabī al-kabīr. Dirāsah muqārinah*, Cairo, 1971.

ʿAbd al-fattāh, Nabīl. *al-Yūtūbyā wa-l-jahīm: qadāyā 'l-hadāthah wa-l-ʿawlamah fī Misr*, Cairo, 2001.

ʿAbd al-karīm, Mamdūh. *al-Qānūn al-duwalī al-khāss wifq al-qānūnayn al-ʿirāqī wa-l-muqāran*, Baghdad, 1972.

ʿAbd allāh, Ismāʿīl Sabrī, William Qilādah & Muhammad Salīm al-ʿAwwā. *al-Muwātanah: Tārīkhīyᵃⁿ, dustūrīyᵃⁿ, fiqhīyᵃⁿ*, Cairo, 1998.

ʿAbd allāh, ʿIzz al-dīn. *al-Qānūn al-duwalī al-khāss*, 9th ed., Cairo, 1986.

ʿAbd allāh, Sāmī. *al-Jinsīyah al-lubnānīyah, muqāranaᵗᵃⁿ bi-l-jinsīyah al-ʿarabīyah al-sūrīyah wa-l-faransīyah*, Beirut, 1986.

ʿAbd allāh, ʿUmar. *Ahkām al-mawārīth fī 'l-sharīʿah al-islāmīyah*, Cairo, 1966.

ʿAbd al-rahmān, ʿAbd al-hakīm Mustafà. *Jinsīyat al-marʾah al-mutazawwijah wa-ʾāthāruhā fī muhīt al-usrah fī 'l-qānūn al-misrī wa-l-faransī wa-l-sūdānī. Dirāsah muqārinah*, Cairo, 1991.

— *al-Jinsīyah al-sūdānīyah*, Cairo, 1992.

ʿAbd al-rahmān, Jābir Jād. *al-Qānūn al-duwalī al-khāss al-ʿarabī*, Cairo, 1958.

— *Majmūʿat qawānīn al-jinsīyah fī 'l-duwal al-ʿarabīyah*, Cairo, 1980.

ʿAbduh, Muhammad & Muhammad Rashīd Ridā, *Tafsīr al-Manār*, Cairo, 1947-1960.

abū Dīb, Badawī. *al-Jinsīyah al-lubnānīyah*, 2nd ed., Beirut, 2001.

abū Hassān, Muhammad. *Turāth al-badw al-qadāʾī: Nazarīyᵃⁿ wa-ʿamalīyᵃⁿ*, Amman, 1987.

— *Ahkām al-jarīmah wa-l-ʿuqūbah fī 'l-sharīʿah al-islāmīyah*, al-Zarqāʾ, 1987.

abū Zahrah, Muhammad. 'al-ʿAlāqāt al-duwalīya fī 'l-islām', *Majallat al-ʿulūm al-qānūnīyah wa-l-iqtisādīyah*, 1964.

ʿAdhbī al-Sabāh, Amal Yūsuf al-. *al-Hijrah ilà 'l-Kuwayt min ʿām 1957 ilà ʿām 1975. Dirāsah fī jughrāfīyat al-sukkān*, Kuwait, 1987.

Afghānī, Jamāl al-dīn al-. 'al-Jinsīyah wa-l-diyānah al-islāmīyah', *al-ʿUrwah al-wuthqà*, 2nd ed., Cairo, 1958, 9-12.

Ahmad, Mahdī al-Shaykh ʿAwad. *al-Raqābah al-qadāʾīyah ʿalà 'l-qarārāt al-mutaʿalliqah bi-masāʾil al-jinsīyah. Dirāsah muqārinah*, Cairo, 2002.

Akwaʿ , Muhammad ibn ʿAlī al- (ed.). *Kitāb al-iklīl*, Sanaa, 1990.

— *Sifat jazīrat al-ʿarab*, Sanaa, 1983.

ʿAlī, ʿAlwī Amjad. *al-Qānūn al-duwalī al-khāss li-dawlat al-Imārāt al-ʿarabīyah al-muttahidah. Dirāsah muqārinah*, I: *Fī 'l-jinsīyah wa-l-mawtin wa-tamattuʿ al-ajānib bi-l-huqūq (markaz al-ajānib)*, Dubai, 1991.

ʿAlī, Jawād. *Tārīkh al-ʿarab qabla al-islām*, Baghdad, 1951-1960.

ʿAlī, Salīh A. al-. *al-Tanzīmāt al-ijtimaʿīyah wa-l-iqtisadīyah fī 'l-Basra fī 'l-qarn al-awwal al-hijrī*, Beirut, 1969.

ʿAlī al-Mansūr, ʿAlī. *al-Sharīʿah al-islāmīyah wa-l-qānūn al-duwalī al-ʿāmm*, 2nd ed., Cairo, 1965.

— *Sharīʿat allāh wa-sharīʿat al-insān*, Cairo, 1977.

Alūsī, Mahmūd Shukrī al-. *Bulūgh al-ʿarab fī maʿrifat ahwāl al-ʿarab*, Cairo, 1964.

ʿAlwānī, Tāhā Jābir al-. 'Hawla fikrat al-muwātanah fī 'l-mujtamaʿ al-islāmī', *Qirāʾāt siyāsīyah* 3 (1/1993): 147-159.

ʿAmāra, Muhammad. *Al-Dawlah al-islāmīyah bayna al-ʿilmānīyah wa-l-sultah al-dīnīyah*, Cairo, 1988.

ʿĀmir, Muhammad. *ʿAqd al-dhimmah fī 'l-fiqh al-islāmī*, Cairo, 1979.

Amitī, Khadījah (ed.). *al-Usrah wa-l-muwātanah*, Rabat, 2002.

ᶜAnānī, Ahmad al-. *al-Watan wa-l-ᶜurūba fī 'l-manzūr al-islāmī*, Amman, 1988.

ᶜAnazī, Rashīd Hamad al-. *al-Jinsīyah al-kuwaytīyah: Dirāsah li-l-nazarīyah al-ᶜāmmah li-l-jinsīyah wa-li-l-marsūm al-amīrī raqam 15 li-sanat 1959 bi-sha'n al-jinsīyah al-kuwaytīyah wa-taᶜdīlātih*, Kuwait, 1995.

ᶜAnfī, Rashīd Hamad al-. *'al-Bidūn' fī 'l-Kuwayt. Dirāsah qānūnīyah ᶜan mashrūᶜīyat iqāmatihim*, Kuwait, 1994.

Armanāzī, Najīb. *al-Sharᶜ al-duwalī fī 'l-islām*, Damascus, 1930.

ᶜAshshūsh, Ahmad ᶜAbd al-hamīd. *al-Jinsīyah al-saᶜūdīyah. Turuq iktisābihā, asbāb faqdihā wa-wasā'il istirdādihā (maᶜa istiᶜrād li-qawānīn al-jinsīyah fī duwal majlis al-taᶜāwun al-khalījī)*, Jedda, 1991.

— *Markaz al-ajānib fī 'l-Mamlakah al-ᶜarabīyah al-saᶜūdīyah maᶜa istiᶜrād li-markaz al-ajānib fī qawānīn duwal Majlis al-taᶜāwun al-khalījī*, Jedda, 1991.

ᶜAshshūsh, Ahmad ᶜAbd al-hamīd & ᶜUmar abū Bakr Bākhashab. *Ahkām al-jinsīyah wa-markaz al-ajānib fī duwal Majlis al-taᶜāwun al-khalījī: Dirāsah muqārinah maᶜa al-ihtimām bi-l-nizām al-saᶜūdī*, Alexandria, 1990.

ᶜAwdah, ᶜAbd al-qādir. *al-Tashrīᶜ al-jinā'ī al-islāmī muqāranᵃⁿ bi-l-qānūn al-wadᶜī*, Beirut, 1981.

ᶜĀyish, ᶜAbduh. 'Intikhābāt al-ri'āsah al-yamanīyah shaklīyah wa-thaqāfat al-mujtamaᶜ qitālīyah', *al-Jazīrah* (5 August 2005).

ᶜAyyād, Hānī (ed.). *Hiwārāt hawla al-muwātanah*, Cairo, 2005.

— (ed.). *al-Muwātanah fī 'l-taᶜlīm*, Cairo, 2005.

— (ed.). *Ishkālīyāt al-tahawwul al-dīmuqrātī wa-l-tahdīth fī Misr*, Cairo, 2005.

— (ed.). *al-Misrīyah ka-muwātinah*, Cairo, 2006.

ᶜAzb, Khālid. 'Iᶜādat iktishāf matbaᶜat Būlāq', *al-ᶜArabī* 559 (June 2005): 110-115.

ᶜAzīz, Makkī Muhammad. *al-Khasā'is al-ijtimāᶜīyah wa-l-iqtisādīyah li-l-muhājirīn ilà 'l-Kuwayt*, Kuwait, 1981.

Badrān, Badrān abū al-ᶜAynayn. *al-ᶜAlāqāt al-ijtimāᶜīyah bayna al-muslimīn wa-ghayr al-muslimīn fī 'l-sharīᶜah al-islāmīyah wa-l-yahūdīyah wa-l-masīhīyah wa-l-qānūn*, Beirut, 1968.

Bakhīt, Ahmad Muhammad Ahmad. *al-Jinsīyah wa-dawr al-umm fī jinsīyat awlādihā. Dirāsah muqārinah fī 'l-fiqh al-islāmī wa-l-mawāthīq wa-l-qawānīn al-muᶜāsirah*, Cairo, 2001.

Bāz, Mustafà Muhammad Mustafà al-. *Jinsīyat al-mar'ah al-mutazawwijah fī 'l-qānūn al-duwalī al-khāss al-muqāran wa-l-fiqh al-islāmī wifqᵃⁿ li-ahkām al-naqd wa-l-qadā'. Dirāsah intiqādīyah li-mawqif al-musharriᶜ al-misri*, Alexandria, 2001.

Bustānī, Saᶜīd al-. *al-Jinsīyah wa-l-qawmīyah fī tashrīᶜāt al-duwal al-ᶜarabīyah. Dirāsah muqārinah*, Beirut, 2003.

Cheikho, Louis. *Shuᶜarā' al-nasrānīyah qabla al-islām*, Beirut, 1890-1891.

Darāz, Muhammad ᶜAbd allāh. 'al-Qānūn al-duwalī al-ᶜāmm wa-l-islām', *al-Majallah al-misrīyah li-l-qānūn al-duwalī*, 1949.

Dāwūdī, Ghālib ᶜAlī al- & Hasan al-Haddāwī. *al-Qānūn al-duwalī al-khāss, I: al-Jinsīyah, al-muwātin, marzak al-ajānib wa-ahkāmuhu fī 'l-qānūn al-ᶜirāqī*, Baghdad, 1981.

Dīb, Fu'ād. *al-Qānūn al-duwalī al-khāss: al-jinsīyah*, Damascus, 1999.

Dabbāgh, Salāh al-dīn al-. 'Haqq al-ᶜawdah', *al-Wasā'il al-ᶜamalīyah li-tatbīq al-faqrah 't' min al-dustūr al-lubnānī*, Beirut, 2000, 45-52.

Fahmī, Muhammad Kamāl. *Usūl al-qānūn al-duwalī al-khāss*, Alexandria, 1985.

Fāsī, ᶜAllāl al-. *al-Harakah al-istiqlālīyah fī 'l-maghrib al-ᶜarabī*, Cairo, 1948.

Fayfī, Sulaymān ibn Qāsim al-. *al-ᶜAmālah al-mustaqdamah: mā lahā wa-mā ᶜalayhā*, Riyadh, 1994.

Ghalyūn, Burhān. *al-Dawlah wa-l-dīn. Naqd al-siyāsah*, Beirut-Casablanca, 1996.
Ghannūshī, Rāshid al-. *Huqūq al-muwātanah, huqūq ghayr al-muslim fī 'l-mujtama^c al-islā-mī*, Herndon, 1993.
— *al-Hurrīyāt al-^{c}āmmah fī 'l-dawlah al-islāmīyah*, Beirut, 1993.
Ghazzālī, Muhammad al-. *Huqūq al-insān bayna ta^{c}ālīm al-islām wa-i^{c}lān al-Umam al-muttahidah*, Cairo, 1963.

Haddād, Hafīza al-. *Durūs fī 'l-jinsīyah al-misrīyah*, Cairo, 1994.
— *al-Mūjaz fī 'l-jinsīyah al-lubnānīyah wa-markaz al-ajānib*, Beirut, 2002.
Haddāwī, Hasan al-. *al-Ahkām al-jadīdah fī qānūn al-jinsīyah al-akhīr raqam 43 li-sanat 1963*, Baghdad, 1963.
— *al-Jinsīyah wa-markaz al-ajānib wa-ahkāmuhumā fī 'l-qānūn al-^{c}irāqī*, Baghdad, 1972.
— *al-Jinsīyah wa-markaz al-ajānib wa-ahkāmuhumā fī 'l-qānūn al-kuwaytī*, Kuwait, 1973.
— *al-Jinsīyah wa-ahkāmuhā fī 'l-qānūn al-urdunī*, Amman, 1994.
Hājj, ^{c}Abd al-rahmān al-. 'al-Riddah wa-^{c}uqūbat al-murtadd.. Murāja^{c}ah fī 'l-jadal al-fiqhī al-hadīth', *al-Hayāh* (3 September 2003).
Hakīm, Jacques al-. 'L'implantation des réfugiés palestiniens au Liban', in (2000), *al-Wasā'il al-^{c}amalīyah li-tatbīq al-faqrah 't' min al-dustūr al-lubnānī*, 41-44. Beirut-Bruxelles: CEDROMA-Bruylant.
Hamad, Ahmad. *Fiqh al-jinsīyāt. Dirāsah muqārinah fī 'l-sharī^{c}ah wa-l-qānūn*, Tanta, 1986.
Hassūn, Sālih ^{c}Abd al-zahrah al-. *Huqūq al-ajānib fī 'l-qānūn al-^{c}irāqī ma^{c}a ishārah khāssah li-wad^c al-muwātin al-^{c}arabī fī daw' fikr hizb al-ba^{c}th al-^{c}arabī al-ishtirākī*, Baghdad, 1981.
Hawāmdah, Mūsà. *Shajarī a^{c}là*, Beirut, 1999.
Hubaydah, Muhammad. 'Min ajli usrah muwātinah', in (2002), *al-Usrah wa-l-muwātanah*, Rabat, 75-77.
Husrī, Sāti^c al-. *al-A^{c}māl al-qawmīyah*, 2nd ed., Beirut, 1990.
Hussayn, Wālqīd al-. 'al-Jinsīyah al-maghribīyah bayna al-khusūsīyah wa-l-^{c}ālamīyah: al-Yahūd al-maghāribah namūdhaj^{an}', *al-Majallah al-qānūnīyah al-tūnisīyah* (2000): 167-193.
Huwaydī, Fahmī. *Muwātinūn lā dhimmīyūn*, Cairo, 1985.

Ibrāhīm, al-Sayyid Muhammad. *al-Jinsīyah fī dawlat al-imārāt al-^{c}arabīyah al-muttahidah*, Dubai, 1976.
^{c}Īd, Edouard. *al-Wajīz fī 'l-madkhal li-^{c}ilm al-qānūn*, Beirut, 1978.
^{c}Īd Rūs, Ahmad. *al-Jinsīyah fī tashrī^c al-Yaman al-dīmuqrātī*, Aden, 1984.

Jabartī, ^{c}Abd al-rahmān ibn Hasan Burhān al-dīn al-. *^{c}Ajā'ib al-'āthār fī 'l-tarājum wa-l-akhbār*, Cairo, 1959.
— *Muzhir al-taqdīs bi-zawāl dawlat al-Faransīs*, Cairo, 1961.
Jābirī, Muhammad ^{c}Ābid al-. *al-^{c}Aql al-siyāsī al-^{c}arabī*, Casablanca-Beirut, 1990.
— *Fikr ibn Khaldūn: al-^{c}asabīyah wa-l-dawlah*, Beirut, 1995.
Jaddāwī, Ahmad Qissmat al-. *Nazarīyat al-jinsīyah fī 'l-qānūn al-misrī al-muqārin*, Cairo, 1981.
— *al-Mūjaz fī 'l-jinsīyah wa-markaz al-ajānib*, Cairo, 1983.
— *Mabādi' al-qānūn al-duwalī al-khāss*, Cairo, 1988.
Jamāl al-dīn, Muhammad Salāh al-dīn. *Nazarāt fī 'l-jinsīyah al-misrīyah: Dirāsah muqārinah ma^{c}a 'l-sharī^{c}ah al-islāmīyah*, Cairo, 1998.
— *Nizām al-jinsīyah fī 'l-sharī^{c}ah al-islāmīyah. Dirāsah muqārinah*, Cairo, 2001, and Alexandria, 2004.
Jāsir, Hamad al-. *Jamharat ansāb al-usar al-mutahaddirah fī Najd*, Riyadh, 1988.

Jawdah, Jamāl. *al-Awdā* *al-ijtimā*ʿ*īyah wa-l-iqtisadīyah li-l-mawālī fī sadr al-islām*, Amman, 1989.

Jazāʾirī, Muhammad ibn ʿAbd al-karīm al-. *Tabdīl al-jinsīyah riddah wa-khiyānah*, Paris, 1993.

— *Fadāʾih takshifuhā fikhākh al-dīmuqratīyah fī ʾl-Jazāʾir*, s.l., 1993.

Jazīrī, ʿAbd al-rahmān. *Kitāb al-fiqh* ʿ*alà* ʾl-*madhāhib al-arba*ʿ*ah*, Beirut, 1998.

Kaʿbī, ʿAbd al-hakīm al-. ʾal-Ansab al-ʿarabīyah: Haqīqah am wahm?ʾ, *al-*ʿ*Arabī* 556 (March 2005): 56-59.

Kahhālah, ʿUmar Ridā al-. *Mu*ʿ*jim qabāʾil al-*ʿ*arab: al-qadīmah wa-l-hadīthah*, Beirut, 1985.

Karam, Joseph. *al-Jinsīyah al-lubnānīyah bayna al-qānūn wa-l-wāqi*ʿ, Beirut, 1993.

Kawākibī, ʿAbd al-rahmān. *Umm al-qurà*, Beirut, 1982.

Khalaf allāh, Muhammad Ahmad. ʿ*Urūbat al-islām*, Rabat, 1990.

Khālid, Hishām. *Ahamm mushkilāt qānūn al-jinsīyah al-*ʿ*arabī. Mushkilat dam al-umm al-*ʿ*arabīyah, mushkilat qadāʾ al-jinsīyah al-*ʿ*arabīyah*, Alexandria, 2006.

Khānikī Bek, ʿAzīz. ʾIkhtilāf al-dārayn wa-matà yakūn māniʿan min al-irthʾ, *Majallat al-qānūn wa-l-iqtisād* 1934 (5).

Khayyāt, Ahmad al- & Ahmad al-Zayn. *Qānūn al-jinsīyah al-*ʿ*arabīyah al-sūrīyah*, Damascus, 1980.

Lāfī, Muhammad al-Mabrūk al-. *al-Qānūn al-duwalī al-khāss al-lībī. Dirāsah muqārinah*, I: *al-Jinsīyah wa-markaz al-ajānib*, Tripoli, 2000.

Madkūr, Muhammad Sallām. *al-Qadāʾ fī ʾl-islām*, Cairo, 1964.

— *Ma*ʿ*ālim al-dawlah al-islāmīyah*, Kuwait, 1983.

Mahfūz, ʿAbd al-munʿim. ʿ*Alāqat al-fard bi-l-sultah: al-hurrīyāt al-*ʿ*āmmah wa-damānāt mumārasatihā. Dirāsah muqārinah*, Cairo, 1989.

Majdhūb, Muhammad al-. ʾRafd al-tawtīn wa-haqq al-ʿawdah, wajhān li-qadīyah wāhidahʾ, *al-Wasāʾil al-*ʿ*amalīyah li-tatbīq al-faqrah ʾtʾ min al-dustūr al-lubnānī*, Beirut, 2000, 23-40.

Makhlūf, Hasanayn Muhammad. *Fatāwā shar*ʿ*īyah wa-buhūth islāmīyah*, Cairo, 1965.

Mawdūdī, abū al-Aʿlà al-. *Huqūq ahl al-dhimmah fī ʾl-dawlah al-islāmīyah*, Cairo, 1978.

Mīmī, Hasan al-. *al-Jinsīyah fī ʾl-qānūn al-tūnisī*, Tunis, 1971.

Miqdār, Mahmūd al-. *al-Mawālī wa-nizām al-walāʾ min al-jāhilīyah ilà awākhir al-*ʿ*asr al-umawwī*, Damascus, 1980.

Munīfī, ʿAbd allāh al-. *al-Qānūn al-duwalī al-khāss*, Riyadh, 1974.

Mūsà, ʿAbd al-rasūl ʿAlī al- & Makkī Muhammad ʿAzīz, *al-Khasāʾis al-ijtimā*ʿ*īyah wa-l-iqtisādīyah li-l-muhājirīn ilà ʾl-Kuwayt*, Kuwait, 1981.

Muslim, Ahmad. *Mūjaz al-qānūn al-duwalī al-khāss al-muqārin fī Misr wa-Lubnān*, Beirut, 1966.

Mustafà, Hāmid. *al-Wajīz fī ʾl-qānūn al-duwalī al-khāss: al-jinsīya*, Baghdad, 1962.

— *Mabādiʾ al-qānūn al-duwalī al-khāss min wijhat nazar al-qānūn al-*ʿ*irāqī*, Baghdad, 1970.

Mutawallī, ʿAbd al-hamīd al-. *Mabādiʾ nizām al-hukm fī ʾl-islām*, Cairo, 1966.

Mutʿinī, ʿAbd al-ʿazīm Ibrāhīm al-. ʿ*Uqūbat al-irtidād* ʿ*an al-dīn bayna al-adillah al-shar*ʿ*īyah wa-shibahāt al-munkirīn*, Cairo, 1993.

Nādir, Muthnà Amīn. *Huqūq al-muwātin ghayr al-muslim fī ʾl-dawlah al-islāmīyah*, Khartoum, 1999.

Naʿīm, Edmond. *al-Mūjaz fī ʾl-qānūn al-duwalī al-khāss wifq*ᵃⁿ *li-l-tashrī*ʿ *wa-l-ijtihād fī Lubnān*, Beirut, 1963.

Najīb, Munīr Muhammad al-. *al-Harakah al-qawmīyah fī mīzān al-islām*, al-Zarqāʾ, 1983.

Nāshif, Antoine al-. *al-Jinsīyah al-lubnānīyah bayna al-qānūn wa-l-ijtihād*, Beirut, 1999.
Nijm, Muhammad al-. *al-Bidūn?!*, Kuwait, 1995.
Nimr, abū al-ʿAlā ʿAlī abū al-ʿAlā al-. *Jinsīyat awlād al-umm al-misrīyah: mushkilah tu'arriq al-fikr al-qānūnī*, Cairo, 2002.

Qaradāwī, Yūsuf al-. *Ghayr al-muslimīn fī 'l-mujtamaʿ al-islāmī*, Cairo, 1977.
— *al-Khasā'is al-ʿāmmah li-l-islām*, 3rd ed., Cairo, 1986.
Qasabī, ʿIsām al-dīn al-. *al-Qānūn al-duwalī al-khāss li-dawlat al-imārāt al-ʿarabīyah al-muttahidah. Dirāsah muqārinah*, I: *Fī 'l-jinsīyah*, Dubai, 1995.
Qāsim, ʿAbd al-rahmān al-. *al-Qānūn al-duwalī al-khāss wa-tatbīquhu fī 'l-nizām al-saʿūdī*, Riyadh, 1977.
Qāsim, ʿAwn al-Sharīf. *Mawsūʿat al-qabā'il wa-l-ansāb fī 'l-Sūdān wa-ashhar asmā' al-ʿālam wa-l-amākin*, Khartoum, 1996.

Ramadān, ʿAbd al-ʿazīm. *Jamāʿāt al-takfīr fī Misr*, Cairo, 1995.
Rāwī, Jabir al-. *al-Qānūn al-duwalī al-khāss wifqan li-ahkām al-qānūn al-ʿirāqī wa-l-muqāran*, Baghdad, 1977.
— *Sharh ahkām al-jinsīyah fī 'l-qānūn al-urdunī*, Amman, 1984.
Ridā, Muhammad Rashīd. 'al-Ijtihād fī 'l-dīn wa-qatl al-murtadd', *Majallat al-Manār* 10 (1907).
— 'al-Jawāb ʿan mas'alat hurrīyat al-dīn wa-qatl al-murtadd', *Majallat al-Manār* 23 (1922).
— *Fatāwā*, Beirut, 1970.
Riyād, Fu'ād ʿAbd al-munʿim. *al-Jinsīyah fī 'l-tashrīʿāt al-ʿarabīyah al-muqāranah*, Cairo, 1975.
— *al-Wasīt fī 'l-jinsīyah wa-markaz al-ajānib*, Cairo, 1988.
— *al-Jinsīyah al-misrīyah. Dirāsah muqārinah*, Cairo, 1990.
— *al-Jinsīyah ma-markaz al-ajānib fī 'l-qānūn al-duwalī wa-l-tashrīʿ al-misrī*, Cairo, 1994.
— *Usūl al-jinsīyah fī 'l-qānūn al-duwalī al-khāss wa-l-qānūn al-misrī al-muqāran*, Cairo, 1995.
Riyād, Fu'ād ʿAbd al-munʿim & ʿInāyat ʿAbd al-hamīd Thābit, *Ahkām tanzīm al-jinsīyah fī 'l-qānūn al-muqārin wa-l-qānūn al-yamanī*, Sanaa, 1990.
Riyād, Muhammad ʿAbd al-munʿim. *Mabādi' al-qānūn al-duwalī al-khāss*, Cairo, 1943.

Sābūnī, ʿAbd al-rahmān al-. *Madà hurrīyat al-zawjayn fī 'l-talāq*, Beirut, 1968.
Sadāwī, Māhir Ibrāhīm al-. *al-Jinsīyah fī 'l-qānūn al-muqārin wa-fī tashrīʿ al-jumhūrīyah al-ʿarabīyah al-yamanīyah*, Cairo, 1984.
Sādiq, Hishām ʿAlī. *al-Jinsīyah wa-l-mawtin wa-markaz al-ajānib*, Alexandria, 1977.
— *al-Jinsīyah al-misrīyah*, Alexandria, 2002.
Sādiq, Hishām ʿAlī & Hafīzah al-Haddād, *Mabādi' al-qānūn al-duwalī al-khāss*, Alexandria, 2001.
Saʿīd, Muhammad. *al-Nasab wa-l-qarābah fī 'l-mujtamaʿ al-ʿarabī qabla al-islām*, Beirut-Casablanca, 2006.
Saʿīdī, ʿAbd al-mutaʿālī al-. *al-Hurrīyah al-dīnīya fī 'l-islām*, Cairo, s.d.
Salāmah, Ahmad ʿAbd al-karīm. *Mabādi' al-qānūn al-duwalī al-khāss al-islāmī al-muqārin*, Cairo, 1989.
Sālih, Sharīf Ibrāhīm. *al-Takfīr akhtar bidʿah tuhaddid al-islām wa-l-wahdah bayna al-muslimīn*, Cairo, 1986.
Sallūm, Subhī. *Tashrīʿāt al-jinsīyah al-ʿarabīyah al-sūrīyah*, Damascus, 1983.
Sāmarrā'ī, Nuʿmān ʿAbd al-rāziq al-. *Ahkam al-murtadd fī 'l-sharīʿah al-islāmīyah*, Beirut, 1968.
Sammāk, Muhammad al-. *al-Aqallīyāt bayna al-ʿurūbah wa-l-islām*, Beirut, 1990.

Sanūsī, Ahmad Taha al-. 'Fikrat al-jinsīyah fī 'l-tashrīᶜ al-islāmī al-muqāran', *Majallat Misr al-muᶜāsirah* 288 (4/1957): 15-67.

Sayyid, Ahmad Lutfī al-. *Ta'ammulāt fī 'l-falsafah wa-l-adab wa-l-siyāsah wa-l-mujtamaᶜ*, Cairo, 1946.

Shalabī, Muhammad Mustafâ. *Ahkām al-mawārīth bayna al-fiqh wa-l-qānūn*, Alexandria, 1967.

Shaltūt, Mahmūd. *al-Fatāwā. Dirāsah li-mushkilāt al-muslim al-muᶜāsir fī hayātihi al-yawmīyah wa-l-ᶜāmmah*, Cairo, 1969.

— *al-Islām ᶜaqīdah wa-sharīᶜah*, 12th ed., Beirut, 1985.

Sharābī, Hishām. *al-Naqd al-hadārī li-l-mujtamaᶜ al-ᶜarabī fī 'l-qarn al-ᶜishrīn*, Beirut, 1990.

Shaykh, Fath al-Rahmān ᶜAbd allāh al-. *Tatawwur qawānīn al-jinsīyah fī 'l-Sūdān*, Beirut, 1991.

Shihātah, Shafīq. *al-Tārīkh al-ᶜām li-l-qānūn fī Misr al-qadīmah wa-l-hadīthah*, Cairo, 1926.

Shukrī, ᶜAzīz. *al-Jinsīyah al-ᶜarabīyah al-sūrīyah*, Damascus, 1970.

Suᶜayyid, Shafīq. 'al-Dustūr wa-l-muwātin', in al-Jamᶜīyah al-tūnisīyah li-l-qānūn al-dustūrī (2000), *al-Dustūr al-tūnisī fī dhikrà al-arbaᶜīn li-isdārih 1959-1999*, 65-88. Tunis: ATDC.

Suhayl, Mūsà Zawād. *Akhtār al-hijrah al-ajnabīyah ilà 'l-khalīj al-ᶜarabī*, Baghdad, 1986.

Sultān, Anwar. *al-Mabādi' al-qānūnīyah al-ᶜāmmah*, Beirut, 1978.

Sultān, Hāmid. *Ahkām al-qānūn al-duwalī fī 'l-sharīᶜah al-islāmīyah*, Cairo, 1986.

Thābit, ᶜInāyat ᶜAbd al-hamīd. *ᶜAlà hāmish tashrīᶜ tanzīm al-raᶜawīyah al-yamanīyah. Dirāsah tahlīlīyah intiqādīyah li-tashrīᶜ tanzīm raᶜawīyah al-Jumhūrīyah al-ᶜarabīyah al-yamanīyah*, Sanaa, 1990.

— *Ahkām tanzīm ᶜalāqat al-raᶜawīyah fī 'l-qānūn al-muqārin wa-l-qānūn al-yamanī*, Sanaa, 1993.

Wakīl, Shams al-dīn al-. *Mabādi' al-qānūn al-duwalī al-khāss*, Cairo, 1965.

— *al-Mūjaz fī 'l-jinsīyah wa-markaz al-ajānib*, Alexandria, 1968.

Wizārat al-ᶜadl, *Mujallad al-tashrīᶜāt*, Muscat, 2005.

Wolfensohn, Israel. *Tārīkh al-Yahūd fī bilād al-ᶜarab fī 'l-jāhilīyah wa-sadr al-islām*, Cairo, 1927.

Yassīn, al-Sayyid. *al-Muwātanah fī zaman al-ᶜawlamah*, Cairo, 2002.

Zakārīyā, Fu'ād. *al-Haqīqah wa-l-wahm fī 'l-harakah al-islāmīyah al-muᶜāsirah*, 3rd ed., Cairo-Paris, 1988.

Zakī, Hāmid. *al-Qānūn al-duwalī al-khāss al-misrī*, Cairo, 1940.

Zarūtī, al-Tayyib. *al-Wasīt fī 'l-jinsīyah al-jazā'irīyah. Dirāsah tahlīlīyah muqārinah bi-l-qawānīn al-ᶜarabīyah wa-l-qānūn al-faransī*, Algiers, 2002.

Zaydān, ᶜAbd al-karīm. *Ahkām al-dhimmīyīn wa-l-musta'minīn fī dār al-islām*, Baghdad-Beirut, 1982.

Zaynī, ᶜAlī al-. *al-Qānūn al-duwalī al-khāss al-misrī wa-l-muqarin*, Cairo, 1968.

Zaytūn, ᶜĀdil. 'Jūlyā Dūmnā: ᶜarabīyah ᶜalà ᶜursh Rūmā', *al-ᶜArabī* 558 (May 2005): 58-63.

Zuhaylī, Wahbah Mustafâ al-.'*Āthār al-harb fī 'l-fiqh al-islāmī*, 3rd ed., Cairo, 1983.

— *al-Fiqh al-islāmī wa-adillatuh*, Damascus, 1997.

— *Haqq al-hurrīyah fī 'l-ᶜālam*, Damascus, 2000.

Zūkāghī, Ahmad. *Ahkām al-qānūn al-duwalī al-khāss fī 'l-tashrīᶜ al-maghribī, I: al-Jinsīyah*, Casablanca, 1992.

— *Wathā'iq al-jinsīyah al-maghribīyah*, Rabat, 1994.

In other languages

(1980), *Juifs du Maroc: Identité et dialogue*. Grenoble: La pensée sauvage.

(1980), *Muslim Communities in Non-Muslim States*. London: Islamic Council of Europe.

(1984-1985), *Tanzimat'tan cümhuriyet'e Türkiye ansiklopedisi*. Istanbul: İletişim Yayınları.

(1997), *Droit de citoyenneté des femmes au Maghreb. La condition socio-économique et juridique des femmes, le mouvement des femmes*. Casablanca: Le Fennec.

(2001), *Les cours judiciaires suprêmes dans le monde arabe*. Beirut-Bruxelles: CEDROMA-Bruylant.

(2003), *Droit et Religion*. Bruxelles: Bruylant.

Abdul-Jabar, F. & H. Dawod (ed.) (2001), *Tribes and Power: Nationalism and Ethnicity in the Middle East*. London: Saqi.

Abel, A. (1945), *La Convention de Nedjrân et le développement du «droit de gens» dans l'islam classique*. Bruxelles: Groeninghe.

Ahmed, M. (1975), 'Der Ausschluß der Ahmadiyya aus dem Islam. Eine umstrittene Entscheidung des pakistanischen Parlaments', *Orient* 16: 112-143.

Aland, K. (1961), *Die Säuglingstaufe im Neuen Testament und in der alten Kirche*. Munich: Kaiser.

Aldeeb, S. (1979), *L'impact de la religion sur l'ordre juridique. Cas de l'Egypte. Non-musulmans en pays d'Islam*. Freiburg: Editions Universitaires.

— (1994), *Les musulmans face aux droits de l'homme*. Bochum: Winkler.

— (2001), *Les musulmans en Occident entre droits et devoirs*. Paris: L'Harmattan.

Aleinikoff, A. T. (2000), 'Between Principles and Policies: U.S. Citizenship Policy', in A. T. Aleinikoff & D. Klusmeyer (eds.), *From Migrants to Citizens. Membership in a Changing World*, 119-174. Washington: Carnegie Endowment for International Peace.

Aleinikoff, A. T. & D. Klusmeyer (eds.) (2000), *From Migrants to Citizens. Membership in a Changing World*. Washington: Carnegie Endowment for Peace.

— (2001), *Citizenship today: Global Perspectives and Practices*. Washington, DC: Carnegie Endowment for International Peace.

— (2002), *Citizenship Policies for an Age of Migration*. Washington: Carnegie Endowment for International Peace.

Ali, M. (1951), *The Holy Qur'an. Arabic Text, Translation and Commentary*. Lahore: Ahmadiyyah Anjuman Isha'at Islam.

al-Mawdūdī, A. (1963), *Murtadd ki sazā islāmi qānūn men*. Lahore: Ahmadiyyah Anjuman Isha'at Islam.

al-Sayyid, A. & M. Desserteaux (1925-1926), *Traité théorique et pratique de procédure civile et commerciale égyptienne, spécialement devant les tribunaux mixtes*. Dijon: Berthier.

Aluffi Beck-Peccoz, R. (1990), *La modernizzazione del diritto di famiglia nei paesi arabi*. Milan: Giuffré.

— (1990), 'La riforma del diritto di famiglia in Somalia. Dai concetti di adeguatezza e di parità al principio di uguaglianza', *Oriente Moderno* 70 (1-6): 93-99.

— (1993), 'Cittadinanza e appartenenza religiosa nel diritto internazionale privato. Il caso dei Paesi arabi', *Teoria politica* 9 (3): 97-110.

Aluffi Beck-Peccoz, R. & G. Zincone (eds.) (2004), *The Legal Treatment of Islamic Minorities in Europe*. Leuven: Peeters.

Amari, M. (1863), *I diplomi arabi del Regio archivio fiorentino*. Florence: Le Monnier.

— (1880-1881), *Biblioteca arabo-sicula*. Turin: Loescher.

— (1889), *Appendice*. Turin: Loescher.

Anderson, J. (1954), *Islamic Law in Africa*. London: HM Stationery Office.

Angioi, S. (2003), 'Le dinamiche universalismo-regionalismo nei diritti umani e i loro ri-
flessi sulle relazioni euromediterranee: quali prospettive per un dialogo tra Europa e
mondo arabo?', *Rivista internazionale dei diritti dell'uomo* 16 (1): 44-85.

Armanāzī, N. (1929), *Les principes islamiques et les rapports internationaux en temps de paix
et de guerre.* Paris: Picart.

Arminjon, P. (1904), 'Le Code civile et l'Egypte', in *Livre du Centenarie du Code civil.* Paris:
Dalloz.

Assabghy, A. & E. Colombani (1926), *Questions de Nationalité en Egypte.* Cairo: Misr.

Atiyah, E. (1955), *The Arabs.* Harmondsworth: Penguin.

Ayalon, A. (1987), *Language and Change in the Arab Middle East: the evolution of modern political discourse.* Oxford: Oxford University Press.

Badawi Pacha, A. (1926), 'Aperçu sur la question de la Nationalité Egyptienne', foreword
to A. Assabghy & E. Colombani, *Questions de Nationalité en Egypte.* Cairo: Misr.

Bader, V. (1997), 'Differentiated Egalitarian Multiculturalism', in R. Bauböck (ed.) *Blurred
Boundaries. Migration, Ethnicity, Citizenship,* 185-220. Aldershot: Ashgate.

— (2001), 'Institutions, culture and identity of trans-national citizenship: How much integration and "communal spirit" is needed?', in C. Crouch & K. Eder (eds.), *Citizenship, Markets, and the State,* 192-212. Oxford: Oxford University Press.

— (2007), *Secularism or Democracy? Associational Governance of Religious Diversity.* Amsterdam: Amsterdam University Press.

Bakht, N. (2004), 'Family Arbitration Using Sharia Law: Examining Ontario's Arbitration
Act and its Impact on Women', *Muslim World Journal of Human Rights* 1 (1): 1-24.

Barakat, M. (1912), *Des privilèges et immunités dont jouissent les étrangers en Egypte vis-à-vis
des autorités locales.* Paris: Rousseau.

Bar Penkaye in A. Mingana (ed.-transl.) (1907), *Sources syriaques.* Leipzig: Harrassowitz.

Barrington, L. W. (2000), 'Understanding citizenship in the Baltic States', in A. T. Aleinikoff & D. Klusmeyer (eds.), *From Migrants to Citizens. Membership in a Changing
World,* 253-301. Washington: Carnegie Endowment for International Peace.

Basagana, R. & A. Sayad (1974), *Habitat et structures familiales en Kabylie.* Algiers: SNED.

Bat Ye'or (1991), *Les Chrétientés d'Orient entre jihâd et dhimmitude (viie-xxe siècle).*
Paris: Cerf.

Bauböck, R. (1994), *Transnational Citizenship. Membership and Rights in International Migration.* Aldershot: Edward Elgar.

— (2002), 'Farewell to Multiculturalism? Sharing values and identities in societies of
immigration', *Journal of International Migration and Integration* 3 (1): 1-16.

— (2003a), 'Towards a political theory of migrant transnationalism', *International Migration Review* 37 (3): 700-723.

— (2003b), 'Public culture in societies of immigration', in R. Sackmann, T. Faist & B.
Peters (eds.), *Identity and Integration. Migrants in Western Europe,* 37-57. Aldershot:
Ashgate.

— (2004a), 'Citizenship Policies: International, state, migrant and democratic perspectives', *Global Migration Perspectives* 19.

— (2004b), 'Civic Citizenship – A New Concept for the New Europe', in R. Süssmuth &
W. Weidenfeld (eds.), *Managing Integration. The European Union's Responsibilities towards Immigrants.* Gütersloh: Bertelsmann Stiftung.

Bauböck, R. (ed.) (2006), *Migration and Citizenship. Legal Status, Rights and Political Participation.* Amsterdam: Amsterdam University Press.

Bauböck, R., E. Ersböll, K. Groenendijk & H. Waldrauch (eds.) (2006a), *Acquisition and
Loss of Nationality. Policies and Trends in 15 European Countries.* I: *Comparative Analyses.* Amsterdam: Amsterdam University Press.

— (2006b), *Acquisition and Loss of Nationality. Policies and Trends in 15 European Countries.* II: *Country Analyses.* Amsterdam: Amsterdam University Press.

Bauböck, R., B. Perchinig & W. Sievers (eds.) (2007), *Citizenship Policies in the New Europe.* Amsterdam: Amsterdam University Press.

Baus, K. (1963), *Von der Urgemeinde zur frühchristlichen Grosskirche.* Freiburg: Herder.

Bausani, A. (1980), *L'Islam.* Milan: Garzanti.

Baz, J. (1969), *Etude sur la nationalité libanaise.* Beirut: Biban.

Bedjaoui, M. (1961), *La Révolution algérienne et le droit.* Bruxelles: Association internationale des juristes démocrates.

Beiner, R. (ed.) (1995), *Theorizing Citizenship.* Albany: State University of New York Press.

Belkeziz, A. (1963), *La nationalité dans les Etats arabes.* Rabat: La Porte.

Ben Achour, Y. (1993), *Normes, Foi et Loi.* Tunis: Cérès.

Bendeddouche, J. (1982), *Notion de nationalité et nationalité algérienne.* 2 ed., Algiers: Société nationale d'édition et de diffusion.

Bennouna, M. (1976), 'L'affaire du Sahara occidentale devant la Cour international de justice. Essai d'analyse structurale de l'avis consultatif du 16 octobre 1975', *Revue juridique, politique et économique du Maroc* 1976 (1): 81 ff.

Bentwich, N. (1926), 'Nationality in Mandated Territories Detached from Turkey', *British Yearbook of International Law* 7: 97-103.

Berger, M. (2005), 'Secularizing Interreligious Law in Egypt', *Islamic Law and Society,* 12 (3): 394-418.

Bilmen, Ö. (1949-1952), *Hukûkı İslâmiyye ve Istılahatı Fıkhiyye Kamusu.* Istanbul: İstanbul Matbaacılık TAO.

Blackstone, W. (1793-1795), *Commentaries on the Laws of England.* London: Strahan and Woodfall.

Blochet, E. (1902), 'Les relations diplomatiques des Hohenstraufen avec les sultans d'Egypte', *Revue Historique* 80: 51-64.

Bodin, J. (1986), *Le six livres de la République.* Paris: Fayard.

Boëtsch, G., B. Dupret & J.-N. Ferrié (eds.) (1997), *Droits et Sociétés dans le monde arabe et musulman : perspectives socio-anthropologiques.* Aix-en-Provence: Presses universitaires d'Aix-Marseille.

Boghdadi, H. (1937), *Origine et technique de la distinction des statuts personnels et réels en Egypte.* Cairo: Barbey.

Bonte, P., E. Conte & P. Dresch (eds.) (2001), *Emirs et Présidents: Figures de la parenté et du politique dans le monde arabe.* Paris: CNRS Editions.

Bontems, C. (1976), *Manuel des institutions algériennes de la domination turque à l'indépendence.* Paris: Cujas.

Bordes, J. (1982), *Politeia dans la pensée grecque jusqu'à Aristote.* Paris: Les belles lettres.

Boswell, C. (2003), 'The "external dimension" of EU immigration and asylum policy', *International Affairs* 79 (3): 619-638.

Bosworth, C. (1968), *Sīstān under the Arabs.* Rome: ISMEO.

Boudahrain, A. (1994), *Elements de droit public marocain.* Paris: L'Harmattan.

Bourbousson, E. (1931), *Traité général de la nationalité dans les cinque partie du monde : du statut de la femme mariée, de la naturalisation, de la perte de la nationalité : avec tous les textes en francais (lois, constitutions, décrets, ordonnances, etc.) sur la nationalité.* Paris: Académie diplomatique internationale.

Bousetta, H. & M. Martiniello (2003), 'L'immigration marocaine en Belgique : du travailleur immigré au citoyen transnational', *Hommes et Migrations* 1242: 94-106.

Brand, L. (2006), *Citizens Abroad. Emigration and the State in the Middle East and North Africa.* Cambridge: Cambridge University Press.

Brickner, B. (1930), 'Nationalité juive', *Revue littéraire juive* (September).

Brinton, J. (1930), *The Mixed Courts of Egypt.* New Haven: Yale University Press.

Brubaker, R. (1992), *Citizenship and Nationhood in France and Germany*. Cambridge: Harvard University Press.
— (1994), 'Nationhood and the National Question in the Soviet Union and Post-Soviet Union Eurasia: An Institutionalist Account', *Theory and Society* 23 (1): 47-78.
— (2001), 'The Return of Assimilation', *Ethnic and Racial Studies* 24 (4): 531-548.
Brubaker, R. (ed.) (1989), *Immigration and the Politics of Citizenship in Europe and North America*. New York: University Press of America and German Marshall Fund of the United States.
Brunschvig, R. (1976), *Etudes d'Islamologie*. Paris: G.-P. Maisonneuve et Larose.
Bruschi, C. (1987), 'Droit de la nationalité et égalité des droits de 1789 à la fin du xixᵉ siècle', in S. Laacher (ed.), *Questions de nationalité. Histoire et enjeux d'un code*. Paris: L'Harmattan.
Buhl, F. (1930), *Muhammeds Liv, med en Inledning om Forholdene i Arabien for Muhammeds Optraeden* (Copenhagen: Gyldendal, 1903), German translation by H. Schäder: *Das Leben Muhammeds*. Leipzig: Quelle & Meyer.
Bultmann, P. F. (2002), 'Dual Nationality and Naturalisation Policies in the German Länder, in R. Hansen & P. Weil (eds.), *Dual Nationality, Social Rights and Federal Citizenship in the U.S. and Europe. The Reinvention of Citizenship*, 136-157. New York: Berghahn Books.
Butenschon, N. A., U. Davis & M. Hassassian (eds.) (2000), *Citizenship and the State in the Middle East: Approaches and Applications*. Syracuse: Syracuse University Press.

Caetani, L. (1905-1926), *Annali dell'Islam*. Milan: Hoepli.
— (1911-1914), *Studii di Storia Orientale*. Milan: Hoepli.
Campanini, M. (2004), *Introduzione alla filosofia islamica*. Rome-Bari: Laterza.
Cantarella, E. (1985), *Tacita Muta: La donna nella città antica*. Rome: Editori riuniti.
— (1996), *Passato prossimo: Donne Romane da Tacita a Sulpicia*. Milan: Feltrinelli.
Cantwell Smith, W. (1960), 'Ahmadiyya', *EI²* I: 311. Leiden-Paris: Brill.
Cardahi, C. (1937), 'La conception et la pratique du Droit international privé dans l'Islam: (Étude juridique et historique)', *Recueil des Cours – Hague Academy of International Law* 60 (2): 507-650.
Carens, J. H. (1992), 'Migration and Morality. A Liberal Egalitarian Perspective', in B. Barry & R. E. Goodin (eds.), *Free Movement. Ethical Issues in the transnational migration of people and of money*, 25-47. Pennsylvania: The Pennsylvania State University Press.
Carlier, J.-Y. & M. Verwilghen (eds.) (1992), *Le statut personnel des musulmans. Droit comparé et droit international privé*. Bruxelles: Bruylant.
Castles, S. & A. Davidson (2000), *Citizenship and Migration. Globalization and the Politics of Belonging*. London: Routledge.
Castro, F. (1990), 'Diritto musulmano', *Digesto*, 4th ed., VI. Turin: UTET.
Cerulli, E. (1919), 'Il diritto consuetudinario della Somalia italiana settentrionale (Sultanato dei Migiurtini)', *Bollettino della Società Africana d'Italia*, 38: 1-74.
Cesarani, D. & M. Fulbrook (eds.) (1996), *Citizenship, Nationality and Migration in Europe*. London: Routledge.
Charfi, M. (1987), 'L'influence de la religion dans le droit international privé des pays musulmans', *Recueil des Cours – Hague Academy of International Law*, 203 (3): 321-454.
Charnay, J.-P. (1965), *La vie musulmane en Algérie d'après la jurisprudence de la première moitié du xxᵉ siècle*. Paris: Presses universitaires de France.
Chauvel, G. (1937), *Les Notions d'Etat et de Nationalité au Maroc*. Casablanca: Farairre.
Chebel, M. (2002), *Le sujet en islam*. Paris: Seuil.
Cheikho, L. (1912, 1919 and 1923), *Le christianisme et la littérature chrétienne en Arabie avant l'Islam*. Beirut: Dar el-Machreq.

Chouraqui, A. (1950), *La condition juridique de l'israélite marocain*. Paris: Alliance israélite universelle.

Christiansen, F. & U. Hedetoft (eds.) (2004), *The Politics of Multiple Belonging. Ethnicity and Nationalism in Europe and East Asia*. Aldershot: Ashgate.

Cohen, J. (1900), *Les Israélites d'Algérie et le décret Crémieux*. Paris: Rousseau.

Cohen, R. (1997), *Global Diasporas. An Introduction*. London: UCL Press.

Collot, C. (1987), *Les institutions de l'Algérie durant la période coloniale (1830-1962)*. Paris-Algiers: CNRS-Office des publications universitaires.

Collot, C. & J.-R. Henry (1978-1981), *Le mouvement national algérien. Textes 1912-1954*. Paris-Algiers: L'Harmattan-Office des publications universitaires.

Contuzzi, F. (1885), *La istituzione dei consolati ed il diritto internazionale europeo nella sua applicabilità in Oriente*. Naples: Anfossi.

Cordini, G. (1998), *Elementi per una teoria giuridica della cittadinanza: Profili di Diritto Pubblico Comparato*. Padua: CEDAM.

Corm, G. (1998), *Histoire du pluralisme religieux dans le bassin méditerranéen*. Paris: Paul Geuth.

Costa, P. (1999-2001), *Civitas: Storia della cittadinanza in Europa*. Rome-Bari: Laterza.

Coulson, N. (1964), *A History of Islamic Law*. Edinburgh: Edinburgh University Press.

Crone, P. (1987), *Roman, Provincial and Islamic Law: The Origins of the Islamic Patronate*. Cambridge: Cambridge University Press.

— (1991), 'Mawlā', *EI²* VI: 866. Paris-Leiden: Brill.

Cuniberti, M. (1996), 'Politica dell'immigrazione, condizione dello straniero e garanzie costituzionali: a proposito del recente decreto legge sull'immigrazione', *Diritto Pubblico* 2 (2): 443-489.

— (1997), *La cittadinanza. Libertà dell'uomo e libertà del cittadino nella costituzione italiana*. Padua: CEDAM.

Dahl, R. A. (1989), *Democracy and its Critics*. New Haven: Yale University Press.

Davidson, R. (1963), *Reform in the Ottoman Empire 1856-1876*. Princeton: Princeton University Press.

Davis, U. (1995), 'Jinsiyya versus Muwatana: The Question of Citizenship and the State in the Middle East: The Cases of Israel, Jordan and Palestine', *Arab Studies Quarterly* 17 (1-2): 19-50.

Dawod, H. (2001), 'The «State-ization» of the Tribe and the Tribalization of the State: the Case of Iraq', in F. Abdul-Jabar & H. Dawod (ed.), *Tribes and Power: Nationalism and Ethnicity in the Middle East*: 110-135. London: Saqi.

Dazi-Héni, F. (2001), 'Vers un modèle rénové de la monarchie arabe du golfe Persique? Etude de cas à Bahreïn', *Monde arabe Maghreb-Machreq* 173: 52-59.

De Bruycker, P., C. Schmitter & S. de Seze (2000), 'Rapport de Synthèse sur la Comparaison des Régularisations d'Étrangers Illégaux dans L'Union Européenne', in P. de Bruycker (ed.), *Les Régularisations des Étrangers Illegaux dans l'Union Européenne*, 24-82. Bruxelles: Bruylant.

Decroux, P. (1935), *Essai sur la nationalité marocaine*. Melle: Goussard.

— (1936), 'Condition et nationalité des indigènes musulmans, berbères, israélites et chrétiens au Maroc', *Recueil de législation et de jurisprudence marocaines*.

de Groot, G.-R. (1989), *Staatsangehörigkeitsrecht im Wandel*. Köln: Heymans.

— (2003), 'Loss of Nationality. A Critical Inventory', in D. A. Martin & K. Hailbronner (eds.), *Rights and Duties of Dual Nationals. Evolution and Prospects*, 201-299. The Hague: Kluwer Law International.

— (2004), 'Towards a European Nationality Law – Vers un droit européen de nationalité', Inaugural lecture delivered on the occasion of the acceptance of the Pierre Harmel chair of professeur invité at the Université de Liège, 13 November 2003. Maastricht: Universiteit Maastricht.

Delanty, G. (2000), *Citizenship in a global age. Society, culture, politics*. Buckingham: Open University Press.

de Maslatrie, L. (1866), Traités de paix et de commerce, et documents divers. Paris: Plon.

D'Emilia, A. (1960), 'Editto di Medina', *Novissimo Digesto Italiano* IV. Turin: UTET.

Deng, F. M. (2001), 'Ethnic Marginalization as Statelessness: Lessons from the Great Lakes Region of Africa', in: A. T. Aleinikoff & D. Klusmeyer (eds.) (2001), *Citizenship today: Global Perspectives and Practices*, 183-208. Washington: Carnegie Endowment for International Peace.

Dennett, D. (1950), *Conversion and the Poll Tax in Early Islam*. Cambridge: Harvard University Press.

Denny, F. (1975), 'The meanings of umma in the Qur'ān', *History of Religions* 15: 34-70.

— (1977), 'Ummah in the Constitution of Medina', *Journal of Near Eastern Studies* 36: 39-47.

Deprez, J. (1988), 'Droit international privé et conflits de civilisations. Aspects méthodologiques. Les relations entre systèmes d'Europe occidentale et systèmes islamiques en matière de statut personnel', *Recueil des Cours – Hague Academy of International Law* 211: 9-372.

Despagnet, F. (1896), *Essai sur les Protectorats*. Paris: Larose.

de Wée, M. (1926a), *La compétence des juridictions mixtes d'Egypte*. Bruxelles: Vandeveld.

— (1926b), *La nationalité égyptienne; commentaire de la Loi du 26 mai 1926*. Alexandria: Whitehead Morris.

Djaït, H. (1986), 'al-Kūfa', *EI²* V: 346-352. Leiden-Paris: Brill.

Dogan, V. (2002), *Türk Vatandaslik Hukuku*. Ankara: Yetkin Basimevi.

Dogliani, M. (1994), *Introduzione al diritto costituzionale*. Bologna: Il Mulino.

Dowty, A. (1987), *Closed Borders. The Contemporary Assault on Freedom of Movement*. New Haven: Yale University Press.

Dumont, P. (1989), 'La période des Tanzîmât (1839-1878)', in R. Mantran (ed.), *Histoire de l'Empire ottoman*: 459-522. Paris: Fayard.

Durkheim, E. (1950), *Leçons de sociologie. Physique des mœurs et du droit*. Paris: Presses Universitaires de France.

Eder, K. & B. Giessen (2001), *European Citizenship. National Legacies and Transnational Projects*. Oxford: Oxford University Press.

Elgeddawi, A. (1971), *Relations entre systèmes confessionnel et laïque en Droit international privé*. Paris: Dalloz.

— (2001), 'L'intervention de la Cour de Cassation égyptienne en matière de statut personnel', in *Les cours judiciaires suprêmes dans le monde arabe*. Beirut-Bruxelles: CEDROMA-Bruylant.

Engelen, E. (2003), 'How to Combine Openness and Protection? Citizenship, Migration and Welfare Regimes', *Politics and Society* 31 (4): 503-536.

Etienne, B. (1968), *Les problèmes juridiques des minorités européennes au Maghreb*. Paris: CNRS.

Evangelides, P. (1996), *The Republic of Cyprus and its Constitution with special regard to the Constitutional Rights*. Bamberg: Difo-Druck.

Evans-Pritchard, E. (1940), *The Nuer, A Description of the Modes of Livelihood and Political Institutions of a Nilotic People*. Cambridge: Clarendon Press.

Everson, M. (2003), '"Subjects", or "Citizens of Erwhon"? Law and Non-Law in the Development of a "British Citizenship"', *Citizenship Studies* 7 (1): 57-84.

Fabietti, U. (1984), *Il popolo del deserto. Gli Shammar del Gran Nefud, Arabia Saudita.* Rome-Bari: Laterza.
— (2002), *Culture in bilico. Antropologia del Medio Oriente.* Milan: Mondadori.
Faist, T. (2000), *The Volume and Dynamics of International Migration.* New York: Oxford University Press.
Faist, T., J. Gerdes & B. Rieple (2004), 'Dual Citizenship as a Path-Dependent Process, *International Migration Review* 38 (3): 913-944.
Farag, W. (1926), *Le rôle des tribunaux mixtes et indigènes d'Egypte en matière de statut personnel.* Paris: Librairie générale de droit et jurisprudence.
Fattal, A. (1958), *Le statut légal des non musulmans en pays d'Islam.* Beirut: Imprimérie catholique.
Fauchille, P. (1921-1926), *Traité de Droit international public.* Paris: Rousseau.
Faulks, K. (2000), *Citizenship.* London: Routledge.
Favell, A. (1998), 'Multicultural Race Relations in Britain: Problems of Interpretation and Explanation', in C. Joppke (ed.), *Challenge to the Nation-State. Immigration in Western Europe and the United States,* 319-349. Oxford: Oxford University Press.
Favell, A. (2001), 'Integration policy and integration research in Europe: a review and critique', in A. T. Aleinikoff & D. Klusmeyer (eds.), *Citizenship Today. Global Perspectives and Practices,* 349-399. Washington: Carnegie Endowment for International Peace.
Favres, A. (2003), 'Histoires de familles, patronage et clientèles dans l'espace politique local au Liban', *Annuaire de l'Afrique du Nord* 41: 37-66.
Fennema, M. (2004), 'Concept and Measurement of Civic Communities', *Journal of Ethnic and Migration Studies* 30 (3): 429-447.
Fennema, M. & J. Tillie (2001), 'Civic community, political participation and political trust of ethnic groups', *Connections* 23 (2): 44-59.
Ferrari, S. (1989), *Diritti dell'uomo e libertà dei gruppi religiosi: problemi giuridici dei nuovi movimenti religiosi.* Padua: CEDAM.
— (2002), *Lo spirito dei diritti religiosi.* Bologna: Il Mulino.
— (ed.) (2000), *Musulmani in Italia: la condizione giuridica delle comunità islamiche.* Bologna: Il Mulino.
Ferrari, S. & T. Scovazzi (eds.) (1988), *La tutela della libertà di religione: ordinamento internazionale e normative confessionali.* Padua: CEDAM.
Ferrari, S. & A. Bradney (eds.) (2000), *Islam and European Legal Systems.* Aldershot: Ashgate.
Ferrari, S. & G. Mori (eds.) (2003), *Religioni, diritti, comparazione.* Brescia: Morcelliana.
Fioravanti, M. (ed.) (2002), *Lo Stato moderno in Europa. Istituzioni e diritto.* Rome-Bari: Laterza.
Fustel de Coulanges, N. (1864), *La Cité antique.* Paris: Hachette.
Fyzee, A. (1955), *Outlines of Muhammadan Law.* London: Oxford University Press.
— (1965), *Cases in the Mohammedan Law of India and Pakistan.* Oxford: Oxford University Press.

Gabrieli, F. (1967), *Maometto e le grandi conquiste arabe.* Rome: Il Saggiatore.
Gannagé, P. (1983), 'Droit intercommunautaire et droit international privé (A propos de l'évolution du droit libanais face aux droits proche-orientaux)', *Jounal de Droit international* 110: 479-508.
Garcia de Herreros, E. (1914), *Les tribunaux mixtes d'Egypte.* Paris: Rousseau.
Gardet, L. (1954), *La cité musulmane: vie sociale et politique.* Paris: Vrin.
— (1967), *L'Islam: Religion et communauté.* Paris: Desclée de Brouwer.
Gatteschi, D. (1865), *Diritto pubblico e privato ottomano.* Alexandria: Posta europea.
Gaudeul, J.-M. (1991), *Appelés par le Christe, ils viennent de l'islam.* Paris: Cerf.

Geddes, A. (1998), 'Race Related Political Participation and Representation in the UK', *Revue Européenne des Migrations Internationales* 14 (2): 33-49.

Geisser, V. (1997), *Ethnicite Républicaine*. Paris: Presses de Sciences Po.

Ghali, P. (1934), *Les nationalités détachées de l'Empire ottoman à la suite de la Guerre*. Paris: Domat Montchrestien.

Ghali, S. (1908), 'Les tribunaux mixtes en Egypte', *Revue de droit international et de législation comparée* 10: 465-480.

Gibb, H. (1962), *Studies in the Civilisation of Islam*. Boston: Beacon.

Gibb, H. & J. Kramers (1974), *Shorter Encyclopedia of Islam*. Leiden: Brill.

Glick Schiller, N., N. Basch & C. Blanc-Szanton (1992), *Towards a Transnational Perspective on Migration. Race, Class, Ethnicity and Nationalism Reconsidered*. Annals of the New York Academy of Sciences 645. New York: New York Academy of Sciences.

— (1994), *Nations Unbound. Transnational Projects, Postcolonial Predicaments, and Deterritorialized Nation-States*. New York: Routledge.

Goitein, S. (1966), *Studies in the Islamic History and Institutions*. Leiden: Brill.

Goldziher, I. (1889), *Muhammedanische Studien*. Halle: Niemeyer.

— (1973), *Le dogme et la loi de l'Islam* (transl. by F. Arin). Paris: Geuthner.

Gosewinkel, D. (2001), *Einbürgern und ausschließen. Die Nationalisierung der Staatsangehörigkeit vom Deutschen Bund bis zur Bundesrepublik Deutschland*. Göttingen: Vandenhoek & Ruprecht.

Grosso, E. (1997), *Le vie della cittadinanza: Le grandi radici, i modelli storici di riferimento*. Padua: CEDAM.

Gsir, S. & M. Martiniello (2004), *Local consultative bodies for foreign residents – A handbook*. Strasbourg: Council of Europe Publishing.

Guest, R. (1912), *The Governors and Judges of Egypt*. Leiden-London: Brill-Luzac.

Guidi, M. (1951), Storia e Cultura degli Arabi fino alla morte di Maometto. Florence: Sansoni.

Guidi, M. & D. Santillana (1919), *Il Mukhtasar o Sommario del diritto malechita*. Milan: Hoepli.

Guiho, P. (1991), *La nationalité marocaine*. Rabat-Paris: La Porte-Médicis.

Guild, E. (1996), 'The legal framework of citizenship in the European Union', in D. Cesarani & M. Fulbrook (eds.), *Citizenship, Nationality and Migration in Europe*, 30-57. London: Routledge.

Guiraudon, V. (1998), 'Citizenship Rights for Non-Citizens: France, Germany, and the Netherlands', in C. Joppke (ed.), *Challenge to the Nation-State. Immigration in Western Europe and the United States*, 272-318. Oxford: Oxford University Press.

Guiraudon, V. & G. Lahav (2000), 'A Reappraisal of the State-Sovereignty Debate. The Case of Migration Control', *Comparative Political Studies* 33 (2): 163-195.

Habermas, J. (1992), 'Citizenship and National Identity: Some Reflections on the Future of Europe', *Praxis International* 12 (1): 1-19.

Haldane, J. (1923), *The Insurrection in Mesopotamia, 1920*. Edinburgh-London: Blackwood.

Hall, W. (1917), *Treatise on International Law*. 7th ed., Oxford: Clarendon Press.

Hamidullah, M. (1945), *Muslim Conduct of State*. Lahore: Ashraf.

Hammar, T. (1990), *Democracy and the Nation State. Aliens, Denizens and Citizens in a World of International Migration*. Aldershot: Ashgate.

Hammar, T. (ed.) (1985), *European immigration policy: a comparative study*. Cambridge: Cambridge University Press.

Hanna, S.& G. Gardner (1966), 'al-Shuʿubiyya Up-dated: A Study of the 20th Century Revival of an Eighth Century Concept', *Middle East Journal* 20: 335-352.

Hansen, R. (2000), *Citizenship and immigration in post-war Britain*. Oxford: Oxford University Press.

— (2002), 'Globalization, Embedded Realism, and Path Dependance. The Other Immigrants to Europe', *Comparative Political Studies* 35 (3): 259-283.

Hansen, R. & P. Weil (eds.) (2001a), *Towards a European Nationality. Citizenship, Immigration and Nationality Law in the EU.* Basingstoke: Palgrave.

— (2001b), 'Introduction: Citizenship, Immigration and Nationality: Towards a Convergence in Europe?', in R. Hansen & P. Weil (eds.), *Towards a European Nationality. Citizenship, Immigration and Nationality Law in the EU,* 1-24. Basingstoke: Palgrave.

— (2002a), *Dual Nationality, Social rights and Federal Citizenship in the U.S. and Europe. The Reinvention of Citizenship.* New York: Berghahn Books.

— (2002b), 'Dual Citizenship in A Changed World: Immigration, Gender and Social Rights', in R. Hansen & P. Weil (eds.), *Dual Nationality, Social Rights and Federal Citizenship in the U.S. and Europe. The Reinvention of Citizenship,* 1-15. New York: Berghahn Books.

Harbi, M. (1992), *L'Algérie et son destin. Croyants et citoyens.* Paris: Arcantère.

Heard-Bey, F. (2005), 'The United Arab Emirates: Statehood and Nation-Building in a Traditional Society', *Middle East Journal* 59 (3): 357-375.

Heater, D. (1999), *What is Citizenship?* London: Polity Press.

— (2004), *A Brief History of Citizenship.* Edinburgh: Edinburgh University Press.

Héchaïmé, C. (1967), *Louis Cheikho et son livre «Le christianisme et la littérature chrétienne en Arabie avant l'Islam».* Beirut: Dar el-Machreq.

Heffening, W. (1993), 'Murtadd', *EI²* VII: 635. Leiden-Paris: Brill.

Herb, M. (1999), *All in the Family: Absolutism, Revolution and Democracy in the Middle Eastern Monarchies.* Albany: State University of New York Press.

Herbst, J. (2000), *States and Power in Africa. Comparative Lessons in Authority and Control.* Princeton: Princeton University Press.

Hitti, P. (1948), *The Arabs: A Short History.* London: Macmillan.

Hoerder, D. (2002), *Cultures in Contact: World Migrations in the Second Millennium.* Durham: Duke University Press.

Homsy, B. (1956), *Les capitulations et la protection des chrétiens au Proche-Orient aux XVIᵉ, XVIIᵉ et XVIIIᵉ siècles.* Harissa: Geuthner.

Hourani, A. (1992), *A History of the Arab Peoples.* New York: Warner.

Human Rights Watch Middle East (1995), *The Bedoons of Kuwait: citizens without citizenship.* New York: HRW.

Hussein, T. (1974), *La grande épreuve = 'Uthmân.* Paris: Vrin.

İnalcık, H. (1971), 'Imtiyāzāt (II)', *EI²* III: 1208-1219. Leiden-Paris: Brill.

Itzigsohn, J. (2000), 'Immigration and the Boundaries of Citizenship: The Institutions of Immigrants' Political Transnationalism', *International Migration Review* 34 (4): 1126-1154.

Jacobson D. (1996), *Rights across Borders. Immigration and the Decline of Citizenship.* Baltimore: Johns Hopkins University Press.

Jawhari, R. (2000), *Wegen Überfremdung abgelehnt.* Vienna: Braumüller.

Jellinek, G. (1892), *System der subjektiven öffentlichen Rechte.* Freiburg: Mohr.

Joffre, A. (1924), *Le mandat de la France sur la Syrie et le Grand-Liban.* Lyon: Bascou.

Joppke, C. (1998), 'Immigration Challenges the Nation State', in C. Joppke (ed.), *Challenge to the Nation-State. Immigration in Western Europe and the United States,* 5-46. Oxford: Oxford University Press.

— (1999), 'How immigration is changing citizenship: a comparative view', *Ethnic and Racial Studies* 22 (4): 629-692.

— (2001), 'The Legal-Domestic Sources of Immigrant Rights', *Comparative Political Studies* 34 (4): 339-366.

— (2004), 'Citizenship without Identity', *Canadian Diversity/ Diversité Canadienne* 3 (2): 85-87.
— (2005), *Selecting by Origin: Ethnic Migration in the Liberal State*. Cambridge: Harvard University Press.
Jordan, B. & F. Düvell (2003), *Migration. The Boundaries of Equality and Justice*. Cambridge: Polity Press.
Joseph, S. (ed.) (2000), *Gender and Citizenship in the Middle East*. Syracuse: Syracuse University Press.
Juda, J. (1983), *Die sozialen und wirtschaflichen Aspekten der Mawālī in frühislamischen Zeit*. Tübingen: s.n.

Kantorowicz, E. (1931), *Kaiser Friedrich der Zweite*. London: Constable.
Karal, E. (1970), *Osmanlı tarihi. Nizam-i cedit ve tanzimat devirleri, 1789-1856*. Ankara: Türk Tarih Kurumu.
— (1954), *Osmanlı tarihi. Ishlahat fermanı devri, 1856-1861*. Ankara: Türk Tarih Kurumu.
— (1956), *Osmanlı tarihi. Ishlahat fermanı devri, 1861-1876*. Ankara: Türk Tarih Kurumu.
Karcic, F. (2005), 'The Issue of Citizenship in Contemporary Islamic Legal Thought', in G. Filoramo (ed.), *Teologie politiche: modelli a confronto*. Brescia: Morcelliana.
Kassir, W. (2002), *Réflexions sur le renvoi en droit international privé comparé. Contribution au dialogue des cultures juridiques nationales à l'aube du xxième siècle*. Bruxelles-Paris: Bruylant.
Kerber, W. (ed.) (1991), *Wie Tolerant ist der Islam?*. Munich: Kindt.
Khadduri, M. (1966), *The Islamic Law of Nations: Shaybānī's siyar*. Baltimore: Johns Hopkins Press.
Khoury, P. & J. Kostiner (eds.) (1990), *Tribes and State Formation in the Middle East*. Berkeley: University of California Press.
Kibreab, G. (2003), 'Citizenship Rights and Repatriation of Refugees', *International Migration Review* 37 (1): 24-73.
Kleger, H. (ed.) (1997), *Transnationale Staatsbürgerschaft*. Frankfurt: Campus.
Kofman, E. (2002), 'Contemporary European Migrations, civic stratification and citizenship', *Political Geography* 21: 1035-1054.
Kondo, A. (2001), 'Comparative Citizenship and Aliens' Rights', in A. Kondo (ed.), *Citizenship in a Global World. Comparing Citizenship Rights for Aliens*, 225-250. Houndsmill: Palgrave.
Kostakopoulou, D. (2000), 'The "Protective Union": Change and Continuity in Migration Law and Policy in Post-Amsterdam Europe', *Journal of Common Market Studies* 38 (3): 497-518.
— (2002), 'Long-term resident third-country nationals in the European Union: normative expectations and institutional openings', *Journal of Ethnic and Migration Studies* 28 (3): 443-462.
— (2003), 'Why Naturalisation?', *Perspectives on European Politics and Society* 4 (1): 85-115.
Kretzmer, D. (1990), *The Legal Status of Arabs in Israel*. Boulder: Westview.
Kurdi, A. (1984), *The Islamic State. A Study based on the Islamic Holy Constitution*. London-New York: Mansell.
Kymlicka, W. (1995), *Multicultural Citizenship. A Liberal Theory of Minority Rights*. Oxford: Oxford University Press.
Kymlicka, W. & W. Norman (1994), 'The Return of the Citizen: A Survey of Recent Work on Citizenship Theory', *Ethics* 104: 352-381.
Kymlicka, W. & A. Patten (eds.) (2003), *Language Rights and Political Theory*. Oxford: Oxford University Press.

Labourt, J. (1904), *Le christianisme dans l'Empire perse sous la dinastie sassanide (224-632)*. Paris: Lecoffre.

Lagarde, P. (1997), *La nationalité française*. 3rd ed., Paris: Dalloz.

Lammens, H. (1921), *La Syrie. Précis historique*. Beirut: Imprimerie catholique.

— (1924a), *L'Arabie occidentale à la veille de l'hégire*. Beirut: Imprimerie catholique.

— (1924b), *La Mecque à la veille de l'hégire*. Beirut: Imprimerie catholique.

Lawrence, T. (1927), *Revolt in the Desert*. London: Cape.

Lee, D. (1921), *The Mandate for Mesopotamia and the Principles of Trusteeship in English Law*. London: The League of Nations Union.

Lefebvre-Teillard, A. (1993), 'Ius sanguinis : l'émergence d'un principe (Éléments d'histoire de la nationalité française)', *Revue critique de droit international privé* 225-250.

Levitt, P. (2001), *The Transnational Villagers*. Berkeley: University of California Press.

Levy, D. & Y. Weiss (eds.) (2002), *Challenging Ethnic Citizenship. German and Israeli Perspectives on Immigration*. Oxford: Berghahn.

Levy, J. (2000), *The Multiculturalism of Fear*. Oxford: Oxford University Press.

Lewis, B. (1961), *The Emergence of Modern Turkey*. London-New York: Oxford University Press.

— (1971), *Race and Color in Islam*. New York: Harper & Row.

— (1988), *The Political Language of Islam*. Chicago: University of Chicago Press.

— (1995), *The Middle East*. London: Weidenfeld & Nicolson.

Linant de Bellefonds, Y. (1952-1973), *Traité de Droit musulman comparé*. Paris-The Hague: Mouton et Cie.

Little, D., J. Kelsay & A. Sachedina (eds.) (1988), *Human Rights and the Conflict of Cultures: Western and Islamic Perspectives on Religious Liberty*. Columbia: University of South Carolina Press.

Locke, J. (2002), *Essays on the Law of Nature*. Oxford: Clarendon Press.

Lockwood, D. (1996), 'Civic Stratification and Class Formation', *The British Journal of Sociology* 47 (3): 531-550.

Lombardi, G. (1967), *Contributo allo studio dei doveri costituzionali*. Milan: Giuffré.

— (1970), *Potere privato e diritti fondamentali*. Turin: Giappichelli.

— (1979), *Principio di nazionalità e fondamento della legittimità dello Stato*. Turin: Giappichelli.

— (1986), *Premesse al corso di diritto pubblico comparato: Problemi di metodo*. Milan: Giuffré.

Longva, A. (2002), 'The Apostasy Law in Kuwait and the Public Predicament', *Cultural Dynamics* 14 (3): 257-282.

Lucassen, L., D. Feldman & J. Oltmer (eds.) (2006), *Paths of Integration. Migrants in Western Europe (1880-2004)*. Amsterdam: Amsterdam University Press.

Luciani, G. (ed.) (1990), *The Arab State*. London: Routledge.

Luquet, J. (1923), *Les mandats A et l'organisation du mandat français en Syrie*. Paris: Editions de la Vie universitaire.

MacDonald, D. (1913), 'Dhimma', *EI*[1] I: 999. Leiden-Leipzig: Brill.

Mahiou, A. (2005), 'La nationalité en Algérie', in *Mélanges Cyrille David*. Paris: Librairie générale de droit et jurisprudence.

Mahmood, S. (1982), 'The Somali Experiment with Family Law Reform', *International and Comparative Law Quarterly* 31: 250-266.

Maktabi, R. (2000), 'State Formation and Citizenship in Lebanon: The Politics of Membership and Exclusion in a Sectarian State', in N.A. Butenschon, U. Davis & M. Hassassian (eds.), *Citizenship and the State in the Middle East: Approaches and Applications*: 146-178. Syracuse: Syracuse University Press.

Maïmonide, M. (1961), *Le livre de la connaissance*. Paris: Presses Universitaires de France.

— (1987), *Le livre des commandements*. Lausanne: L'age d'homme.

Mandaville, P. (2001), *Transnational Muslim Politics – Reimagining the Umma*. London: Routledge.

Mandouze, A. (1962), *La révolution algérienne par les textes*. 3rd ed., Paris: Maspero.

Mantran, R. (ed.) (1989), *Histoire de l'Empire ottoman*. Paris: Fayard.

Marrus, M. & R. Paxton (1981), *Vichy et les Juifs*. Paris: Calmann-Levy.

Marshall, T. H. (1965), 'Citizenship and Social Class', in T. H. Marshall, *Class, Citizenship, and Social Development. Essays by T. H. Marshall*. New York: Anchor Books.

Marsilius of Padua (2005), *Defender of the Peace*. Cambridge: Cambridge University Press.

Martin, D. A. & K. Hailbronner (eds.) (2003), *Rights and Duties of Dual Nationals: Evolution and Prospects*. The Hague: Kluwer Law International.

Martin, D.-C. (ed.) (1994), *Cartes d'identité. Comment dit-on nous en politique ?* Paris: Presses de la Fondation nationale de Sciences politiques.

Martiniello, M. (1992), *Leadership et pouvoir dans les communautés d'origine immigrée*. Paris: CIEMI-L'Harmattan.

— (1997), 'Quelle participation politique?', in M.-T. Coenen & R. Lewin (eds.), *La Belgique et ses immigrés – Les politiques manquées*, 101-120. Bruxelles: De Boeck Université.

— (1998), 'Les immigrés et les minorités ethniques dans les institutions politiques: ethnicisation des systèmes politiques européens ou renforcement de la démocratie?', *Revue Européenne des Migrations Internationales* 14 (2): 9-17.

Massignon, L. (1934-1937), 'Explication du plan de Kufa', in *Mélanges Maspero* III: 337-360. Cairo: Institut français d'archéologie orientale.

— (1954), 'Explication du plan de Basra', F. Meier (ed.), *Westöstliche Abhandlungen*, 154-174. Wiesbaden: Harrassowitz.

Masson, P. (1911), *Histoire du commerce français dans le Levant au xviiie siècle*. Paris: Hachette.

Meehan, E. (1993), *Citizenship and the European Community*. London: Sage.

Mélamède, G. (1934), 'The Meetings at al-'Aḳaba', *Monde Orientale* 28: 17-58.

Messina, S. (1928), *Traité de droit civil égyptien mixte*. Alexandria: Molco.

Meyer, G. (1930), *L'Egypte contemporaine et les capitulations*. Paris: Presses Universitaires de France.

Mezghani, A. (2003), 'Le juge français et les institutions du droit musulman', *Journal de Droit international* 130: 721-765.

Micaud, C. (1964), *Tunisia, the Politics of Modernization*. London: Dunmow.

Michael the Syrian (1899-1910), *Chronique*. Paris: Leroux.

Michon, L. & J. Tillie (2003), *Amsterdamse Polyfonie. Opkomst en stemgedrag van allochtone Amsterdammers bij de gemeenteraads- en deelraadsverkiezingen van 6 maart 2002*. Amsterdam: IMES.

Miller, M. J. (1981), *Foreign Workers in Western Europe. An emerging political force*. New York: Praeger.

Moch, L. P. (1992), *Moving Europeans. Migration in Western Europe since 1650*. Urbana: Indiana University Press.

Mondaini, G. (1939), 'Il problema della cittadinanza ai sudditi coloniali', *Rivista delle Colonie* 13 (1): 51-73.

Monroe, J. (1970), *The Shuʿūbiyya in al-Andalus: The Risāla of Ibn Garcia and Five Refutations*. Berkeley: University of California Press.

Montagne, R. (1947), *La civilisation du désert. Nomades d'Orient et d'Afrique*. Paris: Hachette.

Montgomery Watt, W. (1953), *Muhammad at Mecca*. Oxford: Clarendon Press.

— (1956), *Muhammad at Medina*. Oxford: Clarendon Press.

Morand, M. (1931), *Etudes de droit musulman et de droit coutumier berbère*. Algiers: Carbonel.

Moret, A. & G. Davy (1923), *Des clans aux empires: L'Organisation sociale chez les primitifs et dans l'Orient ancien.* Paris: La Renaissance du livre.

Morimoto, K. (1981), *The Fiscal Administration of Egypt in the Early Islamic Period.* Kyoto: Dohosha.

Morris, L. (2001a), *Managing Migration: Civic Stratification and Migrants' Rights.* London: Routledge.

— (2001b), 'The Ambigous Terrain of Rights. Civic Stratification in Italy's Emergent Immigration Regime', *International Journal for Urban and Regional Research* 25 (3): 497-518.

— (2003), 'Managing Contradictions: Civic Contradiction: Civic Stratification and Migrants' Rights', *International Migration Review* 37 (1): 74-100.

Mottahedeh, R. (1976), 'The Shuᶜûbîyah Controversy and the Social History of Early Islamic Iran', *Internationl Journal of Middle Eastern Studies* 7: 167-170.

Moulay Rchid, A. (1992), 'Le droit international privé du Maroc indépendent en matière de statut personnel', in J.-Y. Carlier & M. Verwilghen (eds.), *Le statut personnel des musulmans. Droit comparé et droit international privé.* Bruxelles: Bruylant.

Münz, R. & R. Ohliger (eds.) (2003), *Diasporas and Ethnic Migrants: Germany, Israel and Post-Soviet Successor States in Comparative Perspective.* London: Frank Cass.

Muranyi, M. (1973), *Die Prophetengenossen in der frühislamischen Geschichte.* Bonn: Orientalischen Seminars der Universität.

Najm, M.-C. (2003), 'Religion et Droit international privé de la famille dans les pays du Proche-Orient', in *Droit et Religion*, 433-449. Beirut-Bruxelles: CEDROMA-Bruylant.

Nallino, C. (1939-1948), *Raccolta di scritti editi e inediti.* Rome: Istituto per l'Oriente.

— (1946), *Vita di Maometto.* Rome: Istituto per l'Oriente.

Nascimbene, B. (ed.) (1996), *Nationality Laws in the European Union.* London-Milan: Butterworths.

Niblock, T. (1982), *Iraq, the Contemporary State.* New York: Saint Martin's Press.

Niboyet, J.-P. (1947), *Traité de droit international privé français.* 2nd ed., Paris: Recueil Sirey.

Nicolas, M. (1928), *La nationalité au Liban d'après le traité de Lausanne.* Lyon: Bosc et Riou.

Nonneman, G., T. Niblock & B. Szajkowski (eds.) (1996), *Muslim communities in the new Europe.* Reading: Ithaca Press.

Nyberg Sørensen, N. & K. F. Olwig (eds.) (2001), *Work and Migration – Life and Livelihoods in a Globalizing World.* London: Routledge.

Okin, S. M. (1979), *Women in Western Political Thought.* Princeton: Princeton University Press.

Oldfield, A. (1990), *Citizenship and Community. Civic Republicanism and the Modern World.* London: Routledge.

Olivier Martin, F. (1948), *Histoire du droit français des origines à la Révolution.* Paris: CNRS.

Oppenheim, L. (1927), *International Law.* London: Longmans.

Pacini, A. (ed.) (1998), *L'islam e il dibattito sui diritti dell'uomo.* Turin: Fondazione Giovanni Agnelli.

Palgrave, W. (1865), *Narrative of a Year's Journey through Central and Eastern Arabia.* London: Macmillan.

Palici di Suni Prat, E. (2002), *Intorno alle minoranze.* 2nd ed., Turin: Giappichelli.

— (2004), *Tra parità e differenza: dal voto alle donne alle quote elettorali.* Turin: Giappichelli.

Paolucci, G. & C. Eid (2005), *I cristiani venuti dall'Islam. Storie di musulmani convertiti*. Casale Monferrato: Piemme.

Parekh, B. (2000), *Rethinking Multiculturalism*. Basingstoke: Macmillan.

Parolin, G. (2003), 'Limiti dell'approccio confessionale alle tematiche di genere: il caso della Giordania', in A. Ligustro & A. Manna (eds.), *Le libertà delle donne in Europa e nel Mediterraneo*: 385-388. Bari: Edizioni Giuseppe Laterza.

— (2004), 'Resistenze al costituzionalismo liberale in Medio Oriente: laicità dello Stato e minoranza cristiana in Giordania', in R. Orrù & L. Sciannella (eds.), *Limitazioni di sovranità e processi di democratizzazione*, 245-250. Turin: Giappichelli.

— (2007), *Dimensioni dell'appartenenza e cittadinanza nel mondo arabo*. Naples: Jovene.

Pélissié du Rausas, G. (1902), *Le régime des capitulations dans l'Empire ottoman*. Paris: Rousseau.

Pellat, C. (1969), *The Life and works of Jāhiz: Translations of selected texts*. London: Routledge.

Penninx, R. & A. van Heelsum (2004), *Bondgenoot of Spelbreker? Organisaties van immigranten en hun mogelijke rol in integratieprocessen*. Utrecht: FORUM.

Penninx, R., M. Berger & K. Kraal (eds.) (2006), *The Dynamics of International Migration and Settlement in Europe*. Amsterdam: Amsterdam University Press.

Perlmann, M. (1965), 'Dönme', *EI²* II: 631. Leiden-Paris: Brill.

Peters, R. & G. De Vries (1976-1977), 'Apostasy in Islam', *Die Welt des Islams* 17: 1-25.

Phillips, A. (1995), *The Politics of Presence*. Oxford: Oxford University Press.

Pitkin, H. F. (1967), *The Concept of Representation*. Berkeley: University of California Press.

Pocock, J.G.A. (1992), 'The Ideal of Citizenship Since Classical Times', *Queen's Quarterly* 99 (1): 35-55. Reprinted in Beiner 1995: 29-52.

Portes, A. (ed.) (2001), 'New Research and Theory on Immigrant Transnationalism', Special Issue, *Global Networks* 1 (3).

Portes, A., L. E. Guarnizo & P. Landolt (1999), 'The study of transnationalism: pitfalls and promises of an emergent research field', *Ethnic and Racial Studies* 22 (2): 217-237.

Pothier, R. (1776-1778), *Traité des personnes*. Paris: Lejay & Dorez.

Preuss, U. K. (1997), 'Probleme eines Konzepts europäischer Staatsbürgerschaft', in H. Kleger (ed.), *Transnationale Staatsbürgerschaft*. Frankfurt: Campus.

— (2003), 'Citizenship and the German Nation', *Citizenship Studies* 7 (1): 37-55.

Preuss, U. K., M. Everson, M. Koenig-Archibugi & E. Lefebvre (2003), 'Traditions of Citizenship in the European Union', *Citizenship Studies* 7 (1): 3-14.

Pufendorf, S. (1967), *De iure naturæ et gentium*. Frankfurt: Minerva.

Rabbath, E. (1980), *Les chrétiens dans l'islam des premiers temps*, I: *L'Orient chrétien à la veille de l'Islam*. Beirut: Université libanaise.

— (1981), *Les chrétiens dans l'islam des premiers temps*, II: *Mahomet: prophète arabe et fondateur d'Etat*. Beirut: Université libanaise.

Rahman, S. (1972), *Punishment of Apostasy in Islam*. Lahore: Institute of Islamic Culture.

Ramadan, S. (1961), *Islamic Law, Its Scope and Equity*. London: Macmillan.

Rechid, A. (1937), 'L'islam et le Droit des gens', *Recueil des Cours – Hague Academy of International Law* 60 (2): 371-506.

Rey, F. (1899), *La protection diplomatique et consulaire dans les Echelles du Levant et de Barbarie*. Paris: Larose.

Riad, F. & H. Sadek (1992), 'Les conflits de lois en droit interne et en droit international privé égyptien dans les matières de statut personnel', in Carlier, J.-Y. & M. Verwilghen (eds.), *Le statut personnel des musulmans. Droit comparé et droit international privé*: 67-108. Bruxelles: Bruylant.

Robertson Smith, W. (1885), *Kinship and Marriage in Early Arabia*. Cambridge: Cambridge University Press.

Rosenthal, E. (1956), *Averroes' Commentary on Plato's Republic*. Cambridge: Cambridge University Press.

Rouillard, G. (1923), *Administration civile de l'Egypte byzantine*. Paris: Presses Universitaires de France.

Rubio-Marín, R. (2000), *Immigration as a Democratic Challenge. Citizenship and Inclusion in Germany and the United States*. Cambridge: Cambridge University Press.

Rummens, J. A. (2003), 'Conceptualising Identity and Diversity: Overlaps, Intersections, and Processes', *Canadian Ethnic Studies* 35 (3): 10-25.

Saba, J. (1931), *L'Islam et la nationalité*. Paris: Librairie de jurisprudence ancienne et moderne.

Sacco, R. (1985), *Le grandi linee del sistema giuridico somalo*. Milan: Giuffré.

— (1992), *Introduzione al diritto comparato*. Turin: Giappichelli.

Sachedina, A. (1988), 'Freedom of conscience and religion in the Qur'an', in D. Little, J. Kelsay & A. Sachedina (eds.), *Human Rights and the Conflict of Cultures: Western and Islamic Perspectives on Religious Liberty*: 53-90. Columbia: University of South Carolina Press.

Saeed A. & H. Saeed (2004), *Freedom of Religion, Apostasy and Islam*. Aldershot: Ashgate.

Safa, E. (1960), *L'émigration libanaise*. Beirut: Université Saint-Joseph.

Saggar, S. (ed.) (1998), *Race and British Electoral Politics*. London: UCL Press.

Salem, E. (1905-1907), 'De la nationalité en Turquie', *Journal de Droit international privé* 32: 585-591, 872-883, 33: 1032-1041, 34: 51-56.

Salhi, M. (2003), 'Entre communauté et citoyenneté: Le local en contestation. Le cas de la Kabylie', *Annuire de l'Afrique du Nord* 41: 11-36.

Santillana, D. (1926), *Istituzioni di diritto musulmano malichita con riguardo anche al sistema sciafiita*. Rome: Istituto per l'Oriente.

Sator, B. (1963), 'Le Code de la nationalité algérienne', *Revue de la Fonction Publique* (Algiers) April.

Schacht, J. (1950), *The Origins of Muhammedan Jurisprudence*. Oxford: Clarendon Press.

— (1964), *An Introduction to Islamic Law*. Oxford: Clarendon Press.

Scholem, G. (1971-1972), 'Doenmeh', *EJ²* VI: 147-152. Jerusalem-New York: Keter-Macmillan.

Schulze, R. (1995), 'Citizens of Islam. The institutionalization and internationalization of Muslim legal debate', in C. Toll & J. Skovgard-Petersen (eds.), *Law and the Islamic World. Past and Present*, special issue of *Historisk-filogiske Meddelelser* 68: 167-184.

Scott, J. (1907), *The Law Affecting Foreigners in Egypt*. Edinburgh: Green.

Sebêos (1904), *Histoire d'Héraclius*. Paris: Leroux.

Shahid, I. (1971), *The martyrs of Najrān*. Bruxelles: Bollandistes.

Shafir, G. (ed.) (1998), *The Citizenship Debates: A Reader*. Minneapolis: University of Minnesota Press.

Shaw, J. (1998), 'The Interpretation of European Union Citizenship', *The Modern Law Review* 61 (3): 293-317.

— (2007), *The Transformation of Citizenship in the European Union. Electoral Rights and the Restructuring of Political Space*. Cambridge: Cambridge University Press.

Sicakkan, H. & Y. Lithman (eds.) (2004), *Envisioning Togetherness: Politics of Identity and Forms of Belonging*. New York: Edwin Mellen Press.

Sicardi, S. (1996), 'L'immigrato e la Costituzione. Note sulla dottrina e sulla giurisprudenza costituzionale', *Giurisprudenza italiana* 148 IV: 313-324.

— (2005), 'Questioni aperte nella disciplina del fenomeno religioso: dalla laicità al sistema delle fonti', *Quaderni di diritto e politica ecclesiastica* 13 (1): 3-29.

Simeant, J. (1997), *La cause des sans-papiers*. Paris: Presses de Science Po.

Sinclair, T. (1952), *A History of Greek Political Thought*. London: Routledge.

Smith, R. (2001), 'Citizenship: Political', in P. B. Baltes & N. J. Smelser (eds.), *International Encyclopedia of the Social and Behavioral Sciences*: 1857-1860.

Soares, L. (2002), 'El carácter "por naturaleza" de la politicidad aristotélica', *Areté* 14 (2): 55-78.

Soininen, M. (1999), 'The "Swedish Model" as an institutional framework for immigrant membership rights', *Journal of Ethnic and Migration Studies*, 25(4): 685-702.

Solomos, J. & L. Back (1991), 'Black political mobilisation and the struggle for equality', *The Sociological Review* 39 (2): 215-237.

Soysal, Y. (1994), *Limits of Citizenship. Migrants and Postnational Membership in Europe*. Chicago: University of Chicago Press.

Spinner-Halev, J. (1994), *The Boundaries of Citizenship. Race, Ethnicity, and Nationality in the Liberal State*. Baltimore: The Johns Hopkins University Press.

Stanton Russell, S. (1990), 'Migration and Political Integration in the Arab World', in G. Luciani (ed.), *The Arab State*: 373-393. London: Routledge.

Stillman, N. (1991), *The Jews of Arab Lands in Modern Times*. New York: Jewish Publication Society.

Stoyanovsky, J. (1925), *Théorie générale des mandats internationaux*. Paris: Presses Universitaires de France.

Straubhaar, T. (2003), 'Wird die Staatsangehörigkeit zu einer Klubmitgliedschaft?', in D. Thränhardt & U. Hunger (ed.), *Migration im Spannungsfeld von Globalisierung und Nationalstaat*, Leviathan Sonderheft 22, 76-89. Wiesbaden: Westdeutscher Verlag.

Strudel, S. (1996), *Votes Juifs. Itinéraires migratoires, religieux et politiques*. Paris: Presses de Sciences Po.

Tellenbach, S. (2001), 'L'Apostasia nel diritto islamico', *Daimon* 1: 53-70.

Temperley, H. (1920-1924), *History of the Peace Conference of Paris*. London: Frowde.

Tetreault, M.A. (2000a), *Stories of Democracy: Politics and Society in Contemporary Kuwait*. New York: Columbia University Press.

— (2000b), 'Gender, Citizenship, and State in the Middle East', in N.A. Butenschon, U. Davis & M. Hassassian (eds.), *Citizenship and the State in the Middle East: Approaches and Applications*: 70-87. Syracuse: Syracuse University Press.

Thomas, Y. (1995), 'Le droit d'origine à Rome. Contribution à l'étude de la citoyenneté', *Revue critique de droit international privé* (2): 253-290.

Thränhardt, D. (2000), 'Tainted Blood: The Ambivalence of "Ethnic" Migration in Israel, Japan, Korea, Germany and the United States', *German Policy Studies/Politikfeldanalyse*, 1.

Tibi, B. (1990), 'The Simultaneity of the Unsimultaneous: Old Tribes and Imposed Nation-States in the Modern Middle East', in P. Khoury & J. Kostiner (eds.), *Tribes and State Formation in the Middle East*, Berkeley: University of California Press.

Tillie, J. (1994), *Kleurrijk kiezen. Opkomst en stemgedrag van migranten tijdens de gemeenteraadsverkiezingen van 2 maart 1994*. Utrecht: Nederlands Centrum Buitenlanders.

— (1998), 'Explaining Migrant Voting Behaviour in the Netherlands. Combining the Electoral Research and Ethnic Studies Perspective', *Revue Européenne des Migrations Internationales* 14 (2): 71-95.

— (2004), 'Social Capital of Organisations and their Members: Explaining the Political Integration of Immigrants in Amsterdam', *Journal of Ethnic and Migration Studies* 30 (3): 529-541.

Toll, C. & J. Skovgard-Petersen (eds.) (1995), *Law and the Islamic World. Past and Present*, special issue of *Historisk-filogiske Meddelelser* 68.

Toynbee, A. (1917), *The Murderous Tyranny of the Turks*. London: Hodder & Stoughton.

— (1922), *The Western Question in Turkey and Greece. A Study in the Contact of Civilisation*. New York: Howard Fertig.

Tsitselikis, K. (2004), 'Personal Status of Greece's Muslims: A Legal Anachronism or an Example of Applied Multiculturalism?', in R. Aluffi Beck-Peccoz & G. Zincone (eds.), *The Legal Treatment of Islamic Minorities in Europe*: 109-132. Leuven: Peeters.

Turroni, G. (2002), *Il mondo della storia secondo Ibn Khaldūn*. Rome: Jouvence.

Tyan, E. (1926), *Le système de responsabilité délictuelle en droit musulman*. Beirut: Imprimerie catholique.

— (1938), *Histoire de l'organisation judiciaire en Pays d'Islam*. Paris: Recueil Sirey.

— (1954), *Institutions du droit public musulman, I: Le califat*. Paris: Recueil Sirey.

— (1956), *Institutions du droit public musulman, II: Sultanat et Califat*. Paris: Recueil Sirey.

Valognes, J.-P. (1994), *Vie et mort des chrétiens d'Orient: des origines à nos jours*. Paris: Fayard.

Vanel, M. (1945), *Histoire de la nationalité française. Évolution historique de la notion de Français d'origine du XVIe siècle au Code civil*. Paris: Imprimerie de la Cour d'Appel.

— (1946), 'Le Français d'origine dans l'Ancien droit', *Revue critique de droit international privé* 35.

van Gunsteren, H. (1998), *A Theory of Citizenship. Organizing Plurality in Contemporary Democracies*. Boulder: Westview Press.

van Heelsum, A. (2002), 'The relationship between political participation and civic community of migrants in the Netherlands', *Journal of International Migration and Integration* 3 (2): 179-199.

van Heelsum, A. & J. Tillie (2000), 'Stemgedrag van migranten in de gemeenteraadsverkiezingen van 1998', in J. Tillie (ed.), *De etnische Stem, opkomst en stemgedrag van migranten tijdens de gemeenteraadsverkiezingen 1986-1998*, 18-42. Utrecht: FORUM.

Vasiliev, A. (1932), *Histoire de l'Empire byzantin*. Paris: Picard.

Venel, N. (2004), *Musulmans et citoyens*. Paris: Presses universitaires de France.

Vermeersch, P. (2002), 'Ethnic mobilisation and the political conditionality of European Union accession: the case of the Roma in Slovakia', *Journal of Ethnic and Migration Studies* 28 (1): 83-101.

Vertovec, S. (2000), *The Hindu Diaspora*. London: Routledge.

von Testa, I. (1869), *Observations sur le mémoire de la Sublime Porte relatif aux capitulations*. Istanbul: s.n.

Waldrauch, H. & D. Çinar (2003), 'Staatsbürgerschaftspolitik und Einbürgerungspraxis in Österreich', in H. Fassmann & I. Stacher (eds.), *Österreichischer Migrations- und Integrationsbericht. Demographische Entwicklungen – Sozioökonomische Strukturen – Rechtliche Rahmenbedingungen*, 261-283. Klagenfurt: Drava.

Walzer, M. (1983), *Spheres of Justice. A Defence of Pluralism and Equality*. New York: Basic Books.

Walzer, R. (1960), 'Aristūtālīs', EI^2 I: 651-654. Leiden-Paris: Brill.

Wanner, P. & G. D'Amato (2003), *Naturalisation en Suisse. Le rôle des changements législatifs sur la demande de naturalisation*. Neuchâtel: FSM.

Wansbrough, J. (1971), 'Imtiyāzāt (I)', EI^2 III: 1207-1208. Leiden-Paris: Brill.

Weber, M. (1904), 'Die "Objektivität" sozialwissenschaftlicher und sozialpolitischer Erkenntnis', *Archiv für Sozialwissenschaft und Sozialpolitik* 19: 22-87.

Weil, Patrick (2001), 'Access to Citizenship. A Comparison of Twenty-Five Nationality Laws', in A. T. Aleinikoff & D. Klusmeyer (eds.), *Citizenship Today. Global Perspectives and Practices*, 17-35. Washington, DC: Carnegie Endowment for International Peace.

— (2002), *Qu'est-ce qu'un Français? Histoire de la nationalité française depuis la Révolution*. Paris: Grasset.

Weiler, J. H. H. (1997), 'To be a European citizen – Eros and civilization', *Journal of European Public Policy* 4 (4): 459-519.

— (1999), *The Constitution of Europe: 'Do the New Clothes have an Emperor?' and Other Essays on European Integration*. Cambridge: Cambridge University Press.

Wellhausen, J. (1884-1889), *Skizzen und Vorarbeiten*. Berlin: Reimer.

Wiener, A. (1997), 'Making sense of the new geography of citizenship: Fragmented citizenship in the European Union', *Theory and Society* 26: 529-560.

Withol de Wenden, C. (1988), *Les immigrés et la politique*. Paris: Presses de la Fondation Nationale des Sciences Politiques.

Wüstenfeld, F. (1857-1861), *Die Chroniken der Stadt Mekka*. Leipzig: Brockhaus.

Young, G. (1905-1906), *Corps de droit ottoman*. Oxford: Clarendon Press.

Young, I. M. (1990), *Justice and the Politics of Group Difference*. Princeton: Princeton University Press.

Ziadeh, F. (1957), 'Equality (*Kafā'ah*) in the Muslim Law of Marriage', *American Journal of Comparative Law* 6: 503-508.

Zincone, G. (1992), *Da sudditi a cittadini: le vie dello Stato e le vie della società civile*. Bologna: Il Mulino.

— (1994), *Uno schermo contro il razzismo: per una politica dei diritti utili*. Rome: Donzelli.

— (ed.) (2000), *Primo rapporto sull'integrazione degli immigrati in Italia*. Bologna: Il Mulino.

— (ed.) (2001), *Secondo rapporto sull'integrazione degli immigrati in Italia*. Bologna: Il Mulino.

Zolo, D. (1994), *La cittadinanza. Appartenenza, identità, diritti*. Rome-Bari: Laterza.

Zorell, F. (1909), *Lexicon hebraicum et aramaicum Veteris Testamenti*. Rome: Pontificium Institutum Biblicum.

General index

Abbasids 21, 53, 62, 65
ᶜAbbūd 91
Abdel-Hakim (affaire) 27, 92
ᶜAbd allāh (Emir, later King) 83, 86-87
ᶜAbduh 112, 121
abū Bakr 43, 46, 52, 67
abū Hanīfah 53, 64
abū Lahab 42-43
abū Tālib 42
abū Yūsuf 24
    Kitāb al-kharāj 24
Abyssinia (Hegira to) 42
acknowledgment (of a child) 34
acquisition of nationality (Arab laws)
96-107
    acquisition of foreign nationality 100-
    106
    ~ of origin 97-100
    by marriage 106-107
    Islamic perspective 113-114
ᶜAdnān 30
adoption 34
affinity 34
ᶜAflaq 118
ahl 23-24
ahl al-kitāb 49-50, 60, 112, 113
Ahlāf 42-43
Ahmadis 54
ajnabī 25, 102
Aksumite Empire 42
al-ᶜAbbās 43-44
al-ᶜAbbūd 118
al-Afghānī 112
Āl al-Dawsarī 116-117
al-ᶜAlwānī 124
al-ᶜAnānī 118
al-Asad (Hāfiz) 88
ᶜAlawis 51-52
al-Bakrī 31
al-Balādhurī 63
al-Basrah 62

al-Bustānī 95-96
Alexander the Great 19-20
al-Fārābī 18, 24
    Virtuous City 18, 24
al-Fustāt 62
al-Ghannūshī 124
al-Ghazzālī 51, 121
    The Median in Belief 51
al-Ghufrān 116
Algeria
    Code de l'Indigenat 94
    Décret Crémieux 94
    Evian Agreements 95
    Loi Jonnart 94
    Loi Lamine-Guèye 94-95
    nationality 94-95
    Senatus Consultum (1865) 94
al-Husrī 118
al-Hutāt ibn Yazīd 44
ᶜAlī (ibn abī Tālib) 48, 50
ᶜAlī Pāshā 73
al-Jabartī 23
al-Jaddāwī 112
al-Jāhilīyah (ᶜasr) 61
al-Jāhiz 68-69
al-Jawharī 31
al-Jazā'irī 126
al-Kindī 18
al-Kūfah 62
al-Māwardī 21, 30-31, 53, 67
    al-Ahkām al-sultānīyah 21, 67
al-Mawdūdī 124
al-Najīb 118
Althusius 22
al-Qalī 31
al-Qalqashandī 30-31
al-Qayrawān 62
al-qurà al-sabᶜ 117
Āl Rammāl 32
al-Sanūsī 92
al-Sarakhsī 113-114

Corrado Bonifazi, Marek Okólski, Jeannette Schoorl, Patrick Simon, Eds.
International Migration in Europe: New Trends and New Methods of Analysis
2008 (ISBN 978 90 5356 894 1)

Maurice Crul, Liesbeth Heering, Eds.
*The Position of the Turkish and Moroccan Second Generation in Amster-
dam and Rotterdam: The TIES Study in the Netherlands*
2008 (ISBN 978 90 8964 061 1)

Marlou Schrover, Joanne van der Leun, Leo Lucassen, Chris Quispel, Eds.
Illegal Migration and Gender in a Global and Historical Perspective
2008 (ISBN 978 90 8964 047 5)

IMISCOE Reports

Rainer Bauböck, Ed.
Migration and Citizenship: Legal Status, Rights and Political Participation
2006 (ISBN 978 90 5356 888 0)

Michael Jandl, Ed.
Innovative Concepts for Alternative Migration Policies:
Ten Innovative Approaches to the Challenges of Migration in the 21st Century
2007 (ISBN 978 90 5356 990 0)

Jeroen Doomernik, Michael Jandl, Eds.
Modes of Migration Regulation and Control in Europe
2008 (ISBN 978 90 5356 689 3)

Michael Jandl, Christina Hollomey, Sandra Gendera, Anna Stepien,
Veronika Bilger
*Migration and Irregular Work in Austria: A Case Study of the Structure
and Dynamics of Irregular Foreign Employment in Europe at the Beginning
of the 21st Century*
2009 (ISBN 978 90 8964 053 6)

IMISCOE Dissertations

Panos Arion Hatziprokopiou
*Globalisation, Migration and Socio-Economic Change in Contemporary
Greece: Processes of Social Incorporation of Balkan Immigrants in
Thessaloniki*
2006 (ISBN 978 90 5356 873 6)

Floris Vermeulen
The Immigrant Organising Process: Turkish Organisations in Amsterdam and Berlin and Surinamese Organisations in Amsterdam, 1960-2000
2006 (ISBN 978 90 5356 875 0)

Anastasia Christou
Narratives of Place, Culture and Identity: Second-Generation Greek-Americans Return 'Home'
2006 (ISBN 978 90 5356 878 1)

Katja Rušinović
Dynamic Entrepreneurship: First and Second-Generation Immigrant Entrepreneurs in Dutch Cities
2006 (ISBN 978 90 5356 972 6)

Ilse van Liempt
Navigating Borders: Inside Perspectives on the Process of Human Smuggling into the Netherlands
2007 (ISBN 978 90 5356 930 6)

Myriam Cherti
Paradoxes of Social Capital: A Multi-Generational Study of Moroccans in London
2008 (ISBN 978 90 5356 032 7)

Marc Helbling
Practising Citizenship and Heterogeneous Nationhood: Naturalisations in Swiss Municipalities
2008 (ISBN 978 90 8964 034 5)

Jérôme Jamin
L'Imaginaire du Complot: Discours d'Extrême Droite en France et aux Etats-Unis
2009 (ISBN 978 90 8964 048 2)

Inge Van Nieuwenhuyze
Getting by in Europe's Urban Labour Markets: Senegambian Migrants' Strategies for Survival, Documentation and Mobility
2009 (ISBN 978 90 8964 050 5)

Nayla Moukarbel
Sri Lankan Housemaids in Lebanon: A Case of 'Symbolic Violence' and 'Everyday Forms of Resistance'
2009 (ISBN 978 90 8964 051 2)